I0813022

IMAGES
of America

WASHITA COUNTY

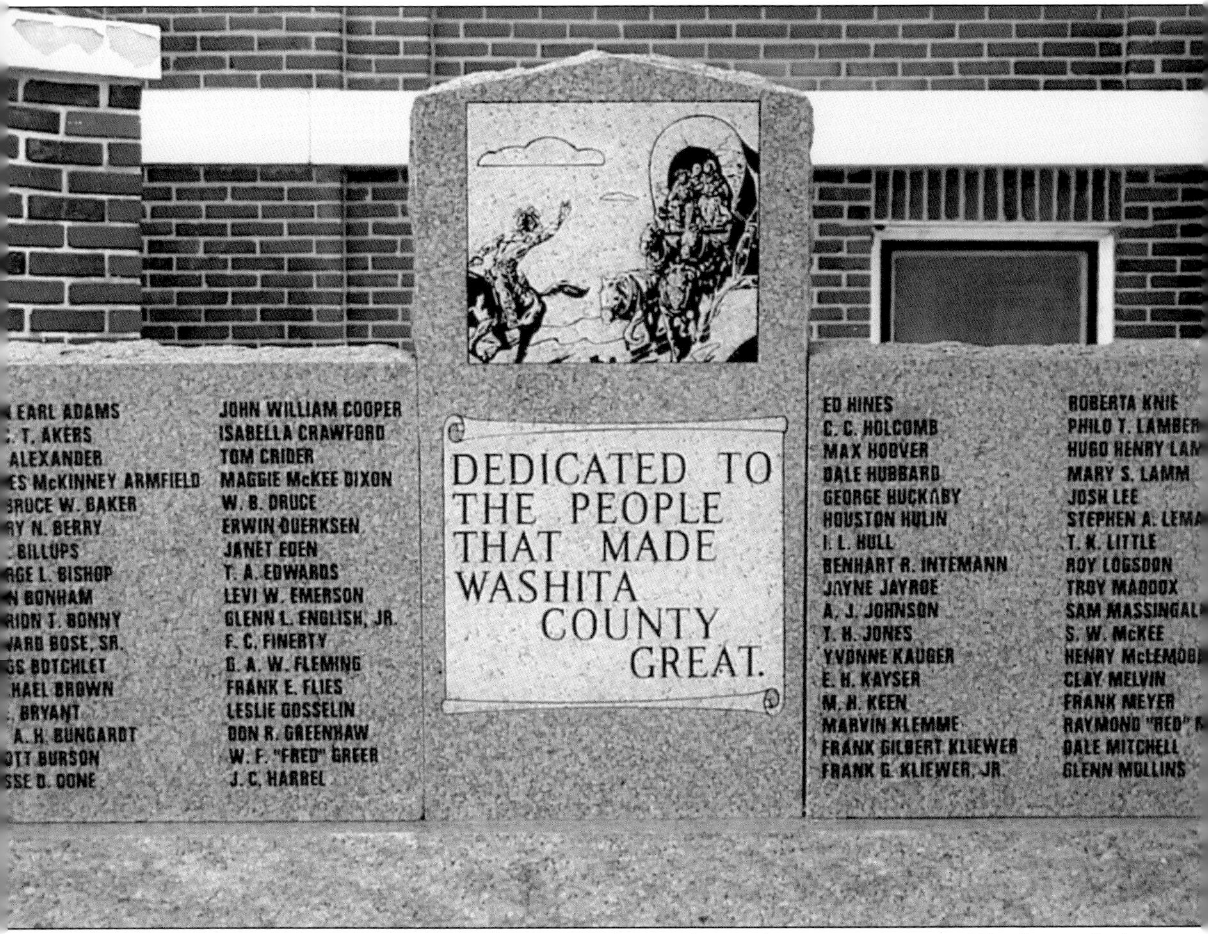

This is a monument dedicated to the people who made Washita County great. The list includes 156 names of names of Washita County people who are recognized as founders and developers of Washita County.

On the cover: Please see page 63. (Courtesy Washita County Museum.)

IMAGES
of America

WASHITA COUNTY

Wayne Boothe

ARCADIA
PUBLISHING

ISBN 978-0-7385-5151-7

Published by Arcadia Publishing
Charleston SC, Chicago IL, Portsmouth NH, San Francisco CA

Printed in the United States of America

Library of Congress Catalog Card Number: 2007929152

For all general information contact Arcadia Publishing at:
Telephone 843-853-2070
Fax 843-853-0044
E-mail sales@arcadiapublishing.com
For customer service and orders:
Toll-Free 1-888-313-2665

Visit us on the Internet at www.arcadiapublishing.com

Contents

ACKNOWLEDGMENTS

The purpose of this book is to record a pictorial history of Washita County, which was founded by a run for homesteads on April 19, 1892. I was born in Washita County 83 years ago, have lived in Washita County most of my life, and am just one generation away from pioneers who established Washita County. My father came to Washita County in a covered wagon as a small child in the 1890s.

Much of the material, such as the vintage images, is from the Washita County Historical Museum files, for which complete access was appreciated. I am indebted to Bob Taylor, one of the nation's best-known agriculture photographers over the past 60 years, who furnished several photographs of Washita County agriculture.

I especially wish to recognize Dr. Linda Wilson, Northeastern Oklahoma State University Education Department, and my daughter Dr. Vickie Foster, an assistant professor of education at Northeastern Oklahoma State University, for their encouragement and challenge in my recording early-day Washita County history in book form.

This book could not have been produced without the help of my granddaughter Kristy Spalding, who spent many hours reproducing photographs and formatting, as this retired farmer is somewhat computer challenged.

I am indebted to the Washita County Oklahoma State University Extension Center, which permitted me access to their high-quality equipment in copying photographs and providing a disk file of all photographs.

Thanks to my wife, Mary, and my family, who gave me encouragement and found themselves living around much clutter while I produced this pictorial history book of Washita County.

I also wish to thank Arcadia Publishing company representatives Ann Marie Lonsdale and John Pearson, who not only tolerated this inexperienced author but also gave me much advice and assistance in the production of the book.

INTRODUCTION

Ten years before the Cheyenne-Arapahoe Indian Reservation was opened for settlement, the first white person to establish a home in what is now Washita County was John H. Seger, an Indian agent for the government from Darlington, Oklahoma Territory. Seger established his home in 1882 at present-day Colony, located on Cobb Creek, which was the first town to be established in Washita County. The government in 1882 leased the Cheyenne-Arapahoe reservation to the cattlemen for $100,000 per year, which was given to the Native Americans. Seger was in charge of building 300 miles of fence around the reservation. The cattlemen were to use the Native Americans to operate the ranches; however, the cattlemen did not live up to their agreement, and in 1885, when Grover Cleveland became president he canceled the rental agreement.

In 1889, Seger brought 500 Native Americans and established the town of Colony. The Sunday morning before they started their journey from Darlington, Seger read the Bible story of the River Jordan and compared their journey to the Bible story. When the group came to the Canadian River, about 40 miles east of Colony, they discarded their native garb, bathed in the river as a symbol of washing away their old life, and dressed in new white men's clothes that the government furnished. They completed the journey and established the town of Colony, which still exists today.

At noon, April 19, 1892, the second run for homesteads in Oklahoma was held, which established County H that later became Washita County. Over 5,000 homesteaders participated in the run that started at noon when the soldiers fired gunshots to begin the run from four different points. Tacola, which later became Cloud Chief, had been established as the county seat of County H by the U.S. Congress and was a town of approximately 20 people; however, by the night of April 19, 1892, it became a tent city of well over 3,000 people. Businesses sprung up by mid-afternoon, operating from tents and wagons.

Within four months, 31 school districts were established. Over the next few years, Washita County had 109 school districts, and no one lived farther than three miles from a school. Today the county has only five school districts, and the students are transported in school buses.

In 1900, the citizens of Washita County voted, by a vote of 1,349 to 283, to move the county seat from Cloud Chief, which was located in the southeast corner of the county, to Cordell, which was a new town located in the exact center of Washita County. The relocation of the county seat was illegal, as only Congress could establish a county seat in a territory. The moving of the county seat resulted in gunplay, one young attorney was tarred and feathered, and it also resulted in a murder. Washita County has had three courthouses, one courthouse at Cloud Chief and two at Cordell. The first courthouse built in Cordell in 1902 was destroyed by a mysterious fire in August 1909. The present courthouse was built in 1911. The architect for the present courthouse was Salomon Andrew Layton, who in 1914 was the architect for the Oklahoma State Capitol in Oklahoma City. Former Oklahoma governor George Nigh referred to the Washita County Courthouse as the grandfather of all county courthouses in Oklahoma.

Washita County is a rich agricultural county. During the 1920s and 1930s, for several years it was the top county in Oklahoma in cotton production. At one time Washita County had 47 cotton gins; today only two cotton gins are operating in the county. Wheat is the largest crop today. During the dust bowl days of the 1930s, cream and eggs kept most families from going hungry. In the 1930s, Cordell had 17 businesses where one could market their cream and eggs.

The Hughes Ranch was established in 1894 and by 1905 was a 20,000-acre spread located in southeast Washita County. The Washita River ran through the ranch, and it was a large producer of corn and livestock. The Hughes Ranch is not remembered as an agricultural ranch, but was well known as a hideout for outlaws. Many posses were shot at and some hit as they attempted an arrest at the ranch for outlaws such as Red Buck, Cole Younger, Ben Casey, Al Jennings, the Daltons, and others.

Many churches in Washita County were established in the 1890s. Most of them started in community schoolhouses. The oldest church in the county was established at Colony as the Dutch Reform Church of New York, in 1890.

Cordell, the present county seat, was established in May 1892, and the post office was established on October 12, 1892. The town was moved about one mile west in 1897 to a site of good water, and a railroad was to come through the new location, but not until 1902.

Washita County now has 44 ghost towns, which once had a post office or a community store. According to postal records, 42 post offices have been established in Washita County since March 1892, of those only 10 are open today.

Modern transportation has had its effect on the many small communities and schools that once were the center of the community. The dust bowl and the depression of the 1930s have impacted the county's population, going from 29,800 in 1930 to only 11,900 in 2000.

One

Establishing Washita County

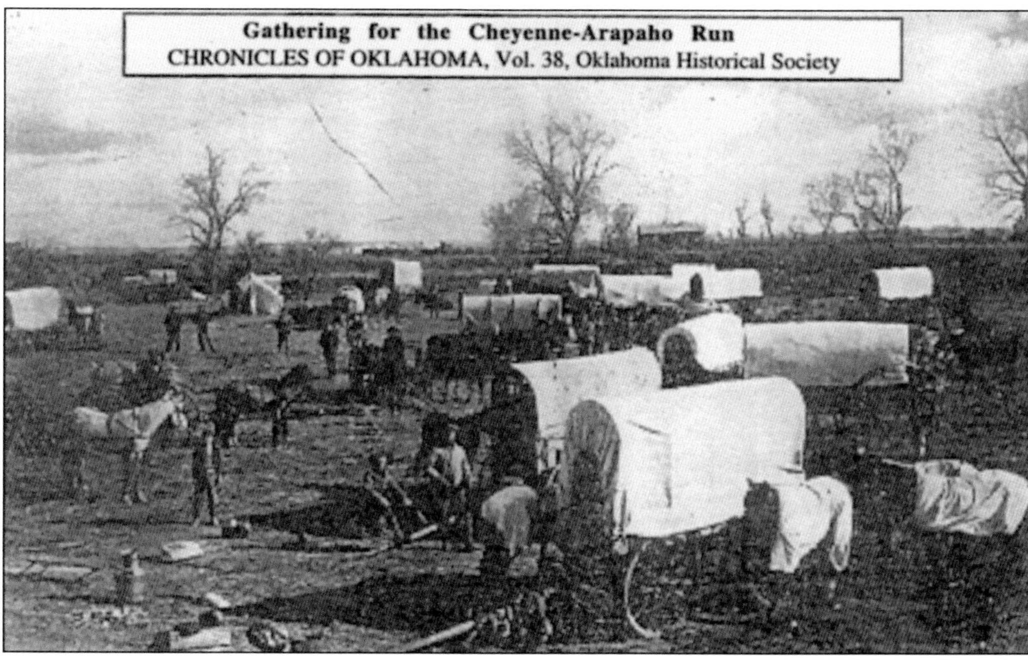

In the late afternoon on April 18, 1892, the homesteaders camped on Cobb Creek, east of Colony, waiting to make the run in order to file on a farm. John Seger, who was in charge of the entry point in northeastern Washita, let those making the run cross Cobb Creek to lessen the chance of an injury before he fired the shot to begin the run. Three additional entry points were a southeast area near Mountain View, south of Cloud Chief, and south of Rocky. Those making the run would replace the surveyor stake with their stake and go to Cloud Chief to register their homestead. (Courtesy Oklahoma Historical Society.)

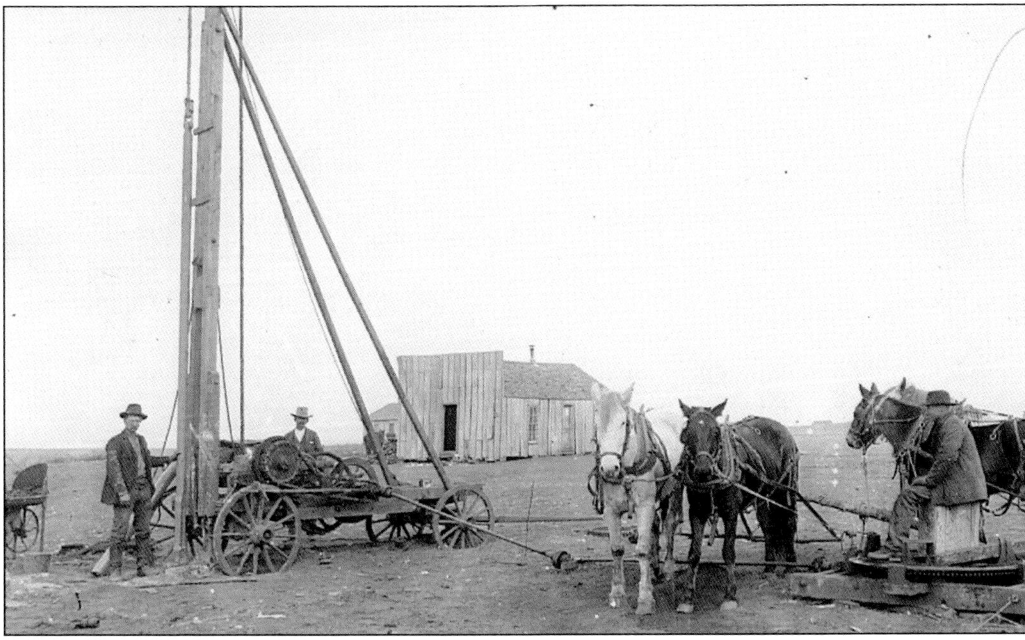

Drilling a water well with a horse-powered rig in front of the courthouse at Cloud Chief in 1893 are head driller Levi Shively, by the rig, and Andy Lewis, driver of the horses that power the drilling rig. An ample supply of water was found, but it was very high in gypsum and hardly drinkable. Most of the water in the Cloud Chief area was poor quality. (Courtesy Washita County Museum.)

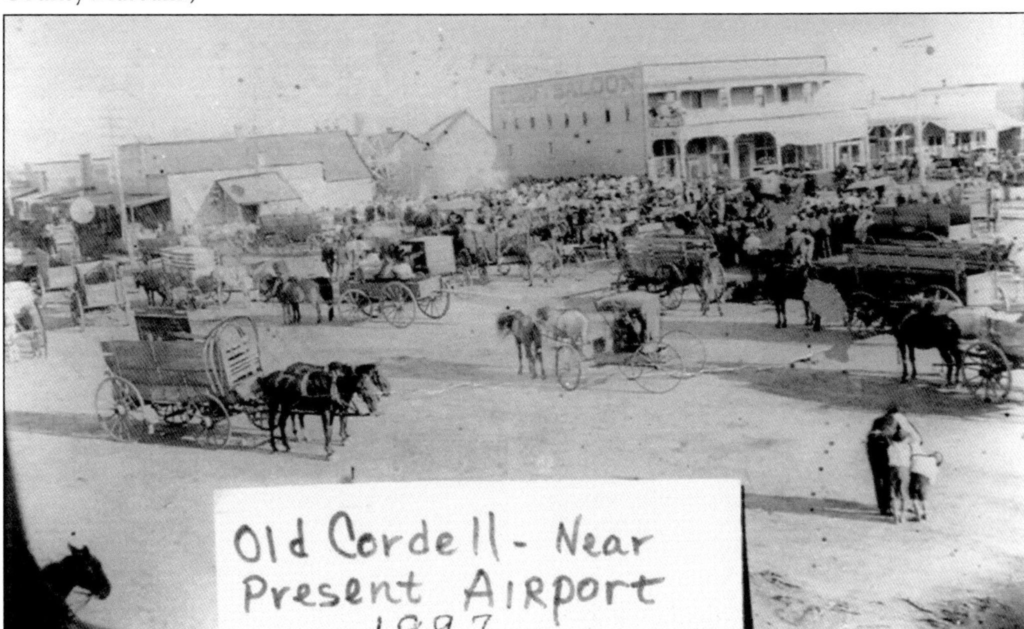

The old Cordell post office was established on October 12, 1892. At the time of this 1897 picture, the population was about 250. However, the town was moved about a mile east to New Cordell in the fall of 1897, when H. D. Young moved his store and post office. (Courtesy Washita County Museum.)

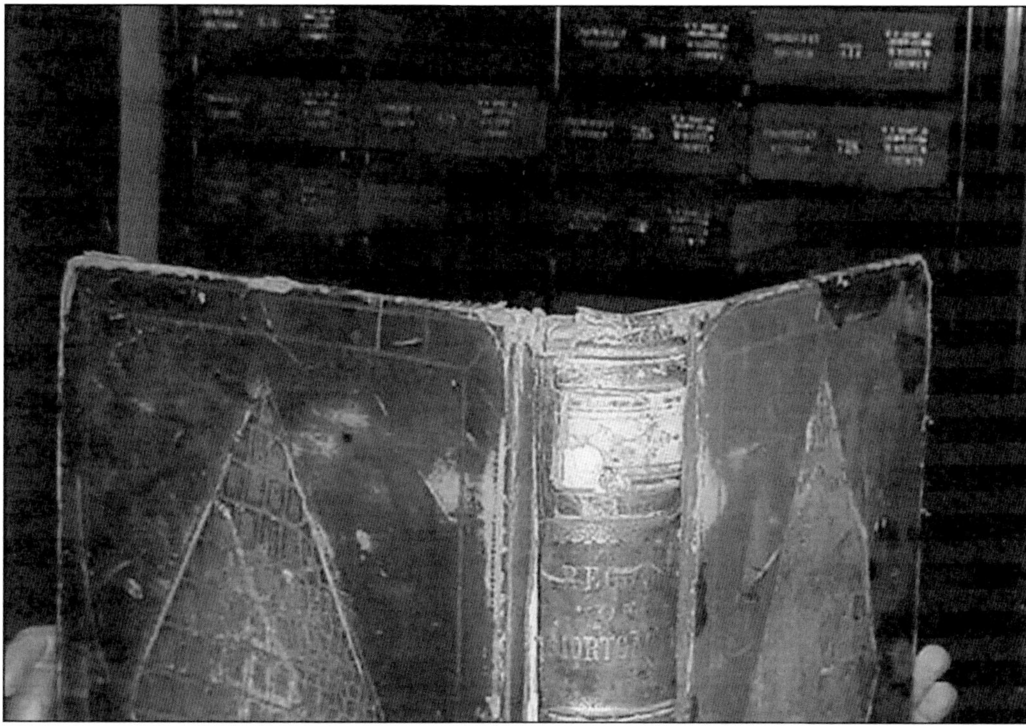

When the records from the courthouse at Cloud Chief were moved to Cordell in August 1900 by county clerk G. E. Wagoner and commissioner Tom Brown, they tried to slip out of Cloud Chief at about 2:30 a.m. without being noticed; however, they were followed, and a gunfight began. The county mortgage book received a bullet hole during the 10-mile race. (Courtesy Washita County clerk.)

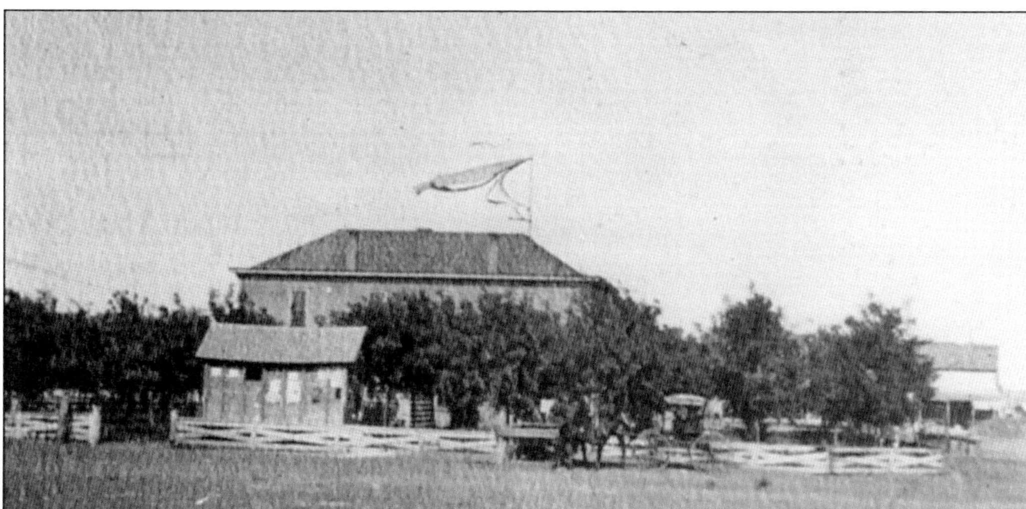

The courthouse at Cordell was built in 1902. It was a two-story, eight-room building and a big improvement over the old one-room Cloud Chief courthouse. On Friday night, August 3, 1909, a mysterious fire started in the courtroom and destroyed the building. Arson was suspected but never proven. (Courtesy Washita County Museum.)

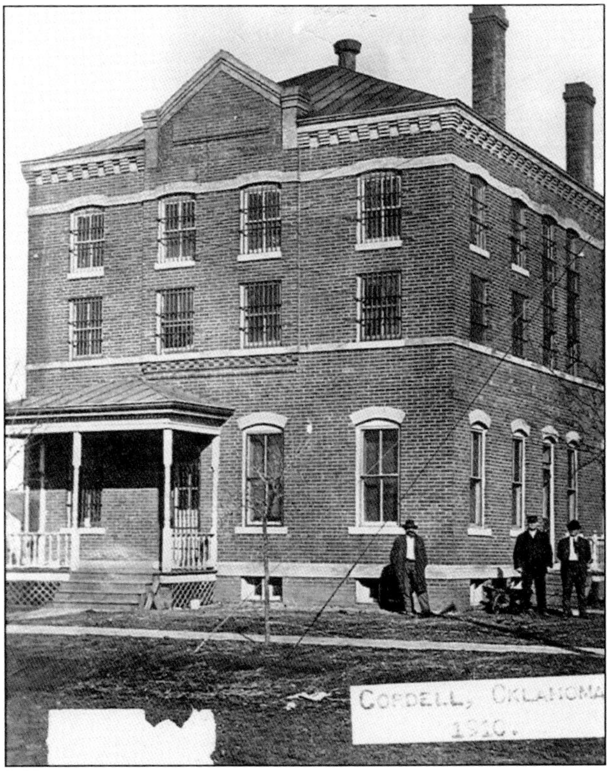

Washita County Jail was built in 1907 at a cost of $20,000. The three-story jail had a hanging gallows inside the top left-hand window. The gallows was taken out in 1936, and the jail was replaced in 1940 as a WPA project. (Courtesy Washita County Museum.)

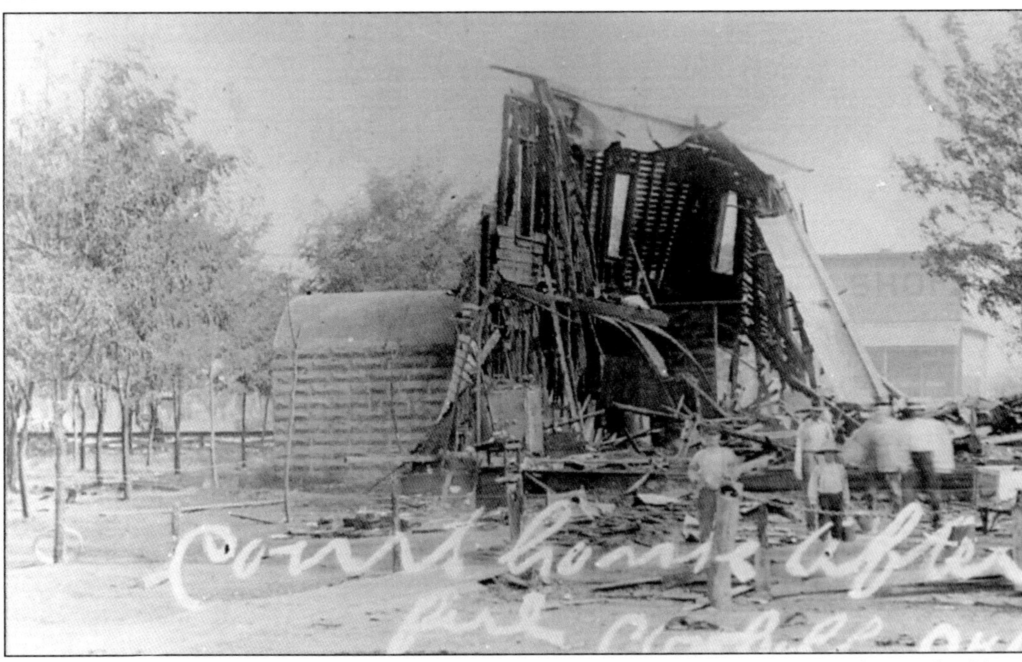

This is what was left of the courthouse after the August 3, 1909, fire. A term of court had been scheduled for Monday, August 6. On the docket were 44 illegal whiskey cases, seven cattle theft cases, and six horse theft cases. After the fire, court was postponed until November when it was held in the meeting room of the New Iron Hotel. (Courtesy Washita County Museum.)

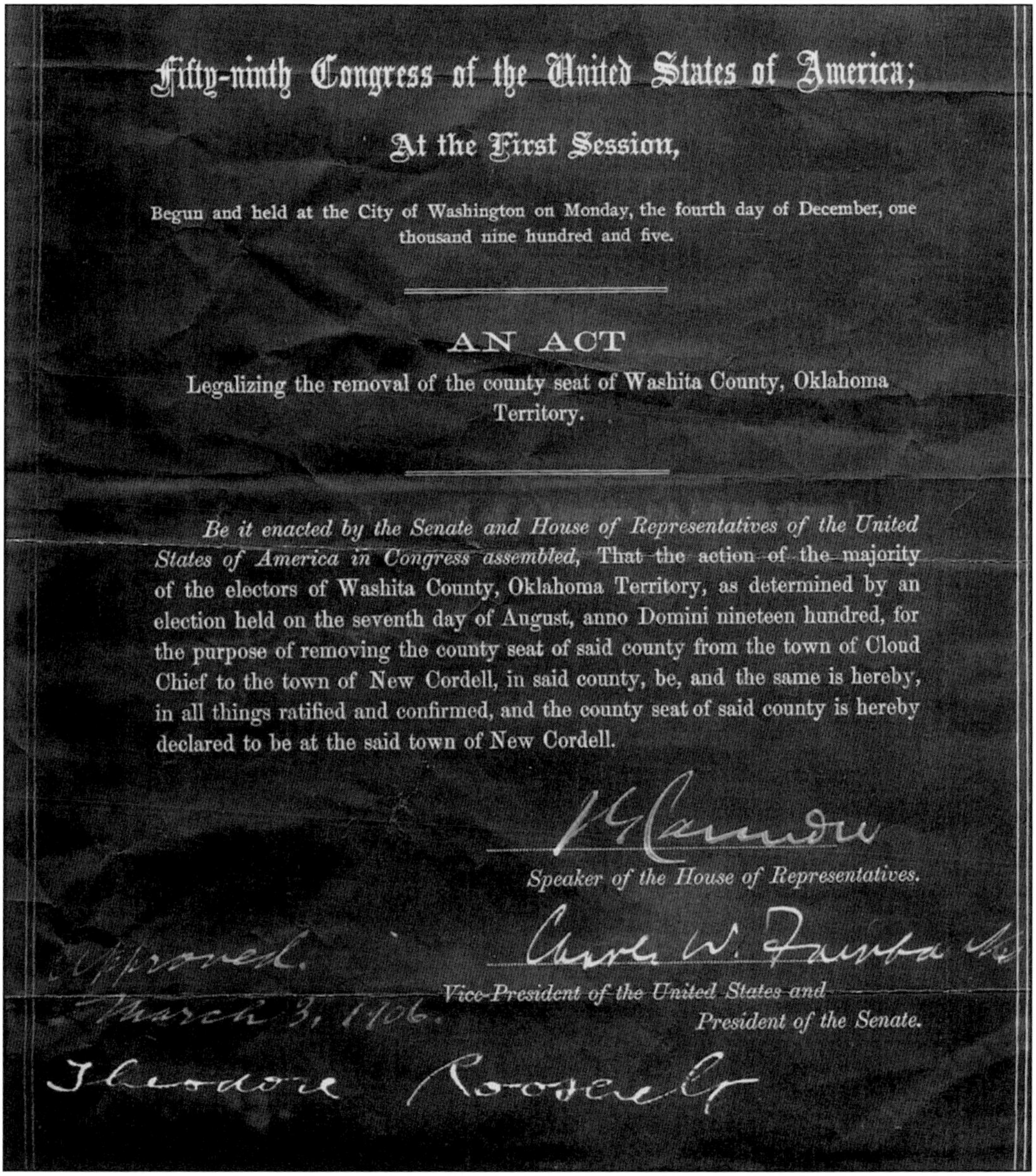

Fifty-ninth Congress of the United States of America;

At the First Session,

Begun and held at the City of Washington on Monday, the fourth day of December, one thousand nine hundred and five.

AN ACT

Legalizing the removal of the county seat of Washita County, Oklahoma Territory.

Be it enacted by the Senate and House of Representatives of the United States of America in Congress assembled, That the action of the majority of the electors of Washita County, Oklahoma Territory, as determined by an election held on the seventh day of August, anno Domini nineteen hundred, for the purpose of removing the county seat of said county from the town of Cloud Chief to the town of New Cordell, in said county, be, and the same is hereby, in all things ratified and confirmed, and the county seat of said county is hereby declared to be at the said town of New Cordell.

Speaker of the House of Representatives.

Vice-President of the United States and President of the Senate.

Approved. March 3, 1906.

Theodore Roosevelt

Shown here is a copy of the bill in congress signed by Theodore Roosevelt in March 1906 that officially made Cordell the county seat of Washita County. Oklahoma Territory Court ruled the courthouse was illegally moved to Cordell and gave six months time to return it to Cloud Chief. Sam Massingale, a Cordell attorney, went to the territory capital at Guthrie to ask for extra time and received a year's stay. Massingale went on to Washington, D.C., and was able to get the bill passed, making Cordell the official county seat. (Courtesy Washita County Museum.)

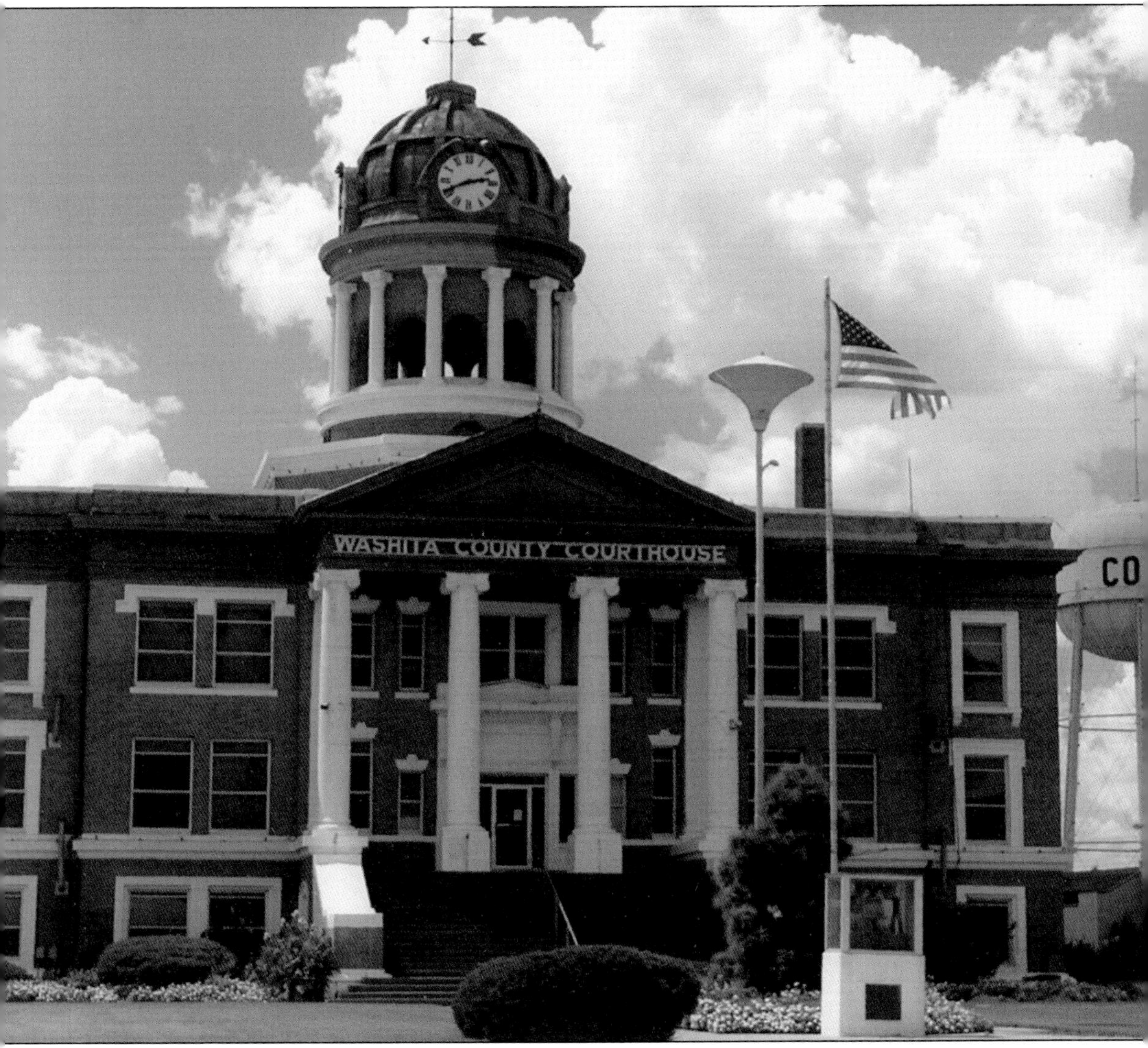

After the fire of August 3, 1909, destroyed the Washita County courthouse, the county commissioners let a $75,000 contract to build a new modern courthouse, and the architecture was a young Salomon Andrew Layton, who was the architect for the new Oklahoma State Capitol, built in Oklahoma City in 1914. For many years the Washita County courthouse was the only county courthouse of the 77 counties in the state that had a clock in its dome that kept time and would strike on the hour. The bell that does the striking came from the Valley View school, which was established in 1892 and consolidated with Cowden in 1911. (Courtesy Washita County Museum.)

Two

EDUCATION AND SCHOOLS

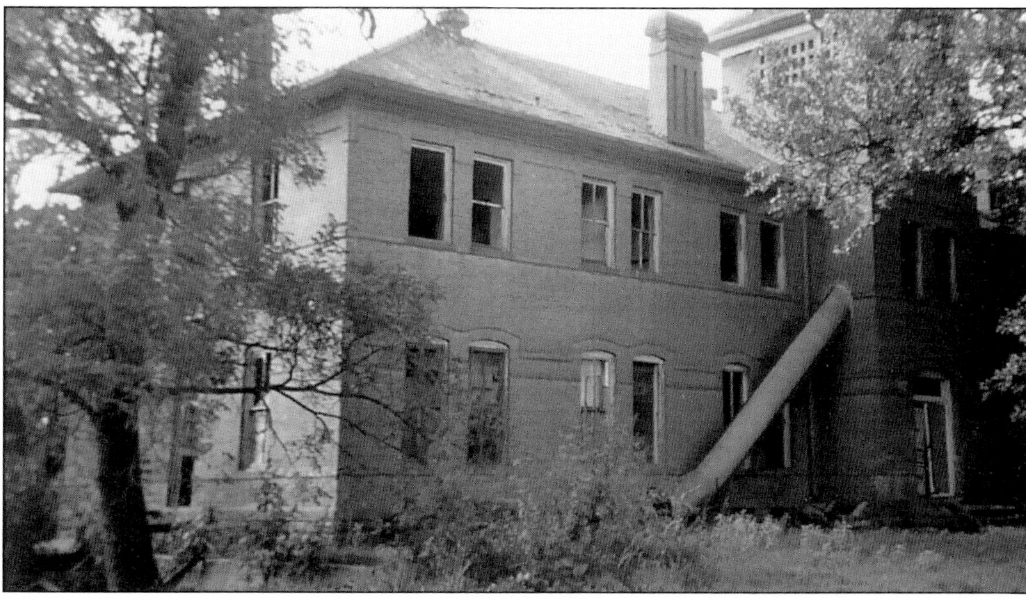

John Seger established the Native American school in 1890, teaching the Native Americans to make bricks. They made all the bricks and constructed the buildings for the school. Seger established the first vo-tech school in Oklahoma, teaching his Indian Colony brick making, construction, and farming. The first wheat produced in Oklahoma Territory was at Colony by Seger and his Native American students. The Seger colony established a livestock operation also and constructed a water tower and water system in 1893. For many years, the Colony School District used the old Native American school building as its school system. The base of the water tower is still standing, 114 years later. The Seger Native American school site is a large beautiful park area today, and each August a weeklong Cheyenne Indian reunion is held there.

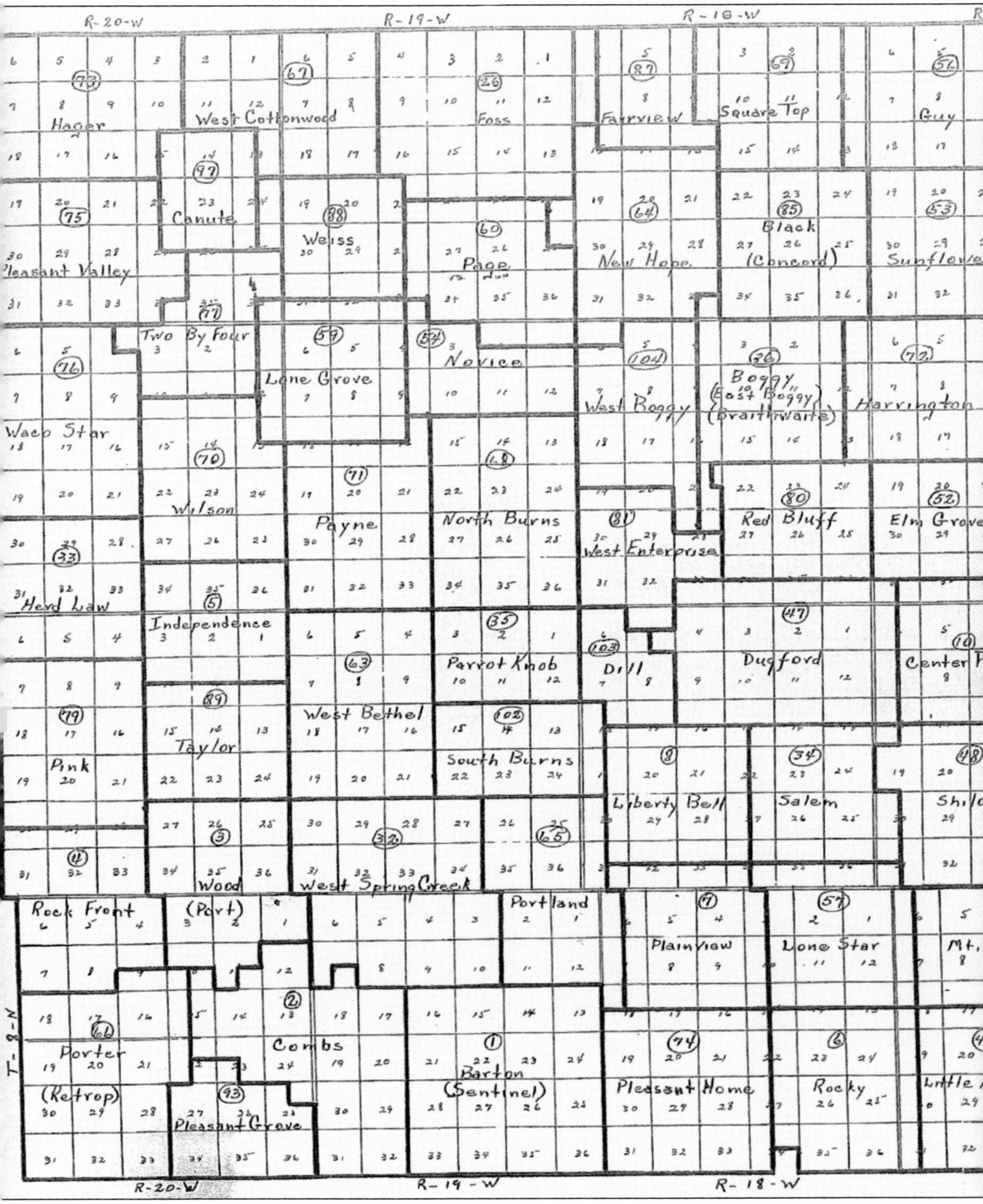

On this map, the 109 Washita County school districts are numbered in the order of their establishment. In the fall of 1892, thirty-one dependent schools were organized. Most of them were housed in dugouts. Barton, which later became Sentinel, was the first district to be

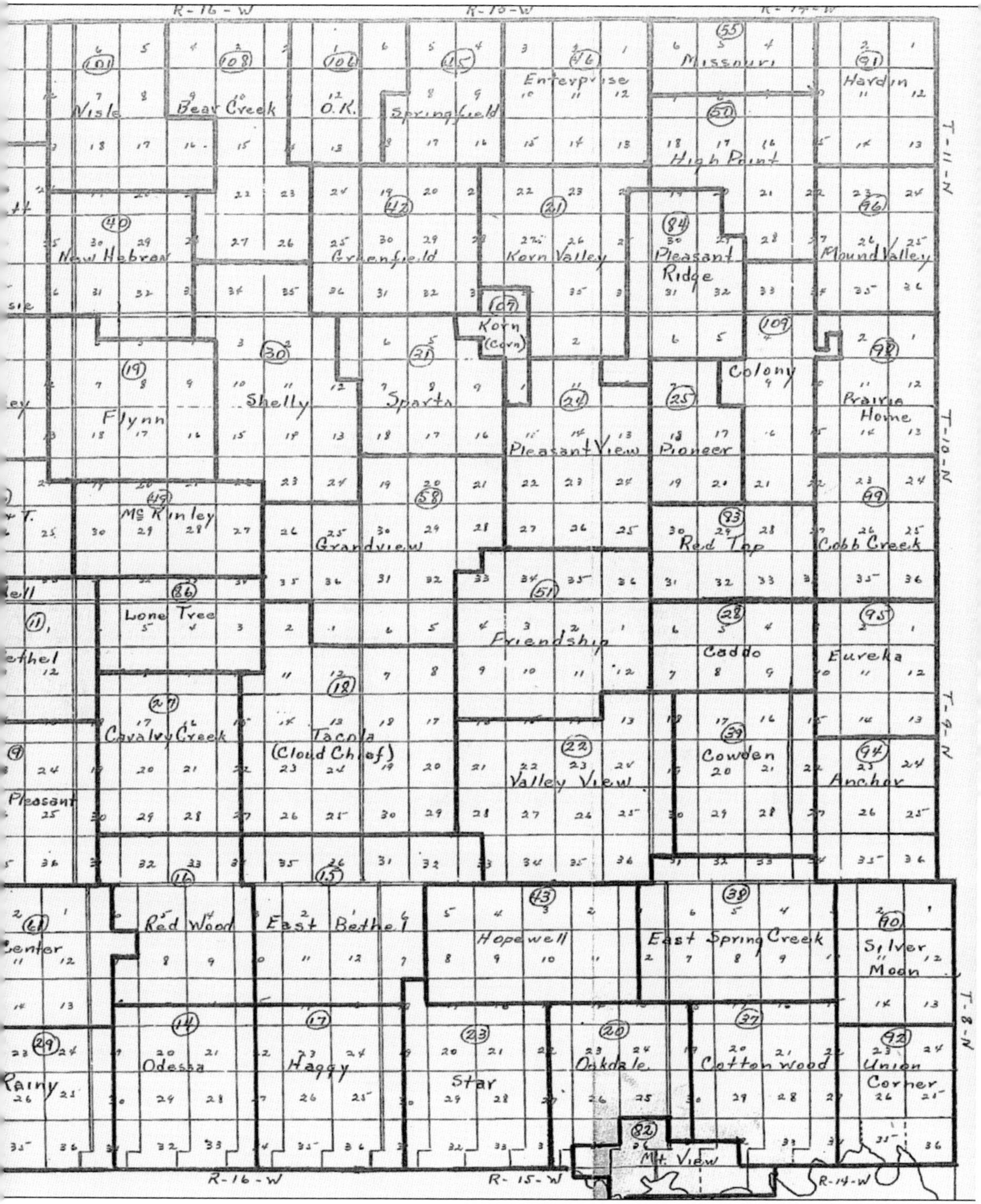

established. By the school term of 1894, another 20 schools were added. Only eight grades were offered. The teacher salary was \$75 to \$100 per school year. In the fall of 1902, Cordell was the first school to offer high school classes. (Courtesy Washita County Museum.)

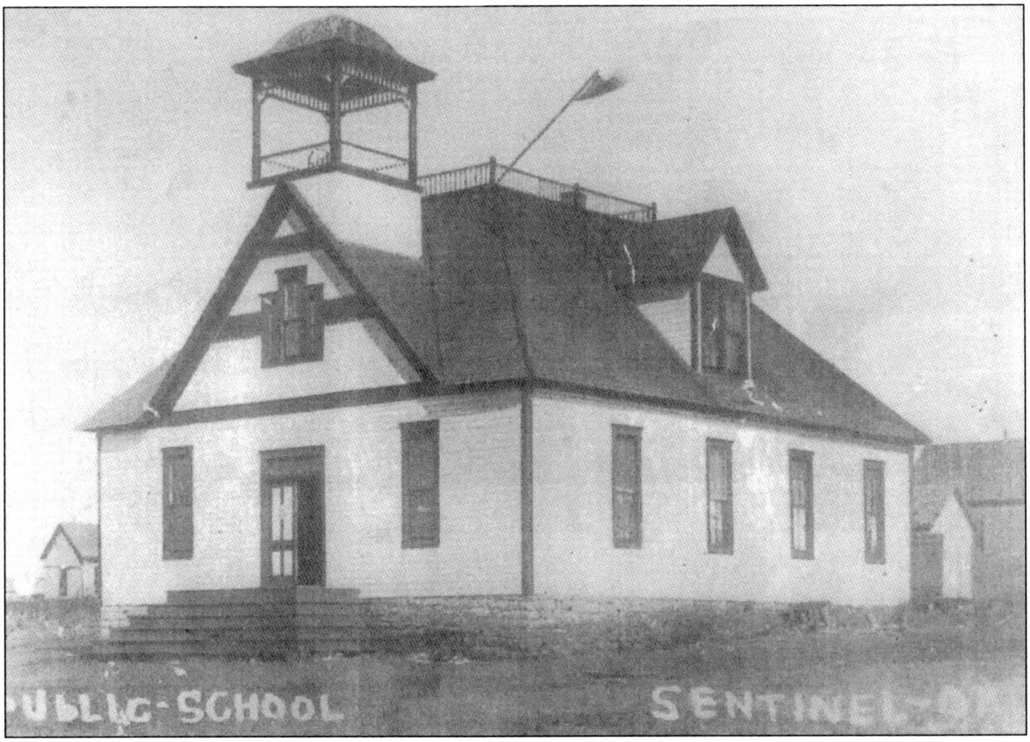

Sentinel school, the first school established in Washita County, was held in dugouts until a one-room building was constructed in 1897. This three-room building was constructed in Sentinel in 1903. The teachers were Professor Blassingame, Maggie Shotwell, and Pearl Smith in 1903. (Courtesy Washita County Museum.)

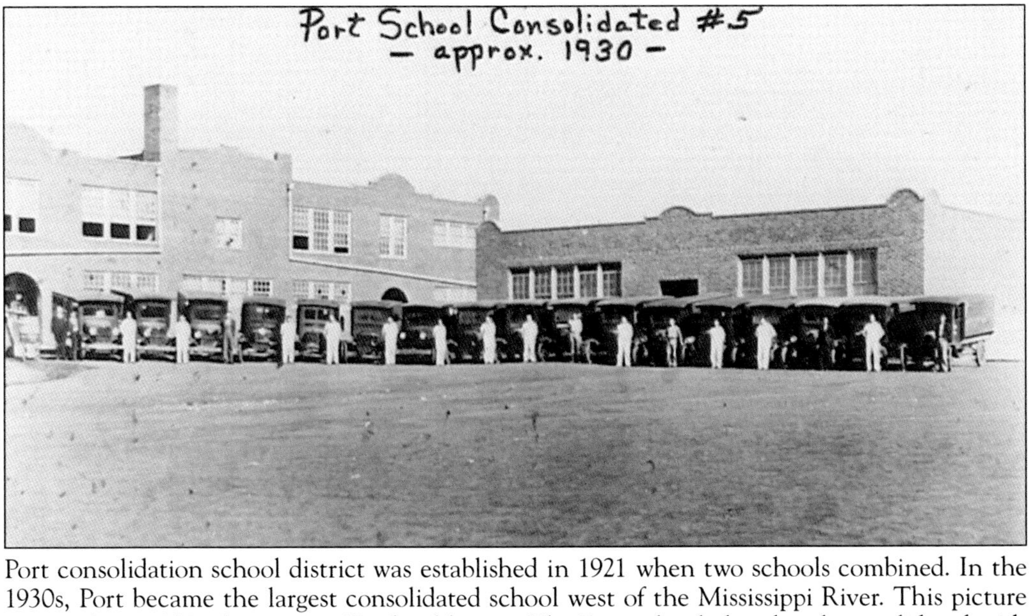

Port consolidation school district was established in 1921 when two schools combined. In the 1930s, Port became the largest consolidated school west of the Mississippi River. This picture was made in 1930 when it ran 17 school busses. The Port school closed and consolidated with Sentinel in May 1966. (Courtesy Washita County Museum.)

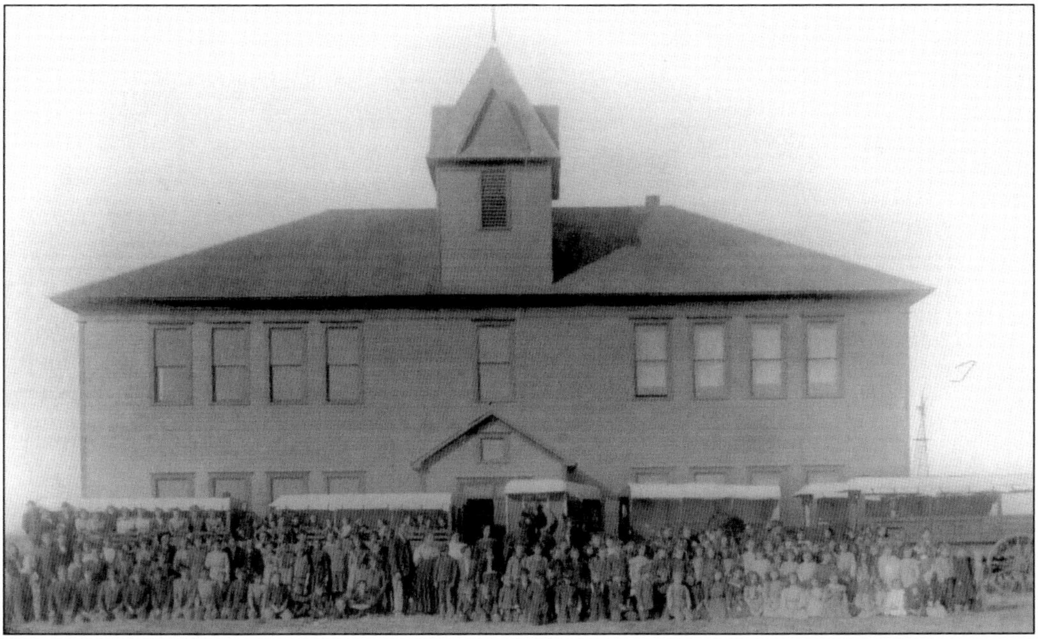

Lake Valley consolidated school was established in 1911 when four schools joined together to form the Lake Valley School District, which was one of the first four schools to consolidate in Oklahoma. This picture in 1916 shows the four horse-drawn wagons to haul students to school, they were called "hooligan wagons." The Lake Valley school closed about 50 years ago. (Courtesy B. E. Bryant.)

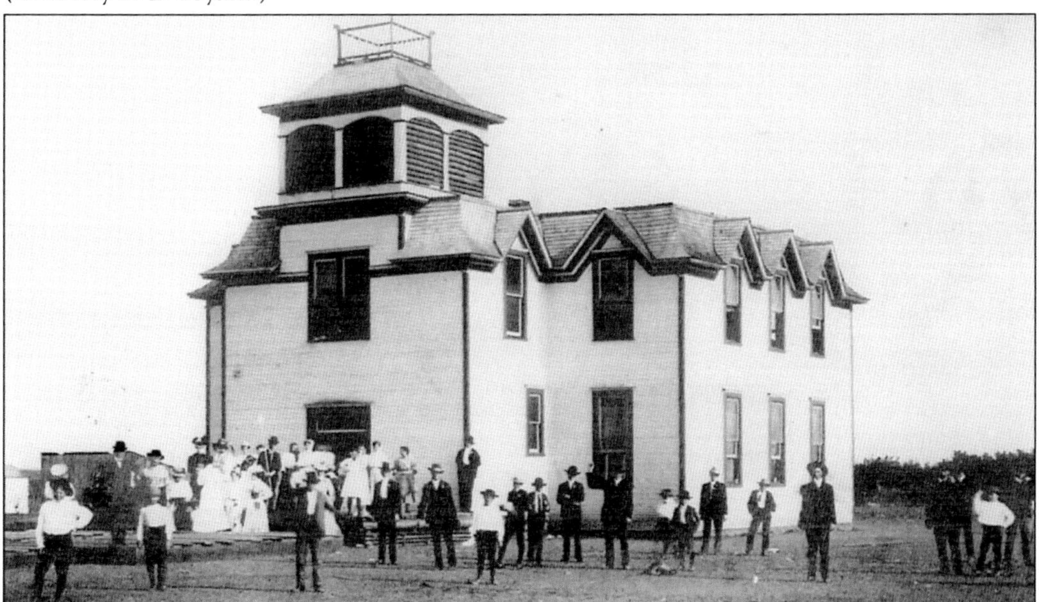

Rocky was the sixth school organized in Washita County in 1892. It was started in a dugout and was known as Orange Blossom school. The large two-story Rocky school building was constructed in 1904. The school continued to grow, and in the late 1930s, a completely new system was built. In 1967, the Rocky school consolidated with Sentinel. (Courtesy Washita County Museum.)

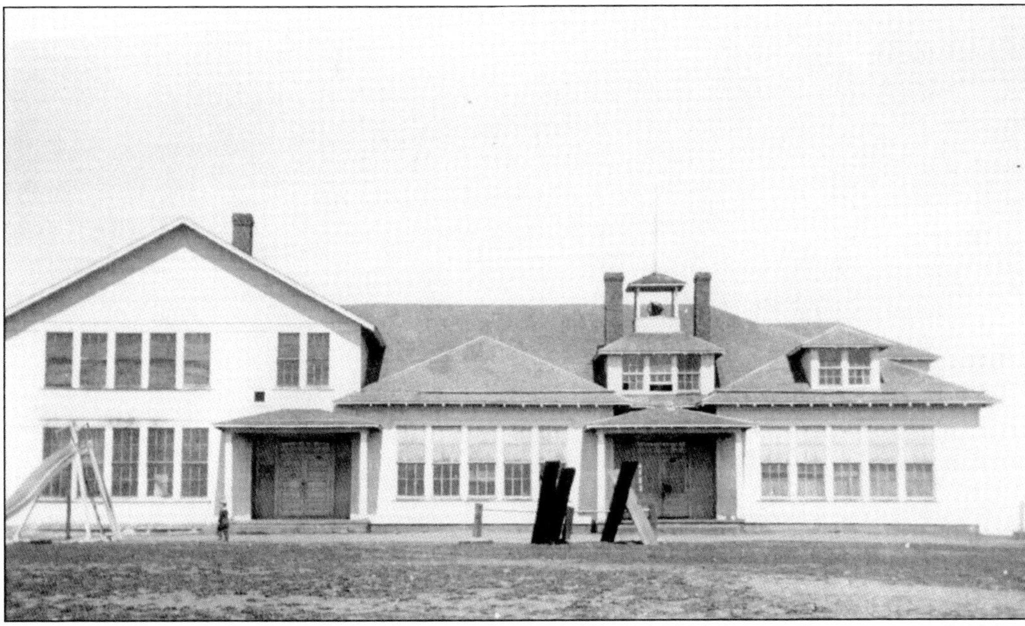

Cloud Chief school was organized in 1892 and started in a half dugout. The two-story building built in 1918 served the district until 1938, when a new set of buildings was constructed and served the district until it closed and annexed to Cordell in 1958. (Courtesy Doyle Fenn.)

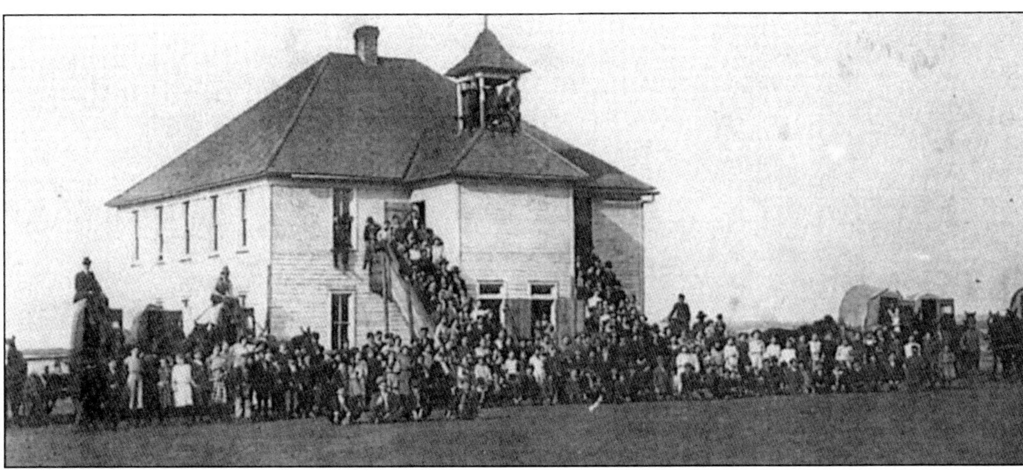

Cowden School District was organized in 1913 when three schools consolidated to form Cowden school. They used horse and wagons for transportation of the students. The school closed in the early 1950s. The school site is where the community center is located today. (Courtesy Washita County Museum.)

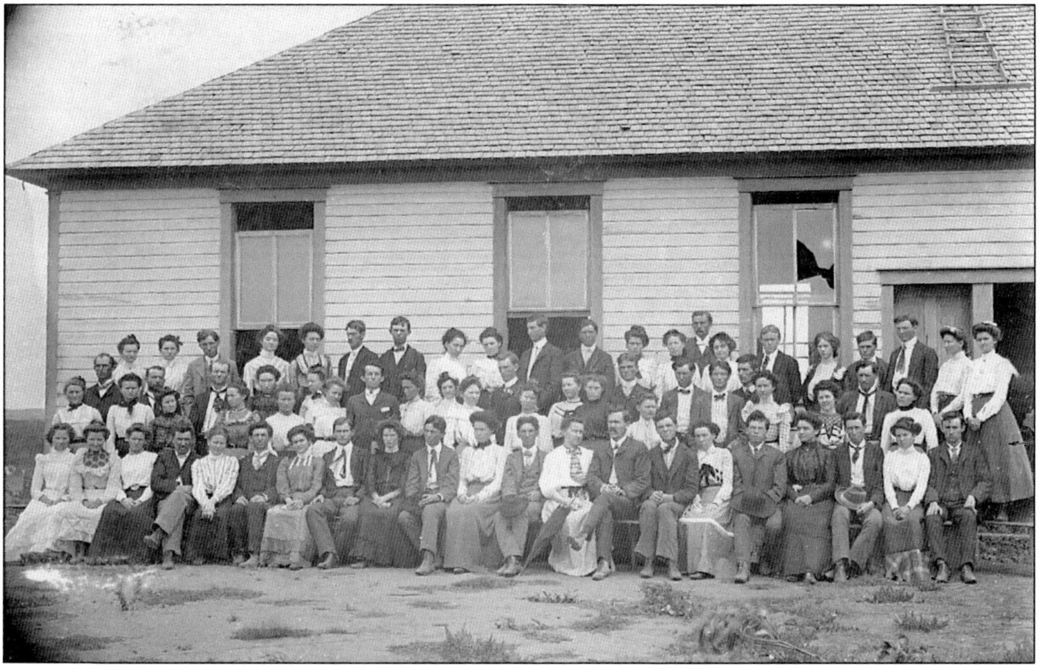

Center school was not formed until 1898, at which time the present building was constructed. The Center school building served as a meeting place for four different church denominations. This picture is of a 1905 county singing school. The school closed in 1949 and consolidated with Rocky school. (Courtesy Fred Greer.)

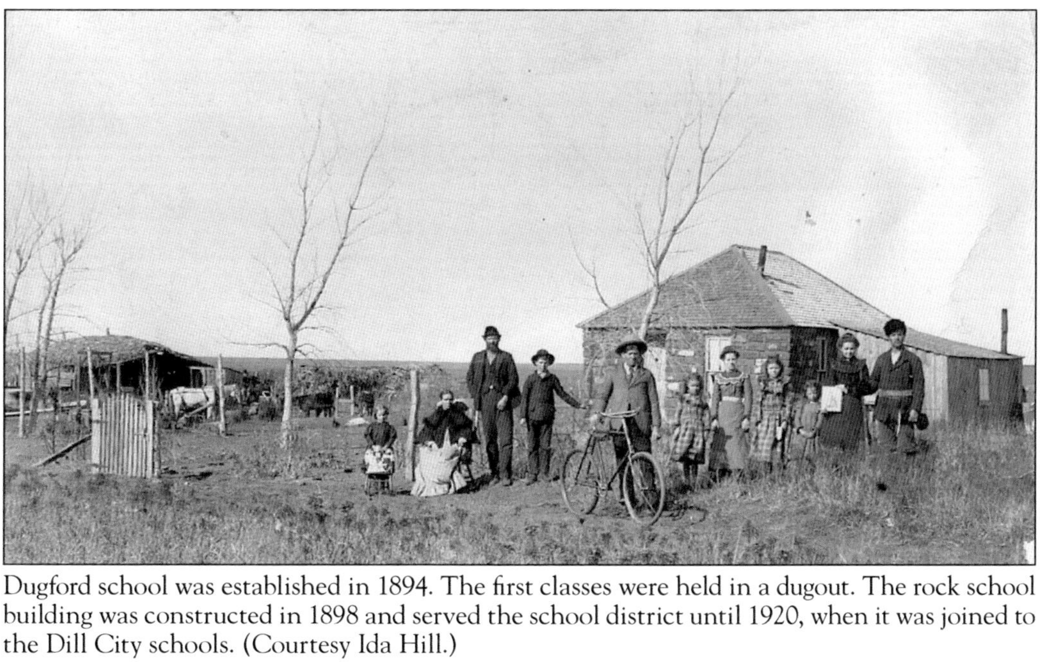

Dugford school was established in 1894. The first classes were held in a dugout. The rock school building was constructed in 1898 and served the school district until 1920, when it was joined to the Dill City schools. (Courtesy Ida Hill.)

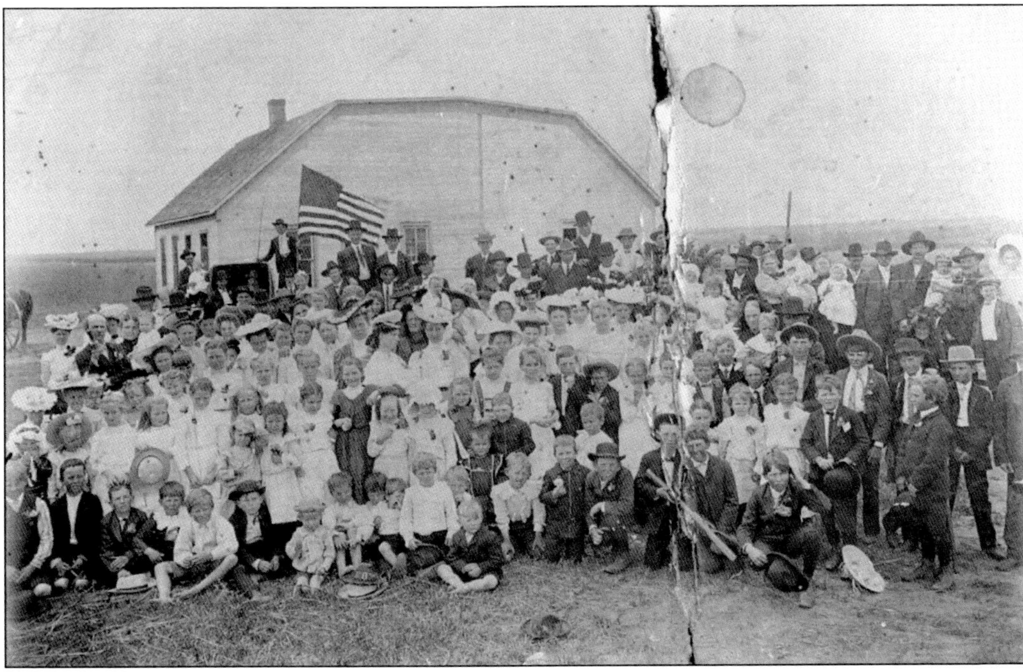

North Burns school was established in 1898. The two-room school building was constructed in 1902. This photograph is an all-school picnic, students and parents, held on July 18, 1903. The North Burns school joined the Burns Flat School District in 1929. (Courtesy Washita County Museum.)

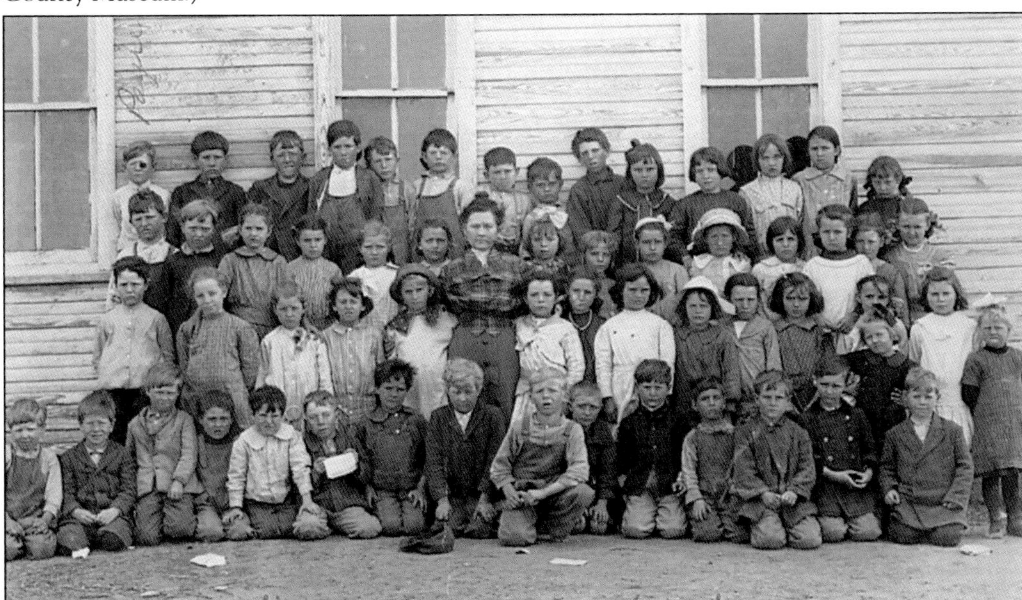

Valley View school was established in 1892 and located in the southeast area of Washita County. Valley View school was at the center of an active community. Three different churches held regular services at the schoolhouse. The bell from the bell tower of the school is today used as the striker for the clock in the county courthouse. Valley View school joined Cowden School District in 1911. (Courtesy Margie Sappington.)

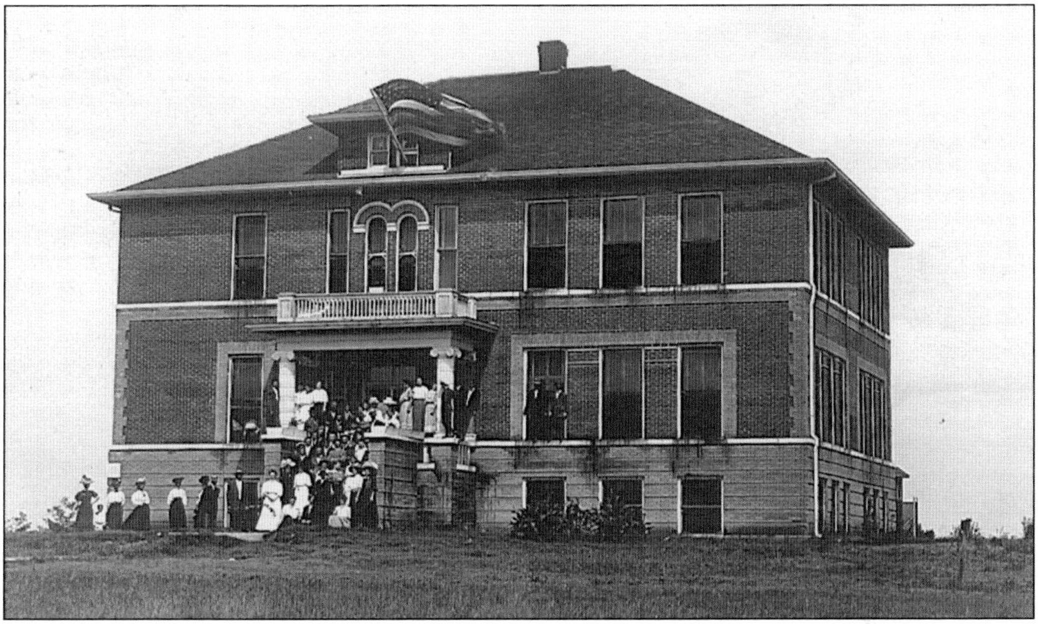

Cordell Academy was to be a high school and junior college. Built by the Dutch Reform Church of New York in Cordell in 1906, the academy held classes until 1911, when it closed. It was purchased by the Cordell School District at a sale in 1914. From 1907 until 1911, a student could receive a high school diploma from Cordell High School, Cordell Academy, or Cordell Christian College. (Courtesy Henry Berry Estate.)

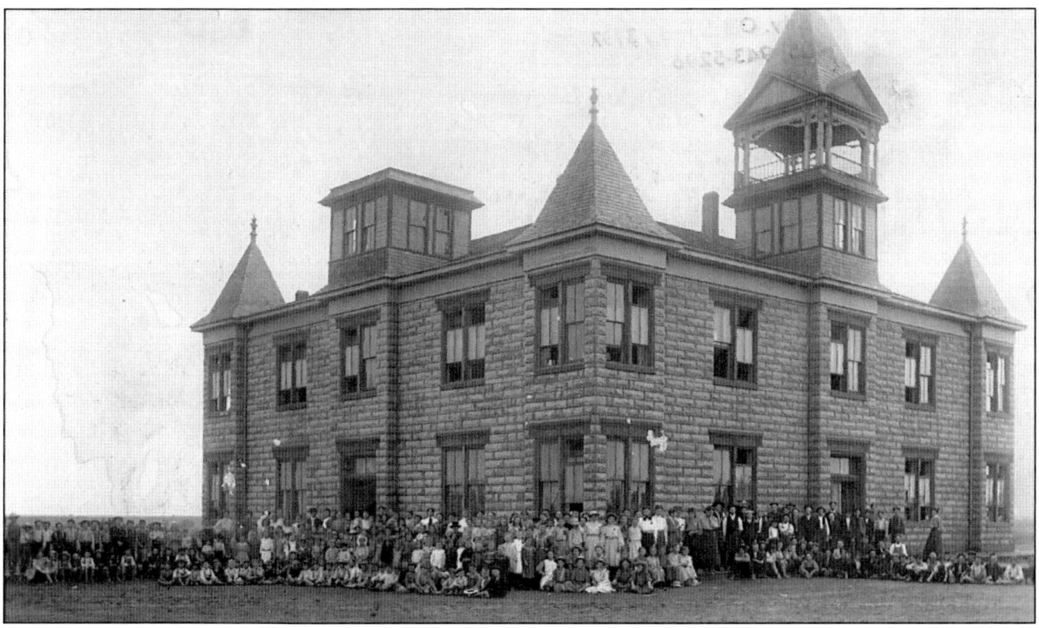

The Cordell school building was built in 1902 in the south part of Cordell. This building served as the only public school building in Cordell until 1908, when a new Lincoln school building was constructed in the north part of town to be used as a junior high and high school. The old 1902 building was built out of homemade blocks, which were inferior, and the building had to be replaced in 1909. (Courtesy Skeet Brayfield.)

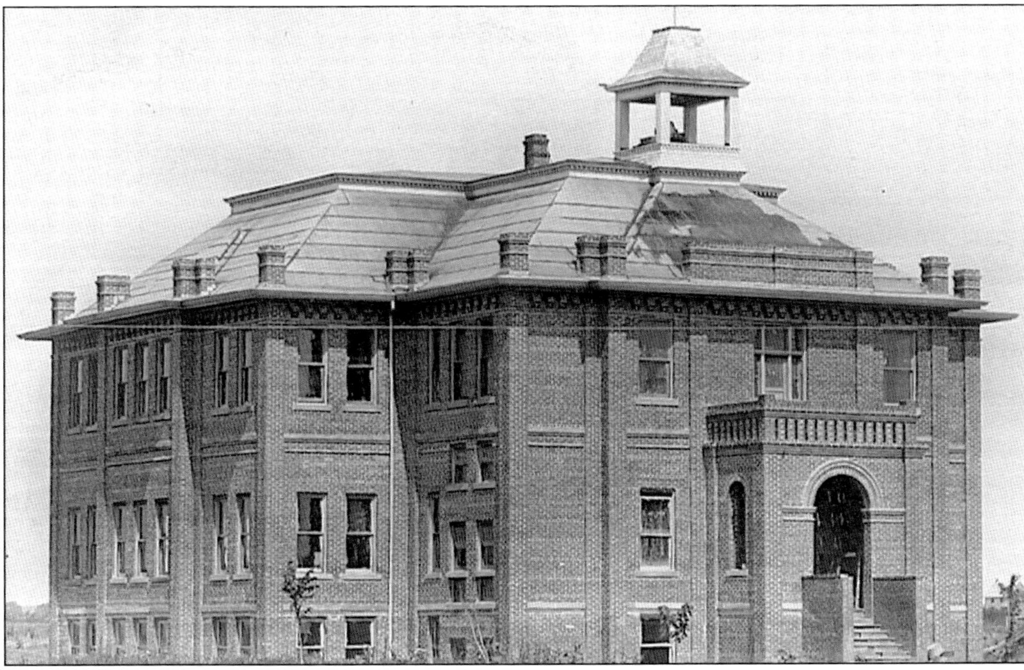

Cordell Christian College was established in 1907, as a Christian grade school, high school, and junior college. In 1918, the school was changed to a college only and named Western Oklahoma Christian College. When the Depression hit in 1931, the college was closed. The Cordell college was the forerunner of the Oklahoma Christian College at Edmond. Its bell is in the bell tower of the Edmond college with a large plaque telling of its start at Cordell. (Courtesy Henry Berry Estate.)

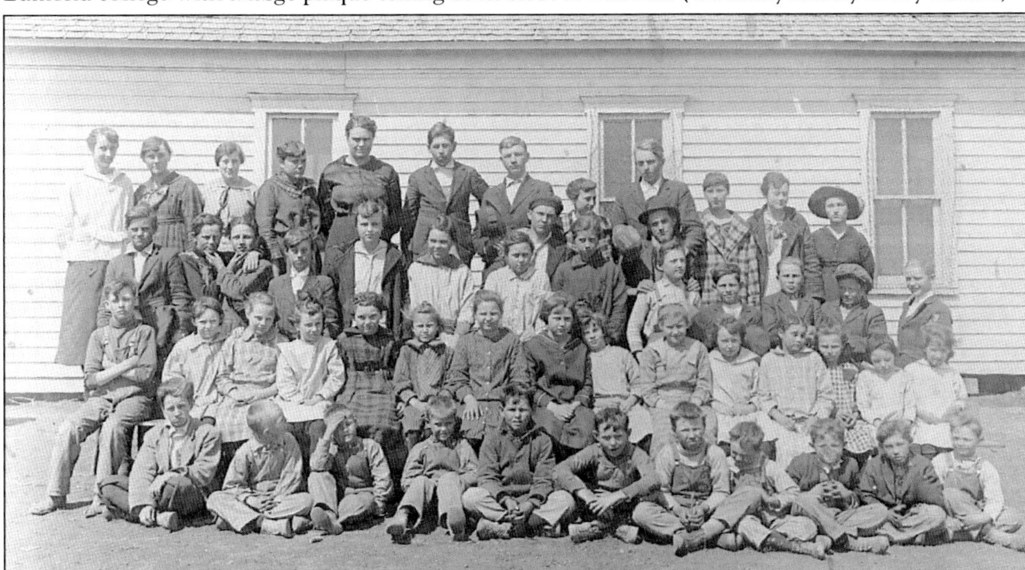

Mount Pleasant school, located six miles southeast of Cordell, was organized in 1892. The Mount Pleasant school was a large two-room school, and in 1949, the district was annexed to the Rocky School District. The school building was moved to Cloud Chief to replace the Methodist church building that was destroyed by fire and is still used as the Cloud Chief Methodist Church today. (Courtesy Tom Crider.)

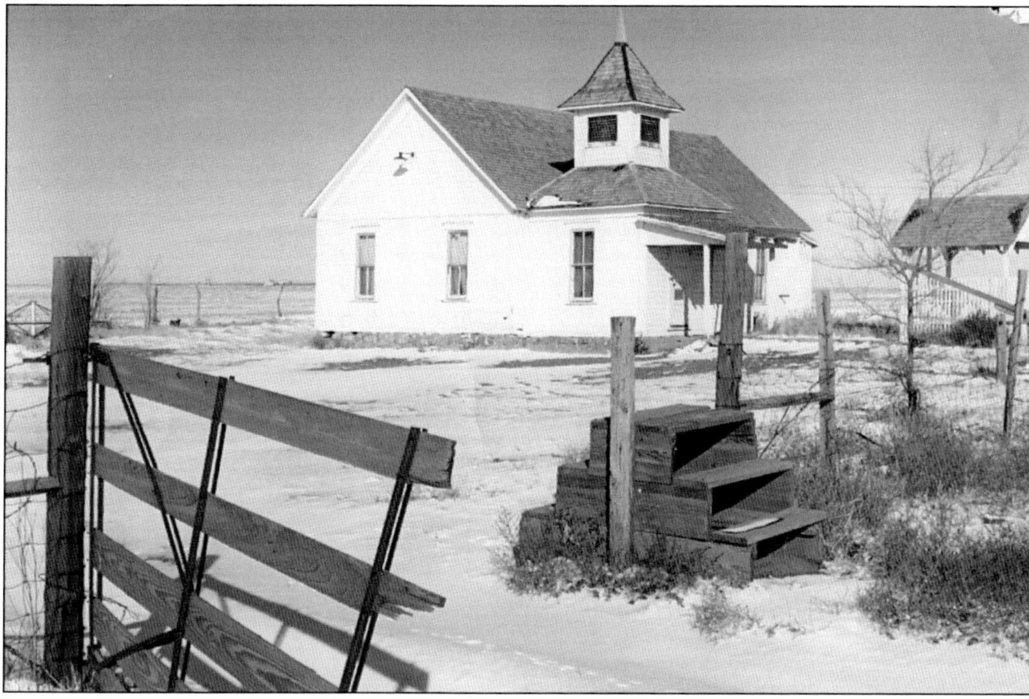

Center Point school was established in 1892 and operated as a dependent school until 1947, when it joined the Cordell schools. The Cordell Church of Christ was organized in 1893 at the Center Point school building. It was located two miles southwest of Cordell. (Courtesy Washita County Museum.)

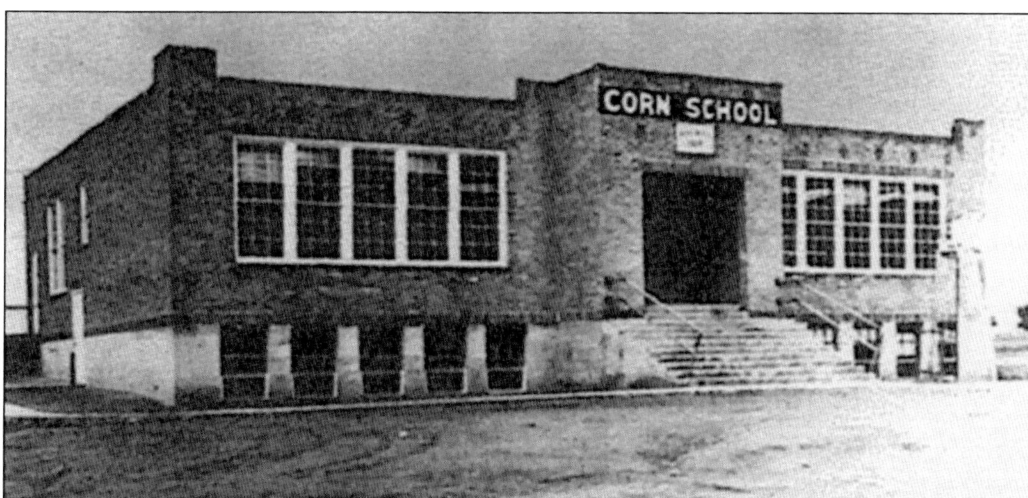

Korn School District was not organized until 1911. Korn Valley school was established in 1892, located a couple miles north of present-day Corn. Korn changed its spelling from Korn to Corn in 1918. This picture is of Corn grade school. In 1929, the upper grades were added, and in 1933, Corn graduated its first senior class. Today the school is known as Washita Heights since Corn and Colony joined their schools. (Courtesy Washita County Museum.)

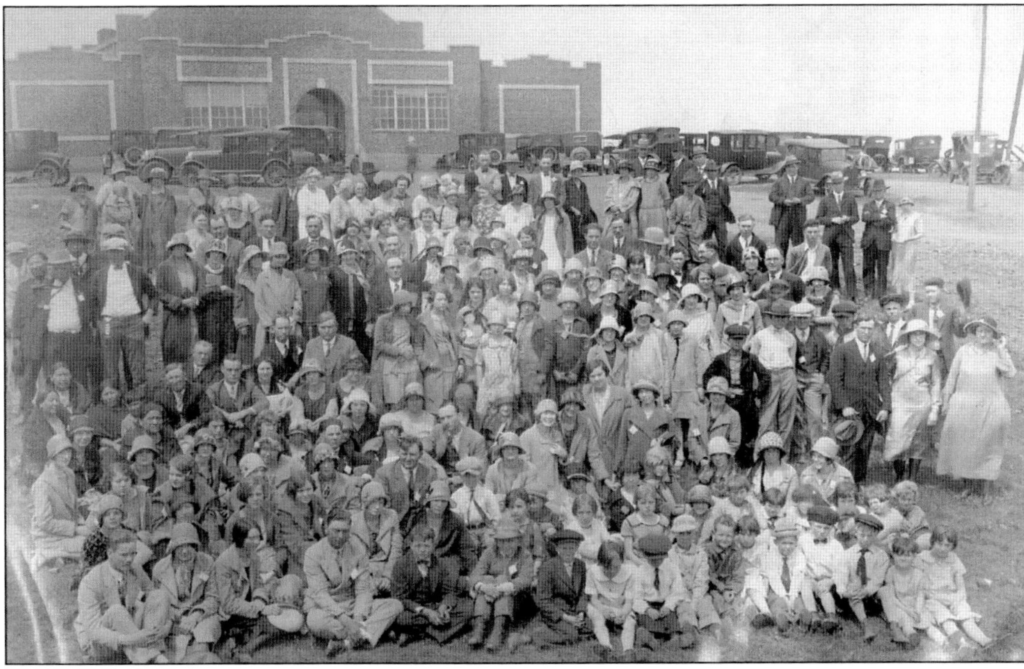

Foss school was organized in 1892. The first school was in Turkey Creek bottom, and a flash flood in 1902 on Turkey Creek washed the school and most of the town away, including the railroad, and drowned several people. The school building was rebuilt on a hill north of town. This picture was taken in 1924 in front of their last school building. The Foss school closed in 1957, annexed to Canute and Burns Flat. (Courtesy Rod Redwine.)

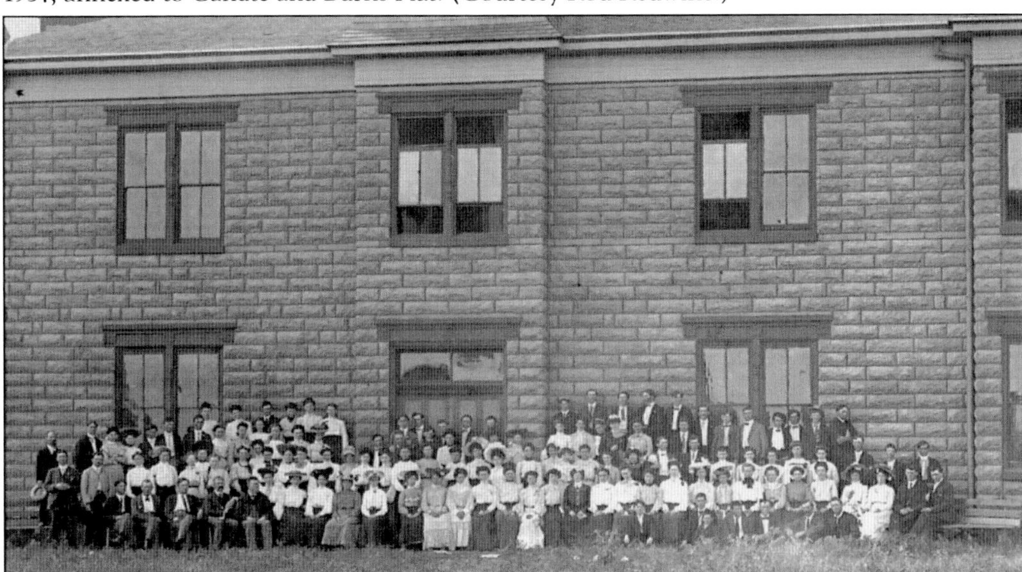

This is Cordell Normal School in 1902. With six weeks training, an eighth-grade graduate could receive a teaching certificate to teach in eight-grade schools. Cordell Normal was held each summer for several years at the Cordell school building that was constructed in 1902. The building was constructed with homemade blocks and had to be replaced in 1909. (Courtesy Fred Greer.)

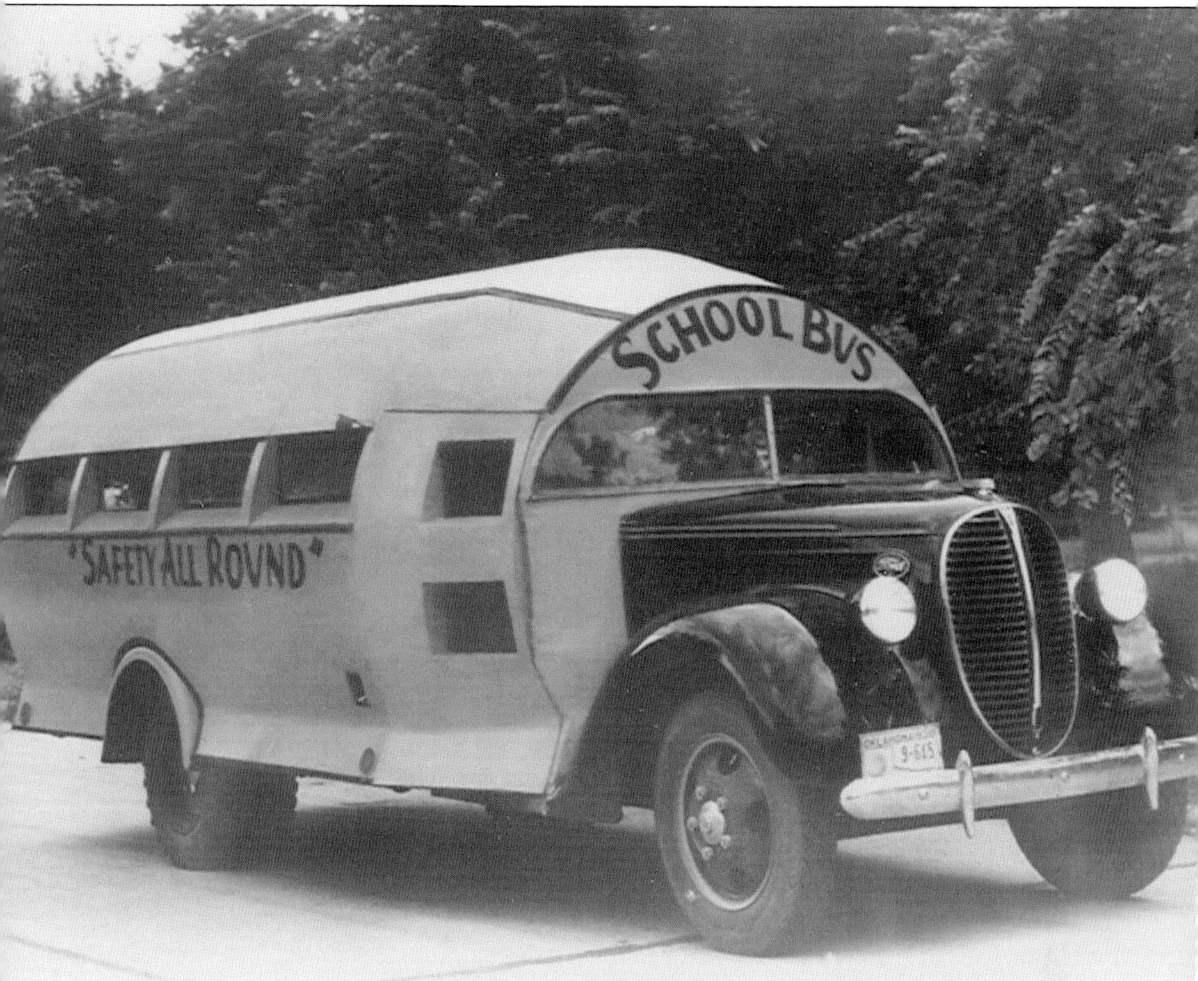

Ferris Safety School Bus had its beginning in 1934. Kirk Farris, who was in charge of transportation for the Port School District, invented and built a school bus that if turned over would roll back on its wheels. During the next 10 to 12 years, all of the busses used by Port school, as well as several other schools, were this new safety design school bus. In 1939, the Port school, 24 seniors with 12 sponsors, took two of the round Port school buses on a 4,000-mile trip to Washington, D.C., and the New York World's Fair, as well as Niagara Falls and Canada. The round buses created a lot of interest. This was during the Depression, and the Port seniors created much envy from the rest of seniors in Washita County. This was when the Port school was in its prime. (Courtesy Washita County Historical Society.)

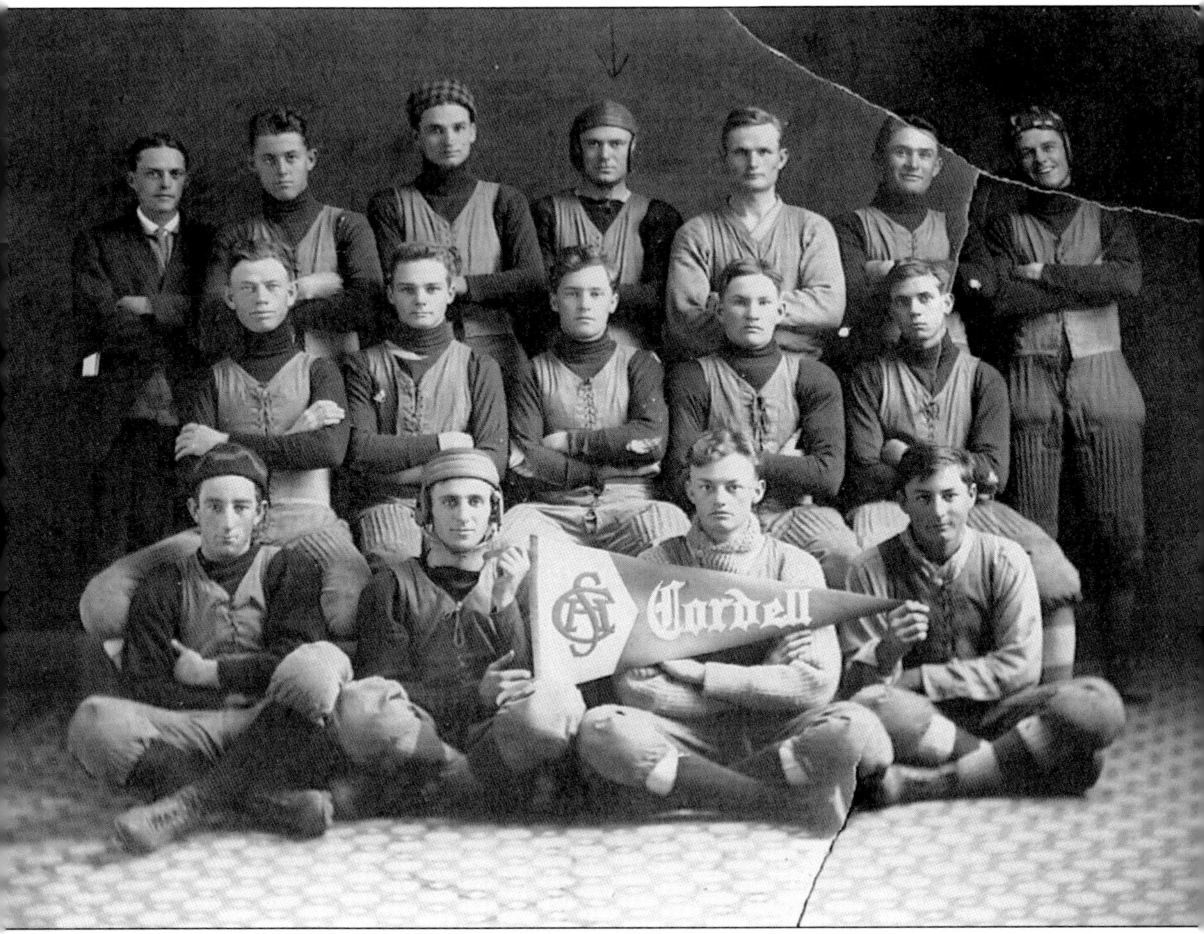

This is the 1914 Cordell High School undefeated football team. Seen here from left to right are (first row) Leon Molen, Herman Lorenz, Shelby Wheeler, and Joe Ames; (second row) Kieth Wooten, John Stone, Virgil Bretton, Frank Ames, and John Brett; (third row) Mr. Fleming (coach), Oran Craven, Stanley Lutz, Joe Taylor, Mervil Miller, Bill Ames, and Major Tarr. The Cordell team played eight games in 1914, scoring a total of 308 points to only 48 points for their opponents. Only two other teams in Oklahoma were undefeated, Oklahoma Central and Muskogee. Oklahoma athletic association denied Cordell to participate in the state playoff. The following report was in the *Cordell Beacon*: "For the championship there were three; Cordell, Oklahoma City and Muskogee; Three is a crowd there is no doubt; So that is why Cordell was left out." (Courtesy Cordell Beacon.)

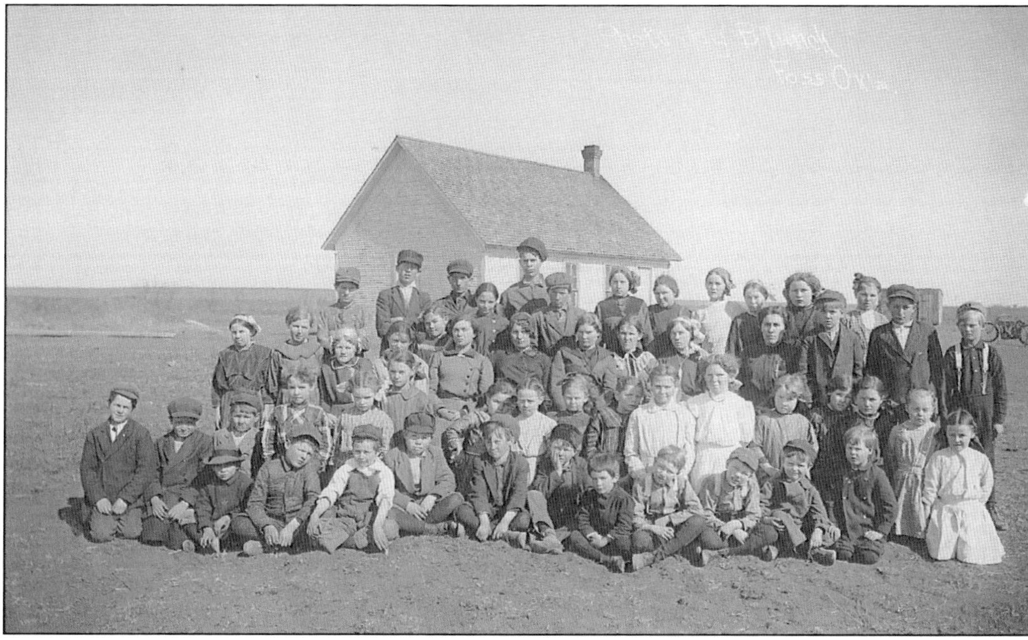

Lone Grove school was established in 1897 and located about five miles southeast of Canute. The school was closed in 1932, when it was attached to the Canute School District. This picture was taken in 1914 when four Harrelson children were attending the school. (Courtesy Brenice [Harrelson] Stafford.)

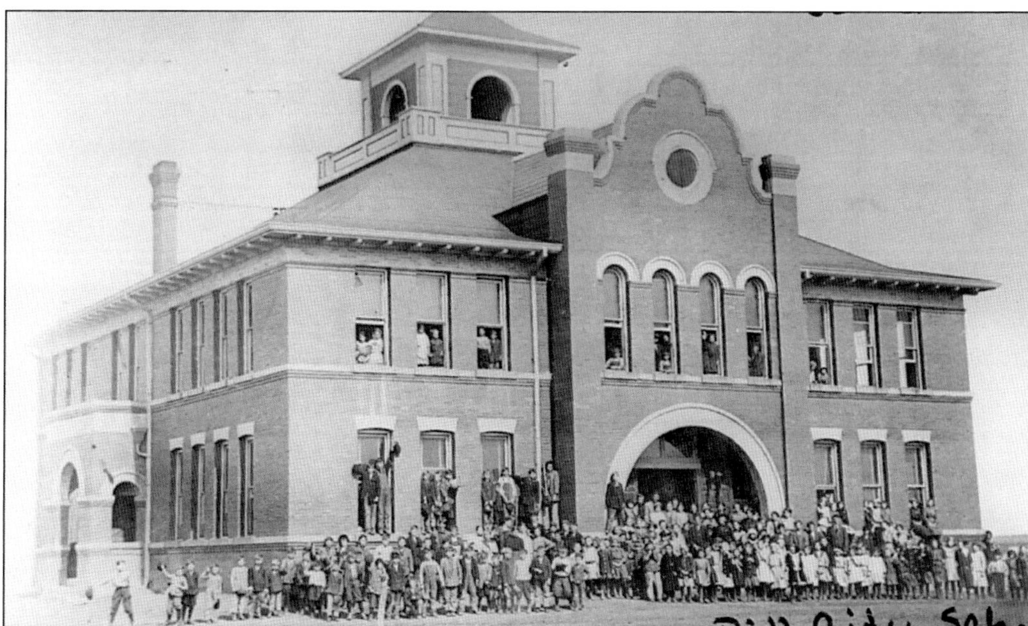

Dill City school was not established until 1903 as the 103rd school district in Washita County. This picture was taken about 1918 or 1919. Dill became an independent school in 1908 when other schools joined them. In the early 1990s, Dill joined the Burns Flat School District to become the Burns Flat-Dill City school. (Courtesy Washita County Museum.)

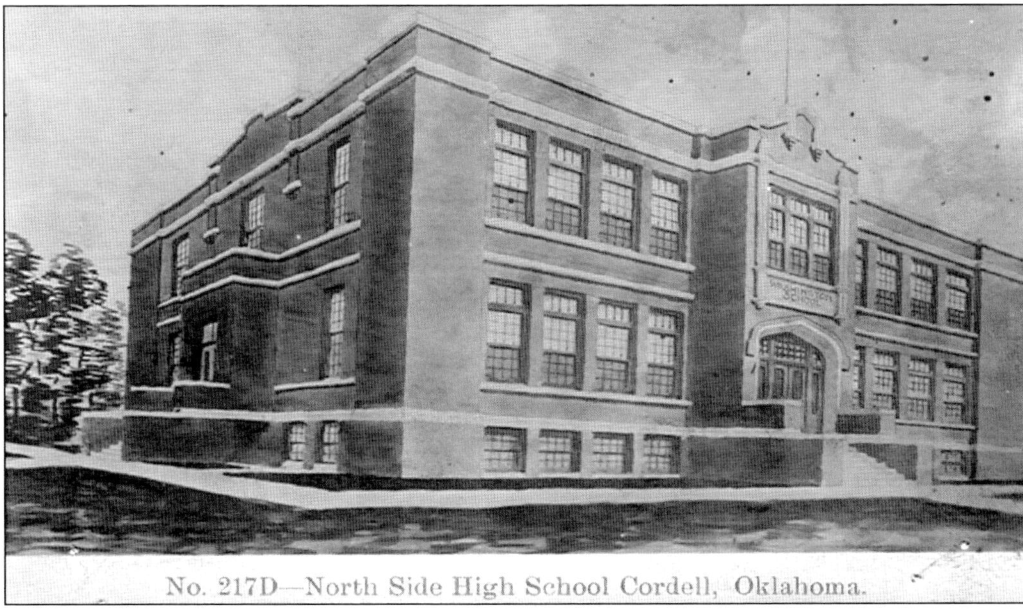

The Cordell Lincoln School was built in 1908, when the original block building in the southern part of the town started to crumble from the homemade blocks. The Lincoln school was destroyed by a fire in 1936 and was replaced with a large single-story building. (Courtesy Washita County Museum.)

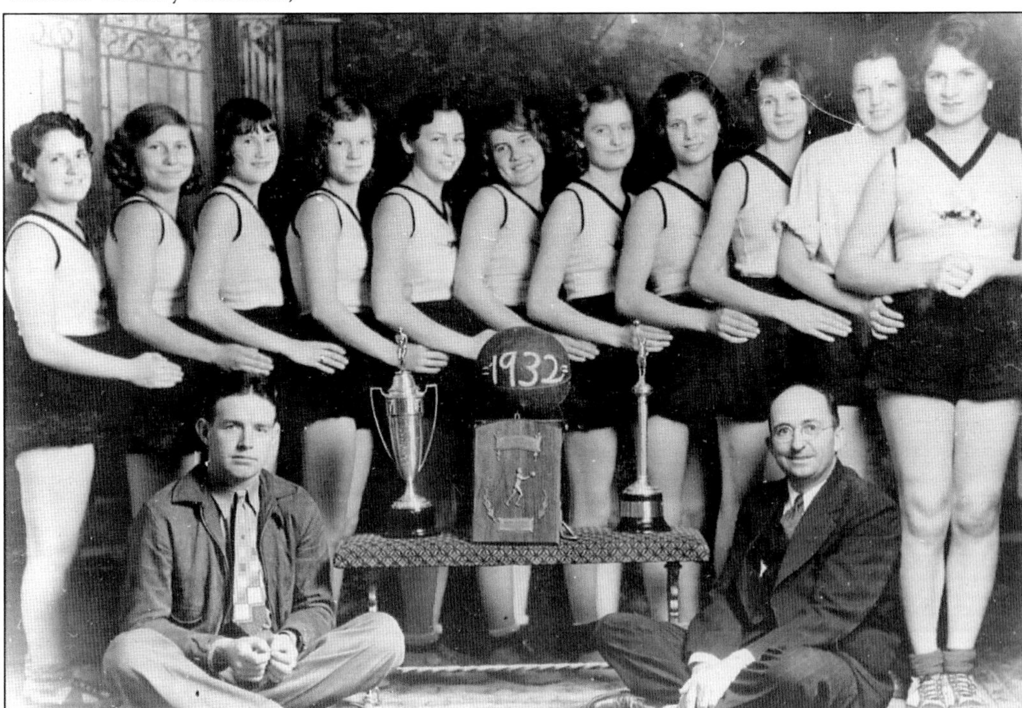

This is the Burns Flat girls' basketball team in 1932. They were runners-up in the county tournament. Coach Fred French is in front on the left and superintendent Elmer Davis on the right. (Courtesy Rod Redwine.)

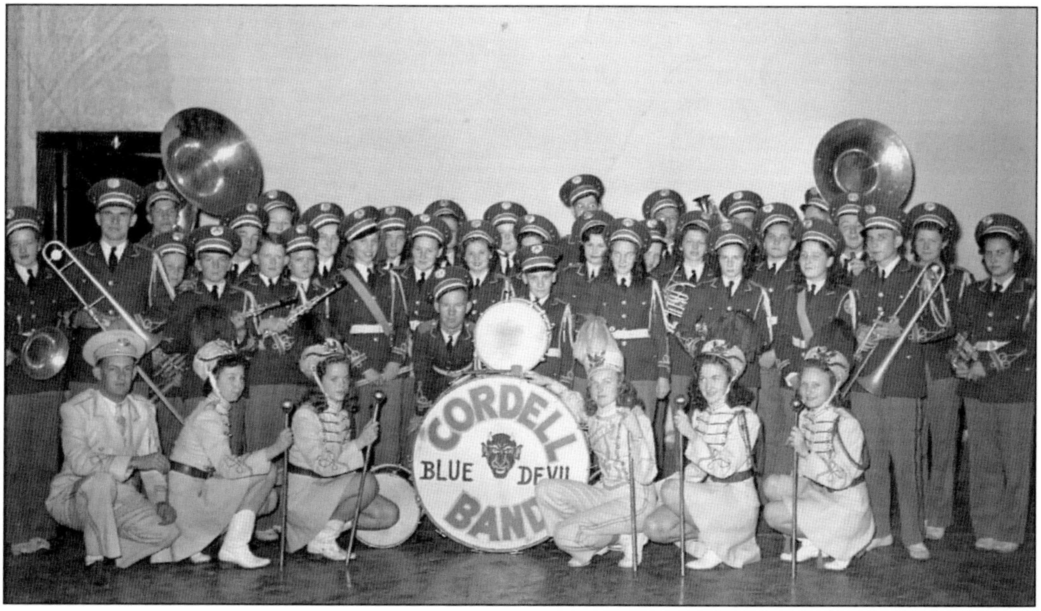

This is the Cordell band. In the front left is band director Mr. Sockwell, along with (from left to right) Charlette Day, Janis Taylor, drum major Francis Shipman, Patty Moore, and Betty Lee Clayton. Cordell has a very strong band program and usually is rated as an outstanding band at the state contest. (Courtesy Cordell Schools.)

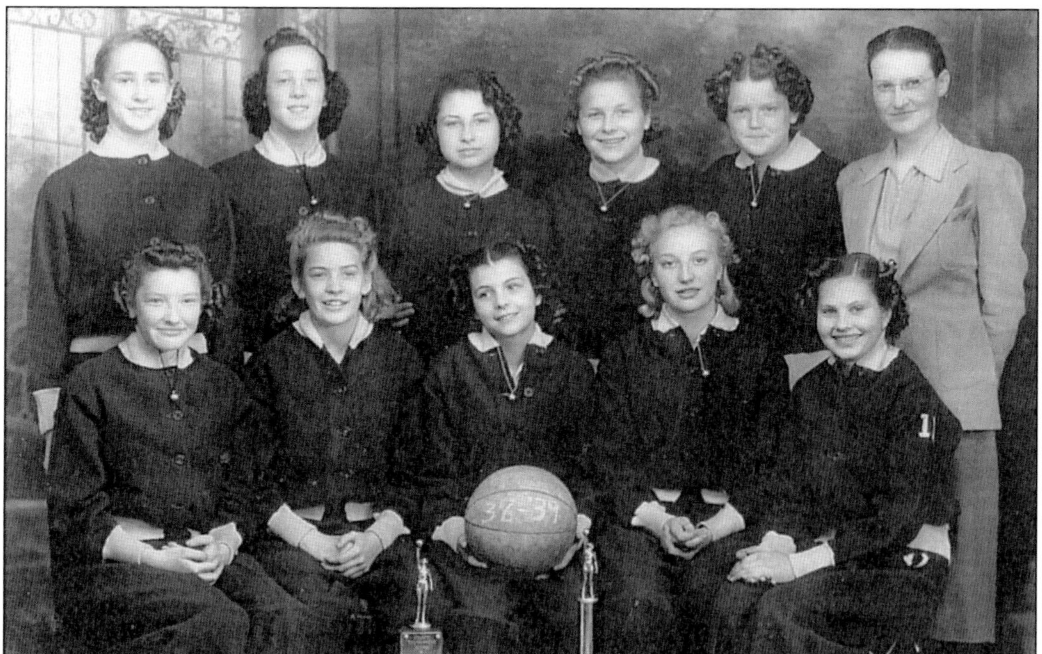

The Cordell girls' basketball team has won the state tournament three times. This 1939–1940 team was beat at state. From left to right, they are (first row) Fanita Brown, Perry Jo Stafford, Zonelle Gregory, Helen Louise Faulkner, and Peggy Buie; (second row) Ina Lee Southworth, Lucille Brown, Mable Winchip, Jimmy Woodward, Kathryn Shipman, and coach Laura McCarty. (Courtesy Washita County Museum.)

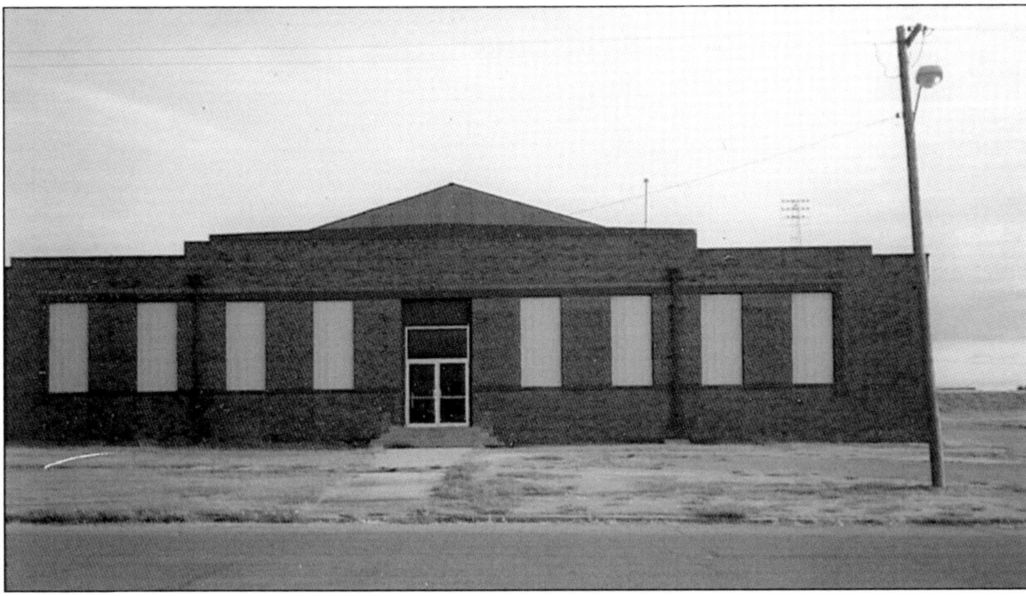

The old Cordell gymnasium was built in 1926. The 1926 Washita County basketball tournament had 63 county school teams entered from eighth grade, junior high, and high school. When built, the gymnasium was said to be the finest basketball faculty between Oklahoma City and Amarillo, Texas. The gymnasium would seat 2,500 people; however, many times more than 3,000 people would be in attendance. (Courtesy Cordell High School.)

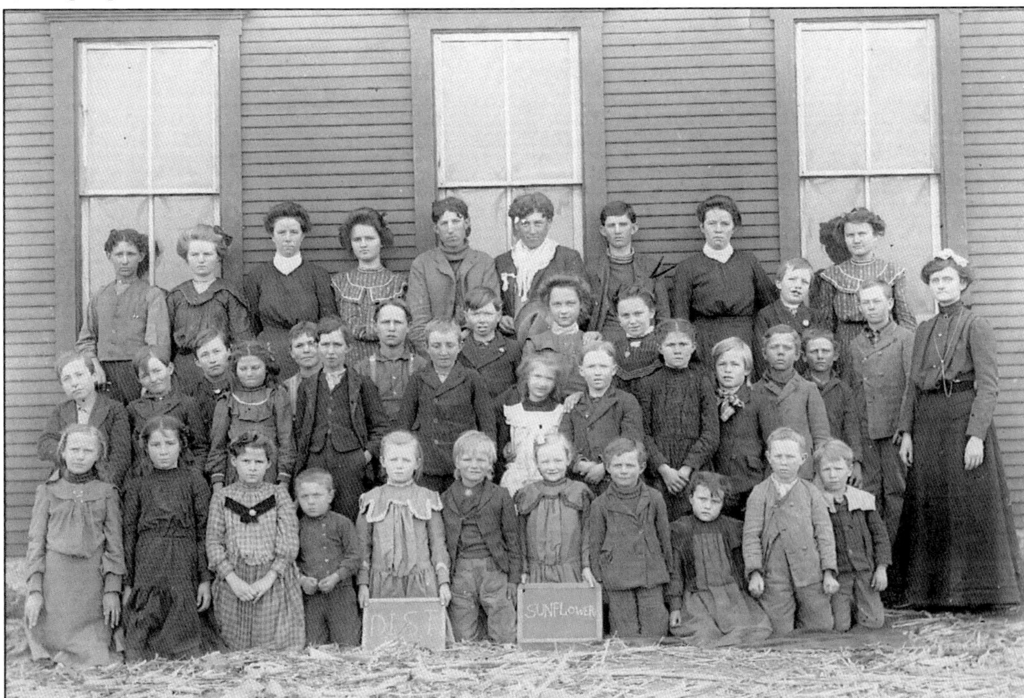

Sunflower school was established in 1896 and located two miles northwest of Bessie. This photograph of the school was taken in 1904. Sunflower was an active one-room school until it was annexed to Bessie School District in 1947. (Courtesy Mary [Wagner] Klump.)

Three

EARLY-DAY CHURCHES

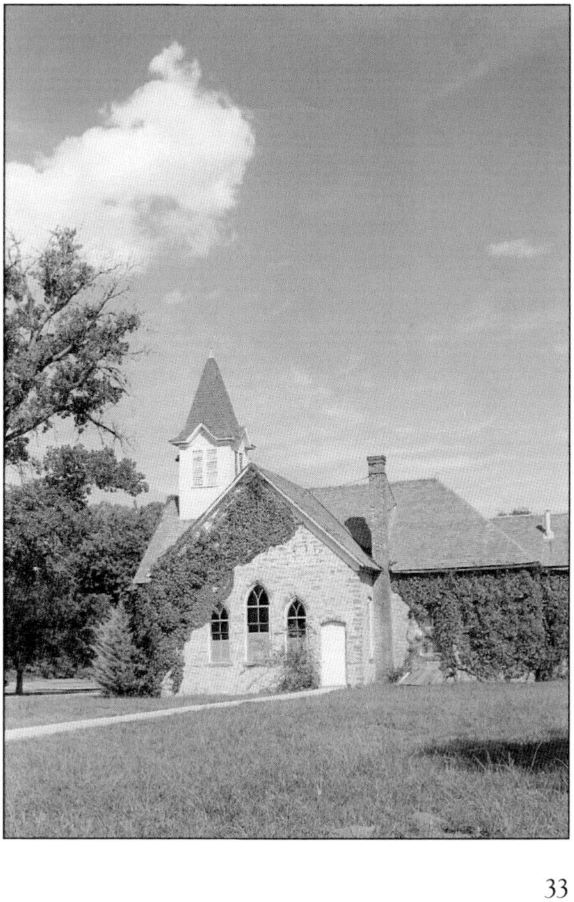

The Columbian Presbyterian Church at Colony began in 1895 as the Columbian Reformed Church, founded by the Dutch Reformed Church of New York, as a mission to the Native Americans. Rev. Dr. Frank Wright was the first pastor, himself a Native American. For several years, the services were translated into the Cheyenne and Arapaho languages. The mission church grew rapidly, and by 1900, 150 families were in the church congregation. The Mohawk Lodge was established around 1900 on the church grounds to give the Native American women a place to buy supplies for their bead work and leather moccasins, as well as a place to sell their work. The Mohawk Lodge is still in operation today and is located just east of Clinton on old highway 66. After the closing of the Indian agencies and the Seger Indian Boarding School in 1932, the church's original mission changed. In that same year, the congregation became Columbian Memorial Presbyterian Church. (Courtesy Washita County Museum.)

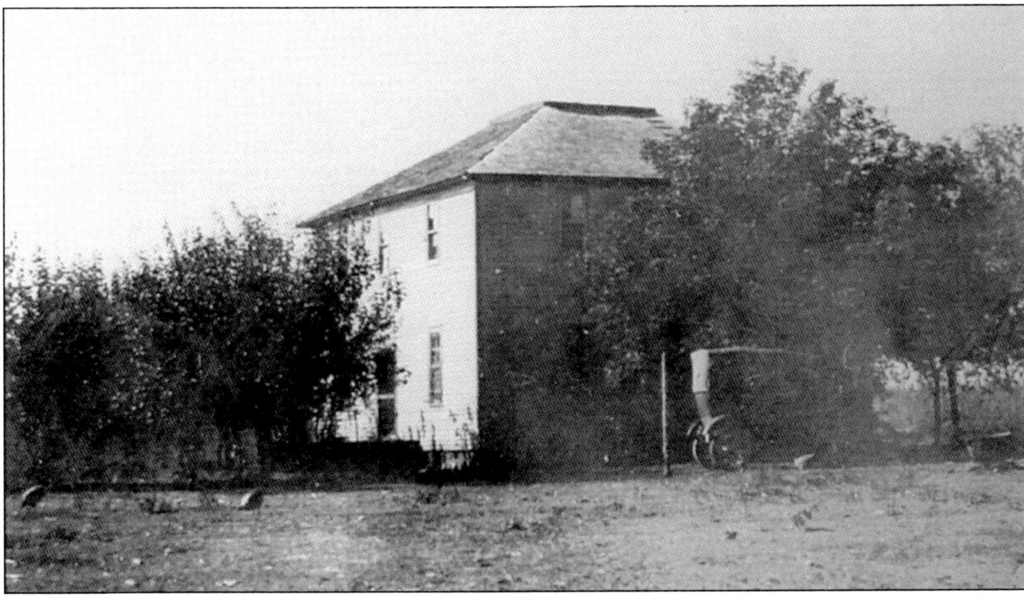

In 1889, the General Mennonite Conference of Kansas sent J. J. Kliewer from Buhler, Kansas, to establish an Native American mission in the Oklahoma Indian Territory. Kliewer established the Shelly Mission, which later became a town located seven miles east and four miles north of Cordell. From this mission the Mennonite churches were established at Corn, Cordell, and Bessie, as well as the Herold and Bergthal churches and the Corn Mennonite Bible Academy. (Courtesy Washita County Museum.)

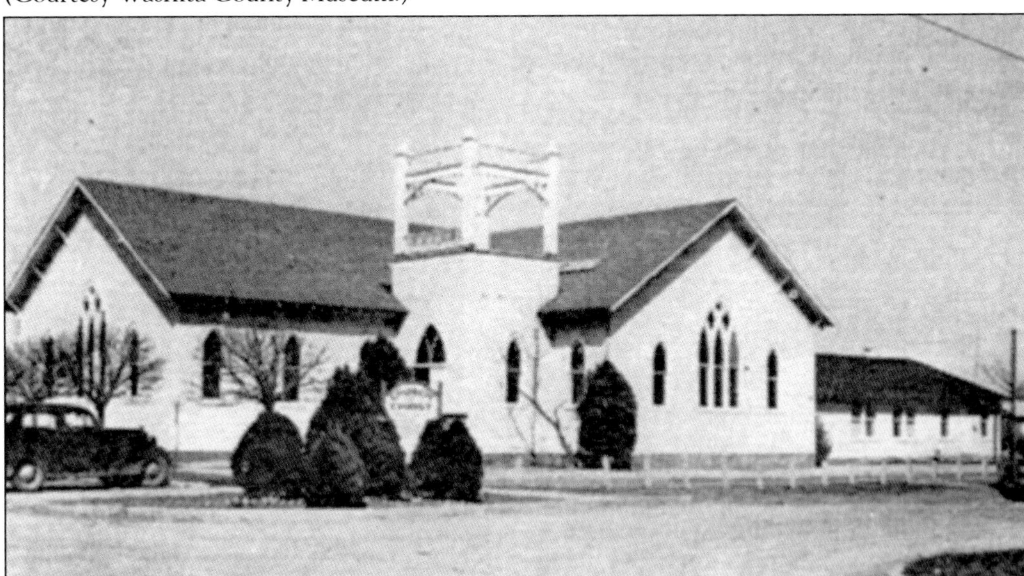

The Cordell Church of Christ was organized in the winter of 1892–1893 at the Center Point school, located one mile west and one mile south of Cordell. J. C. Harrel was one of the charter members. He and his brother from Rocky, a minister, were conducting the services at Center Point when the Cordell church was founded. Harrel gave the land for the church building, at Fourth and College Streets, where the church is located today. The Cordell Church of Christ is one of the oldest congregations in Washita County. (Courtesy Washita County Museum.)

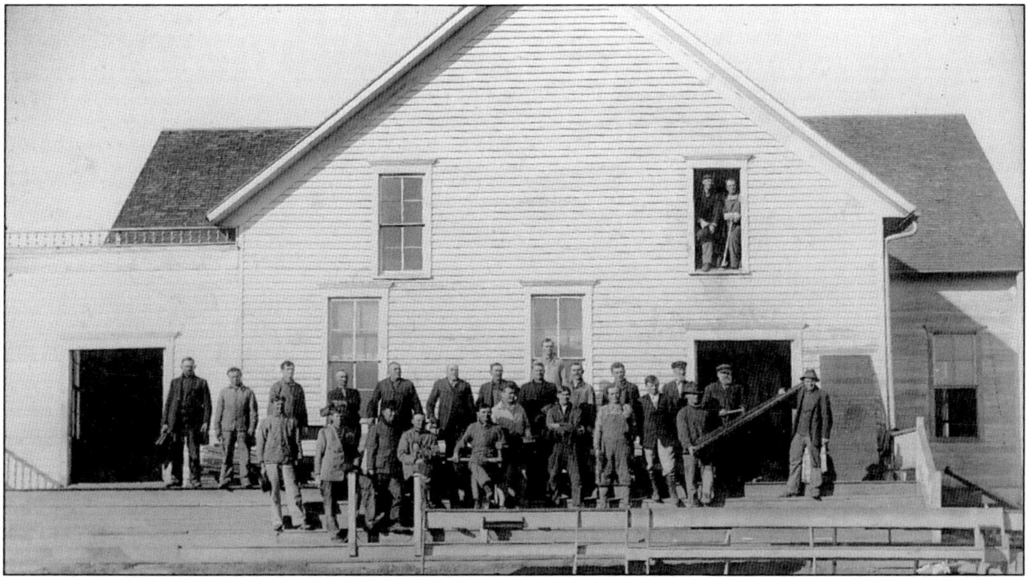

The Washita Mennonite Church, located at Corn, was organized in 1893 with Rev. Abraham Richert as pastor. The congregation built a 20-by-20-foot sod dugout as a meeting place. The land was donated by Peter Bergmann. In 1898, a 60-by-32-foot wooden building was constructed, as shown in this photograph. For many years, the Corn Mennonite Church was the largest Mennonite congregation in the world. Today it has a large, beautiful modern building. (Courtesy Corn Mennonite Church.)

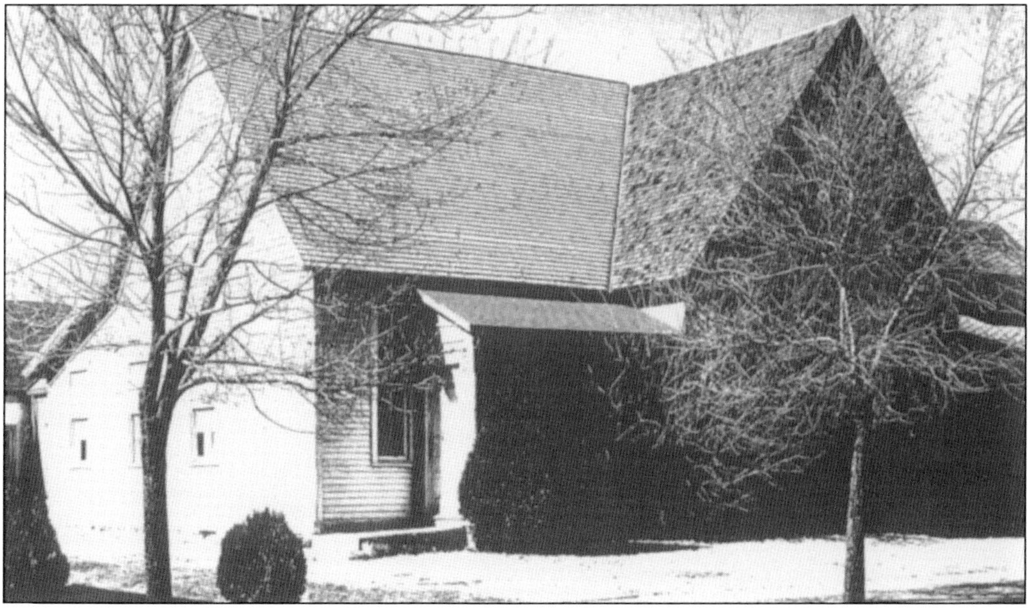

The Cordell Methodist church was organized in the winter of 1892–1893 by F. C. Mabery, Methodist circuit preacher. The church had 11 charter members. A. J. Johnson gave land for the building, which was called the Union Church building and was remodeled as shown in the image above in 1910 and served until 1949 when replaced by the beautiful Cordell Methodist Church building in use today. Other denominations using the old building included Baptist, Dutch Reformed, Methodist Episcopal, and Church of Christ. (Courtesy Doyle Fenn.)

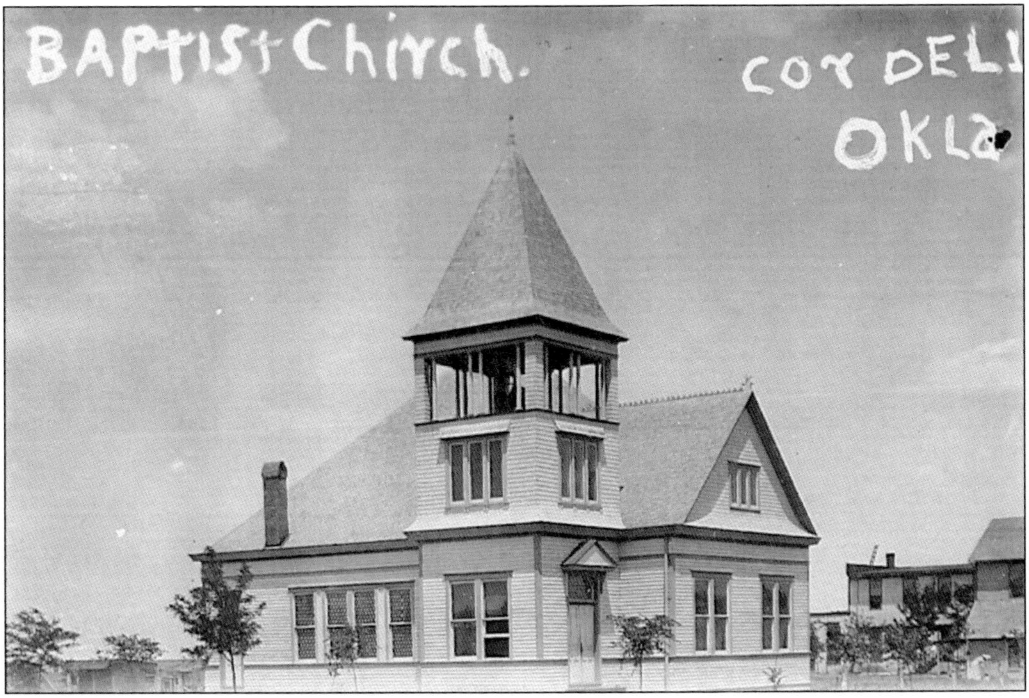

Cordell First Baptist Church was established in 1898 with five families. Rev. J. B. Watson conducted services at the Union Church. It was not until May 1904 that Rev. L. F. Hedge was called as pastor and officially organized and voted to build a church building. This first building was built in 1905, and a basement was added in 1917. Today it has a beautiful church complex covering three-quarters of a block. (Courtesy Washita County Museum.)

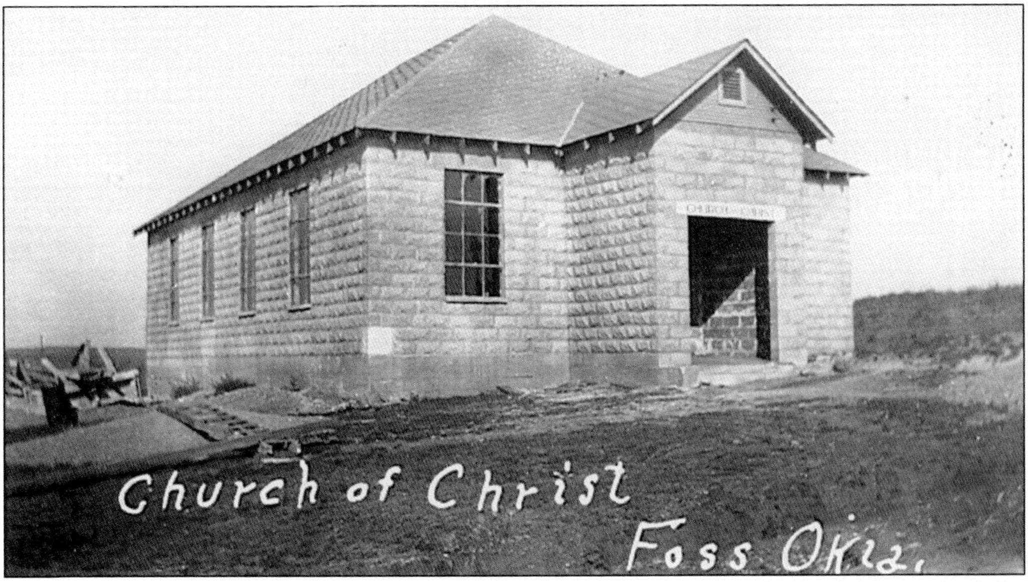

The Foss Church of Christ was organized after the 1902 Turkey Creek flood that washed the community away and caused it to build up the hill from the creek. The Foss Church of Christ is one of the older church buildings in Washita County. The Foss Church of Christ disbanded several years ago. (Courtesy Washita County Museum.)

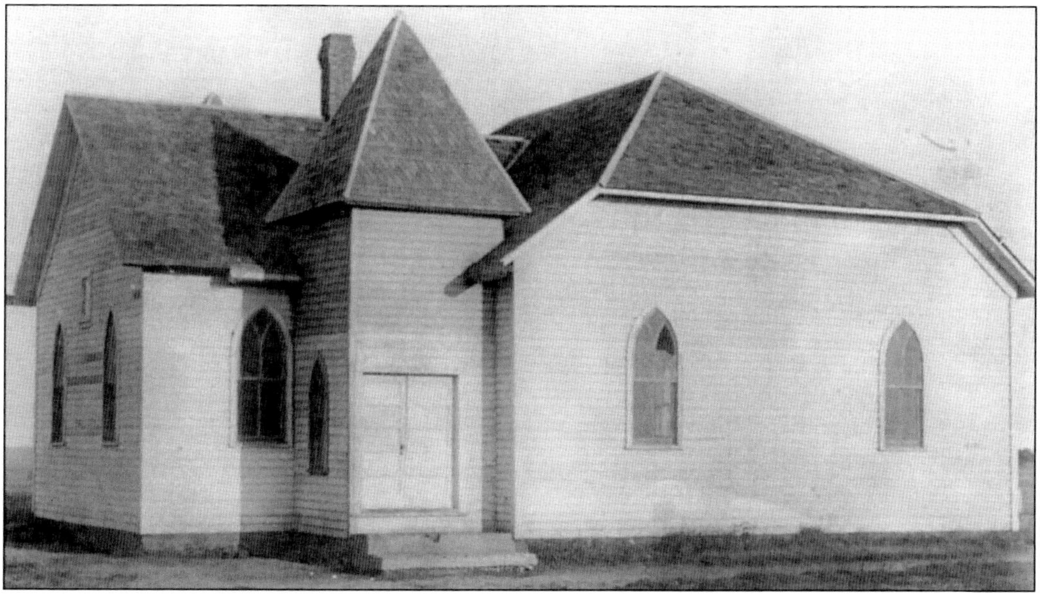

The Sharon Missionary Baptist Church was organized in the fall of 1895 in a half dugout of the Bethel school with seven charter members. In 1905, the Cloud Chief Baptist congregation joined the Sharon congregation by unanimous vote. B. E. Bryant, Washita County delegate to the Oklahoma Constitution Committee, donated land for a church building. Sharon Baptist Church is still an active country church in the same location. (Courtesy Washita County Museum.)

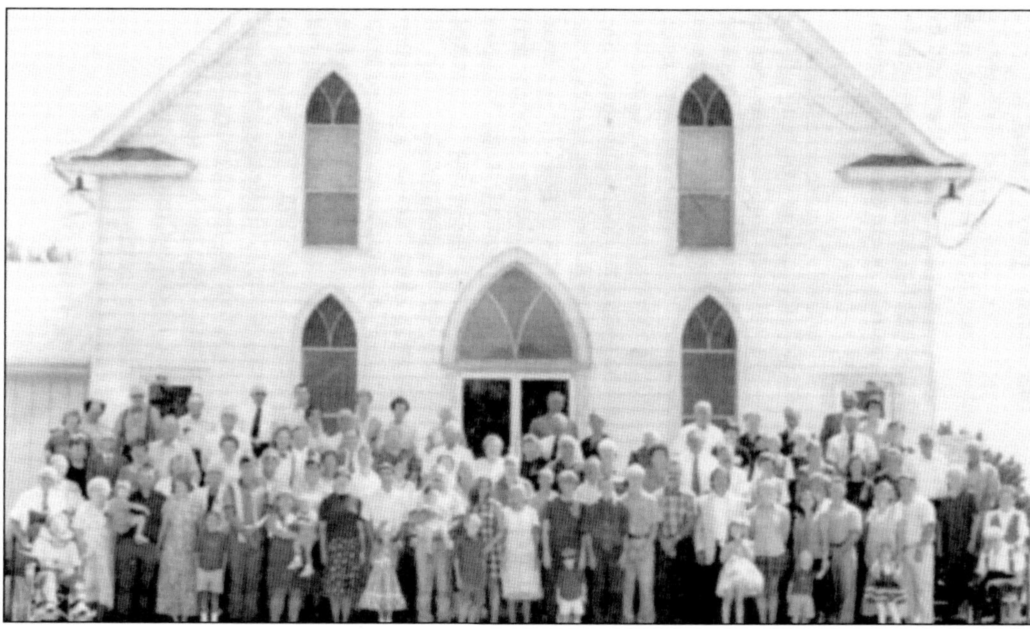

The Herold Mennonite Church was established in 1899 as a result of the Shelly Mennonite Mission and is located seven miles northeast of Cordell. The first building was replaced in 1915 with the present building, shown in this photograph. The building has been well maintained, and a family worship center has been added. The Harold Mennonite is probably the largest country church located in Washita County today. (Courtesy Washita County Museum.)

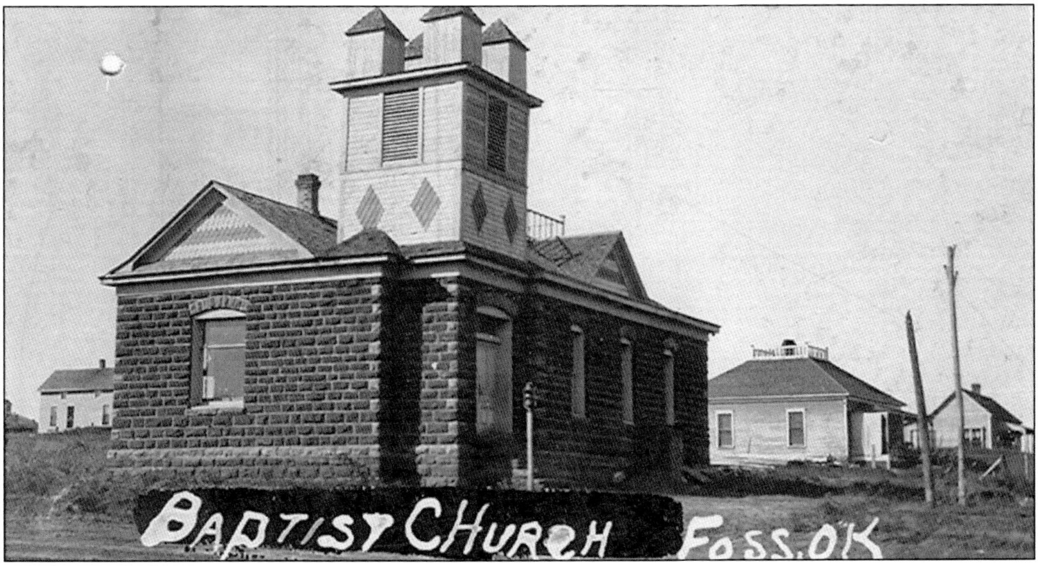

Foss Baptist Church is the oldest church building still being used in Washita County for the congregation's church services. The building was constructed before the famous Foss flood of 1902. It was one of the few buildings in the town that survived the flood. An educational building has been added. The building has been well maintained. (Courtesy Washita County Museum.)

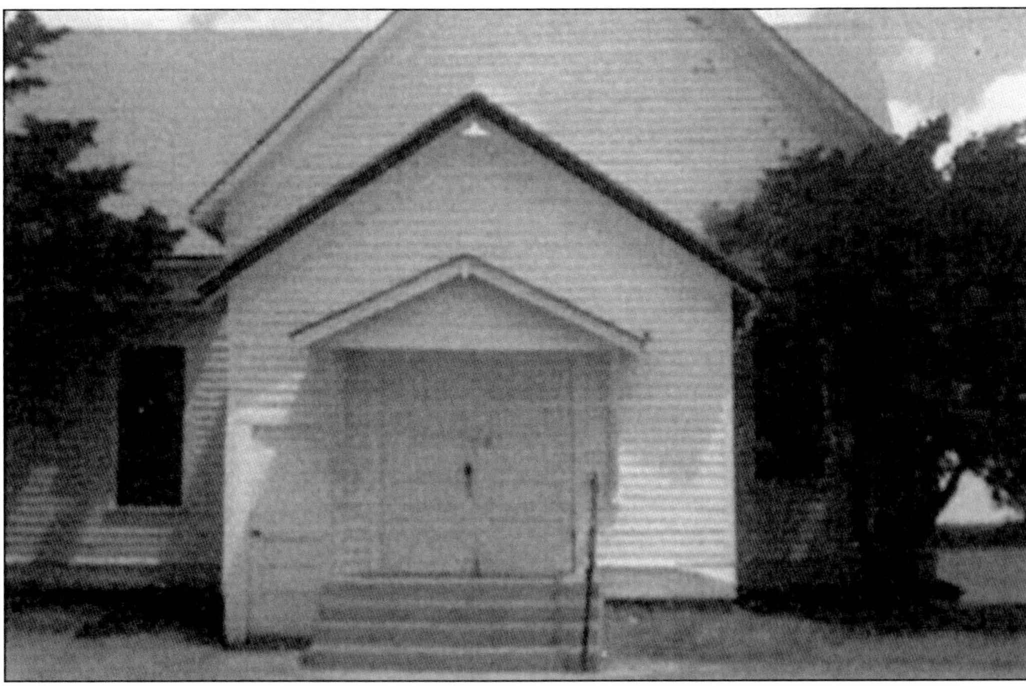

Bergthal Mennonite Church was organized in 1894 as a result of the Shelly Mennonite Mission. It was located two miles west and three miles north of Corn. Bergthal is short for *Bruderberatung*, German for "business meeting place." The last service was held on November 17, 1974, at which time the building was abounded. Vandals destroyed much of the building, and the former members decided to destroy the building. The building was destroyed by burning on June 17, 1906. (Courtesy Harvey Flaming.)

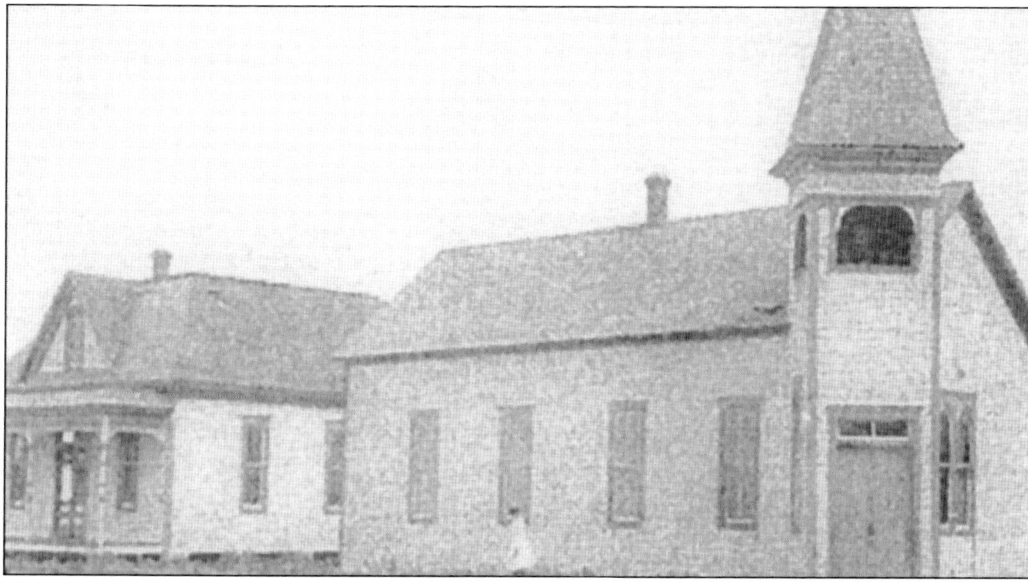

The Cordell First Presbyterian Church was organized in 1902 as the Dutch Reformed Church. In 1911, the Dutch Reformed churches pulled out of Oklahoma, and the healthy congregation voted to become a Presbyterian congregation on March 27, 1911. The building shown in this picture was replaced in 1950 with a beautiful brick building, located at Second and North College Streets. (Courtesy First Presbyterian Church.)

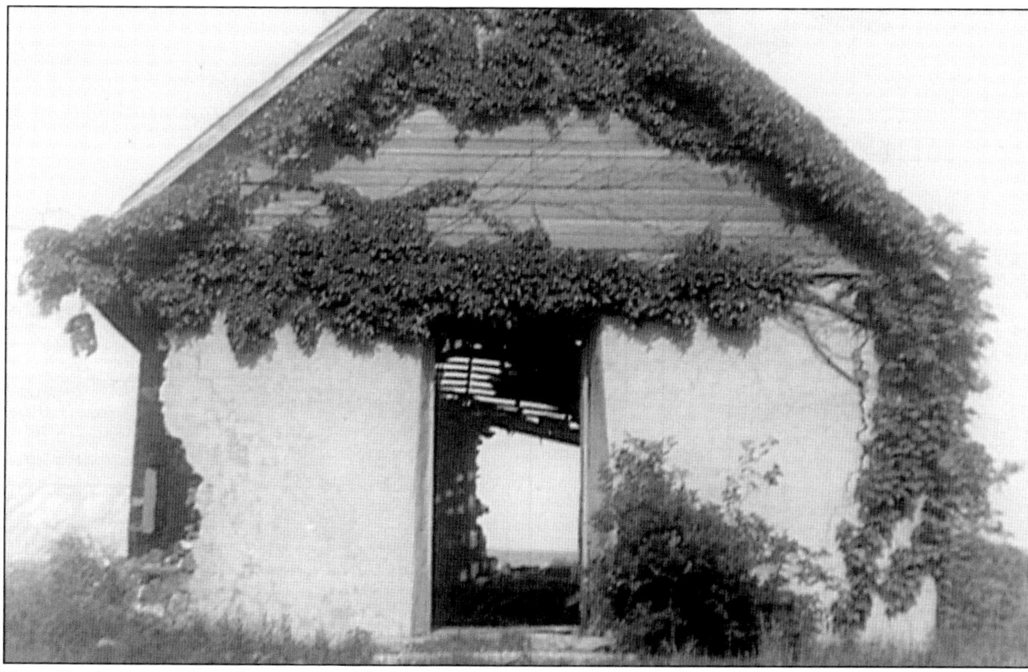

Zion Lutheran Church was established in 1894 by German settlers from Beresina, Russia. The building was located seven miles northwest of Bessie. The church was known as Rock Lutheran church because it was built out of rock held together by mud and straw. The building cost $75, as these pioneers built their own house of worship. The building served as both a church and school until the early 1920s. (Courtesy Washita County Museum.)

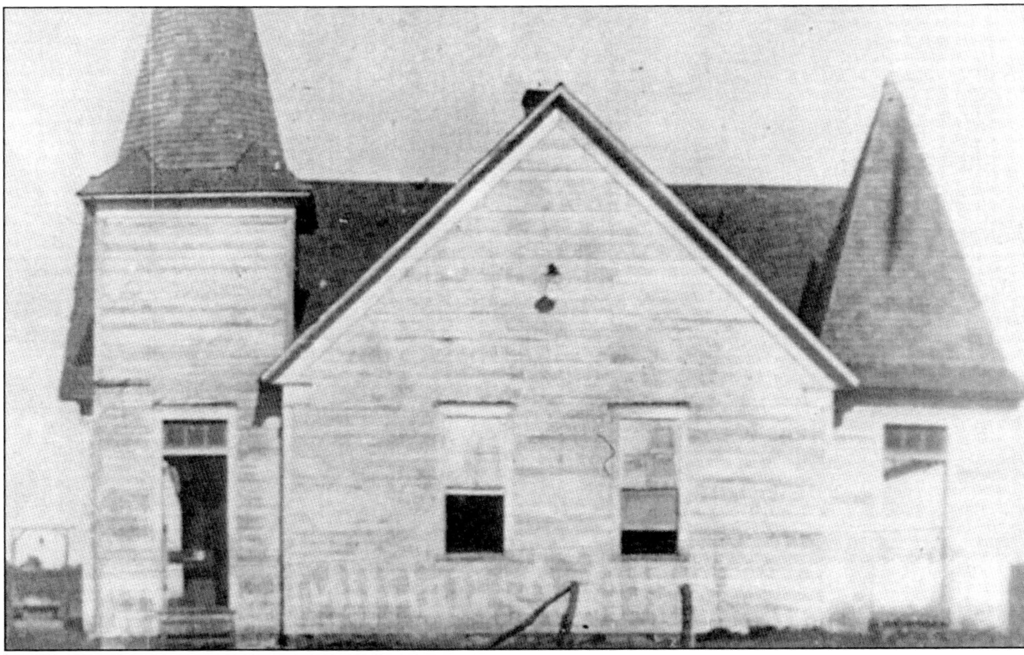

The Delhi Baptist Church was established in November 1898 when seven Christians met in the old Delhi schoolhouse, built of logs, a mile southwest of the Delhi school. The church building shown in this picture was built in 1905. Pastor William Harris preached the first sermon. (Courtesy Cordell Beacon.)

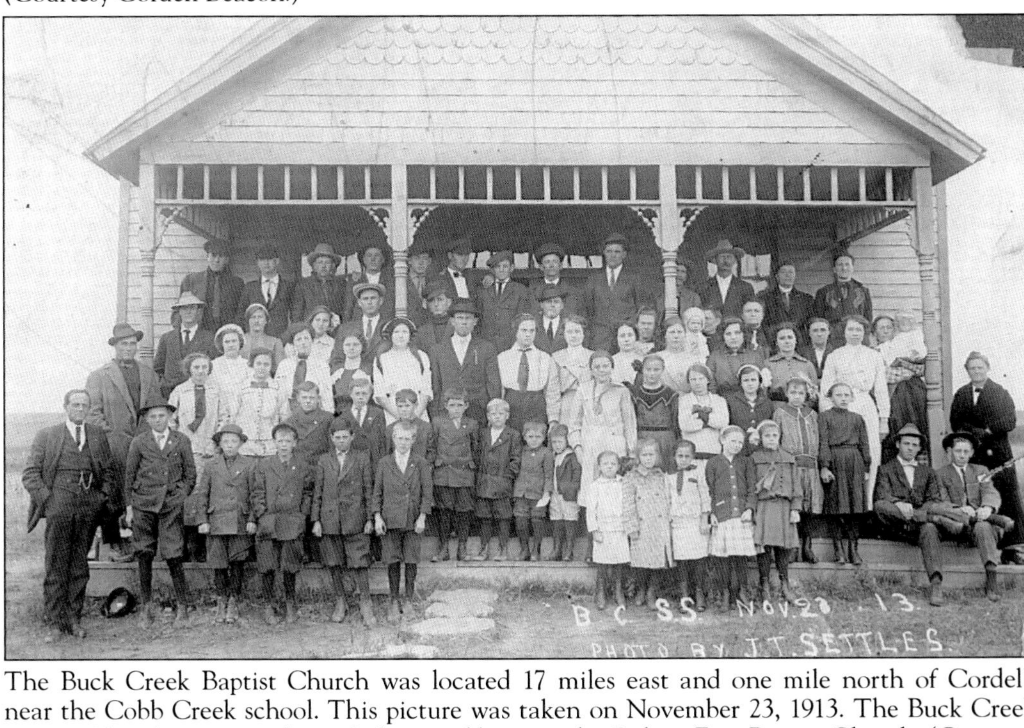

The Buck Creek Baptist Church was located 17 miles east and one mile north of Cordell, near the Cobb Creek school. This picture was taken on November 23, 1913. The Buck Creek Baptist Church was moved into Colony and became the Colony First Baptist Church. (Courtesy Washita County Museum.)

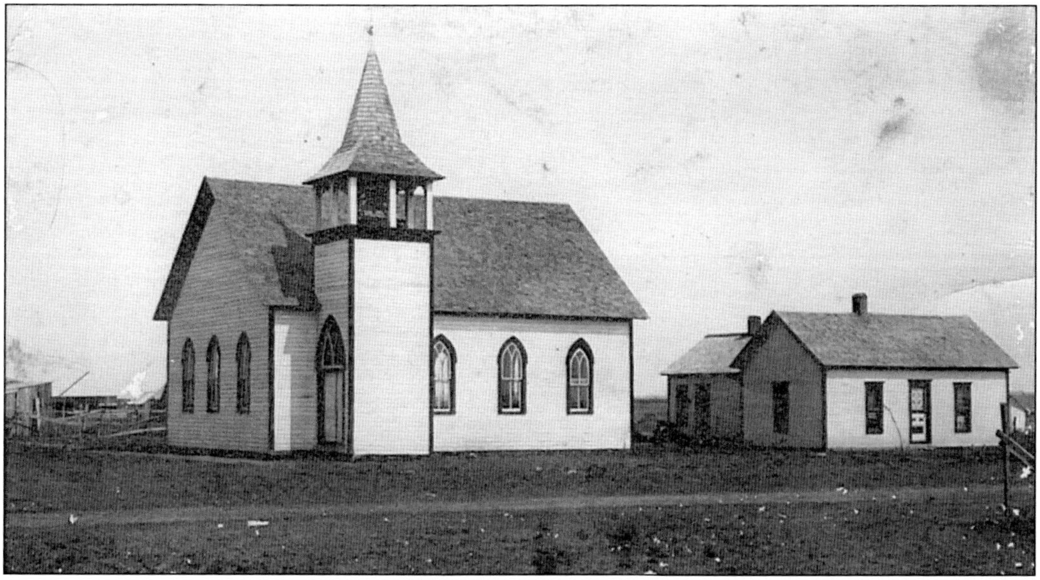

The Rocky Methodist Church was organized in the spring of 1901 when J. E. Veck, Cordell Methodist pastor, conducted services at the Orange Blossom school in Rocky. The church started with 15 charter members. Due to large attendance, the services were moved to Dennison Hall in Rocky in 1901. In 1905, the church built its first building. (Courtesy Su Su Jackson.)

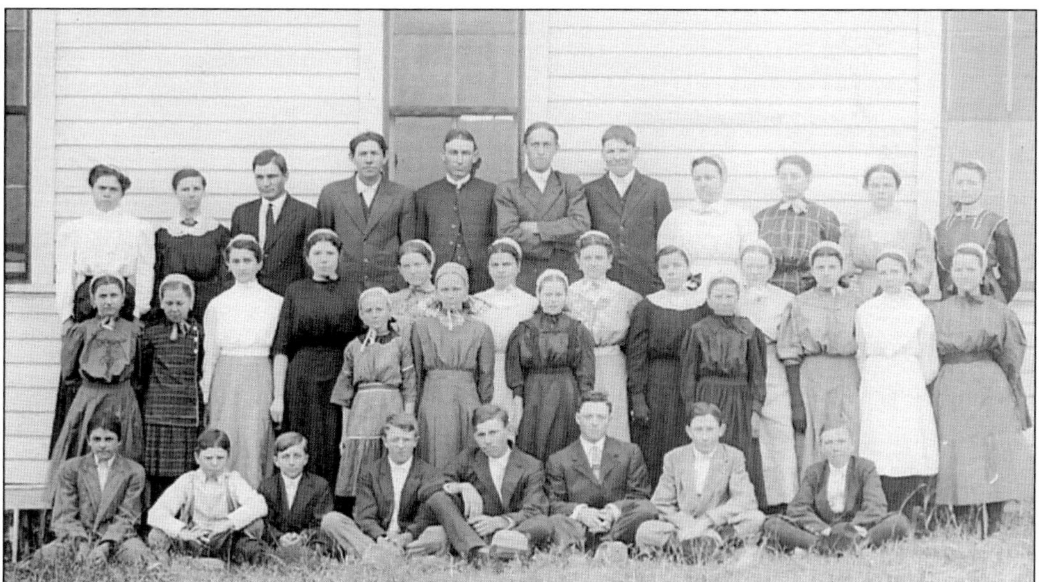

The Washita Church of the Brethren was organized on April 2, 1895, with nine charter members. Meetings were held in homes, mostly dugouts, and as the membership grew, they met at the Calvery Creek and Lone Tree schools. In 1905, the membership had grown to 64, and a church building was constructed. The Brethren Church held its 75th anniversary in 1970 but has since disbanded. (Courtesy Carolyn [Best] Heath.)

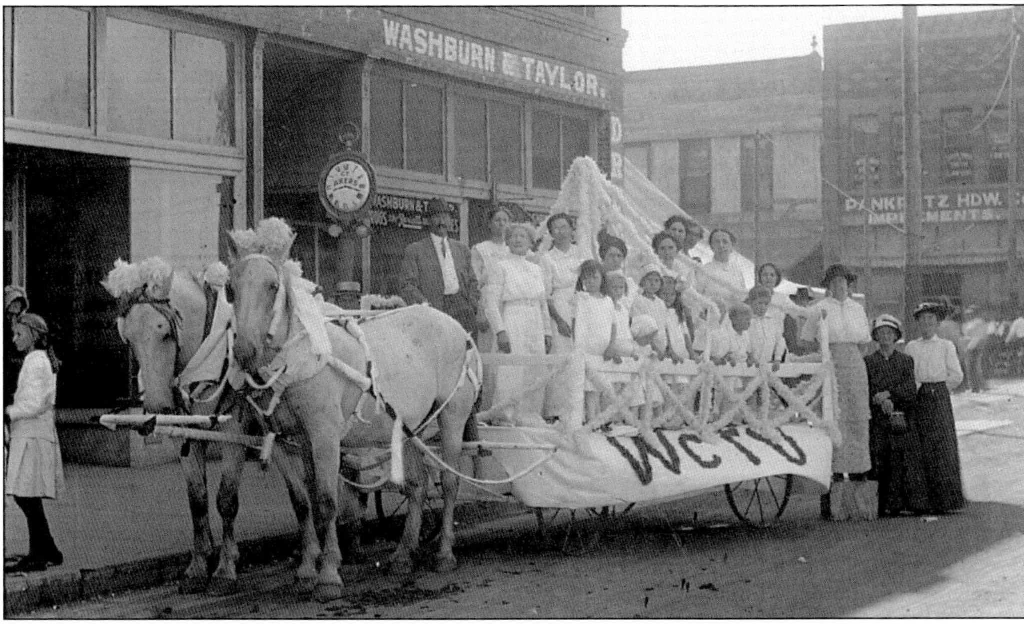

Shown here is the Cordell Women's Christian Temperance Union (WCTU) Christian Women Club. The women were very active in the second decade of the 20th century and the 1920s in Washita County with the WCTU, a group of ladies in opposition of liquor and very active for Prohibition. This photograph of the WCTU parade float was taken in 1912. (Courtesy Washita County Museum.)

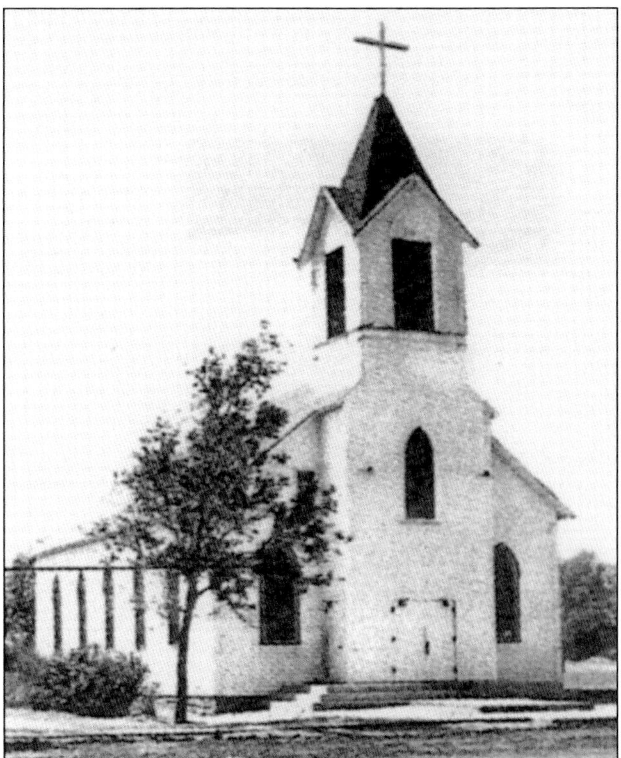

St. Francis Catholic Church, in 1898, was called the "Mother Parish of Western Oklahoma." The father from the St. Francis church and school would serve churches in Beckham, Greer, and Roger Mills Counties. Bishop Victor Reed visited the parish in December 1970 and proclaimed it closed. The St. Francis cemetery is still used. The St. Francis church was located two miles south and two miles east of Canute. (Courtesy Washita County Museum.)

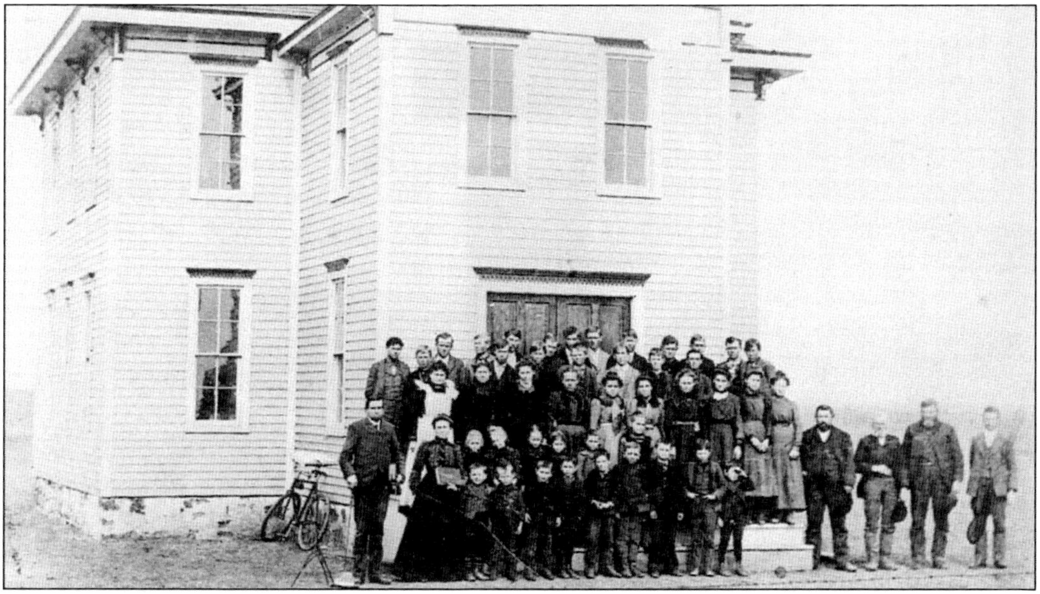

The Corn Bible Academy was established in 1902 on the grounds of the Corn Mennonite Church. At a meeting on March 23, 1895, at the Shelly Mennonite Mission house, the General Mennonite Conference voted to establish a German Christian school; however, it was seven years later that the Corn Mennonite Bible Academy was established. This picture is of the academy students in 1903. The school is active today with well over 100 students. (Courtesy Corn Bible Academy.)

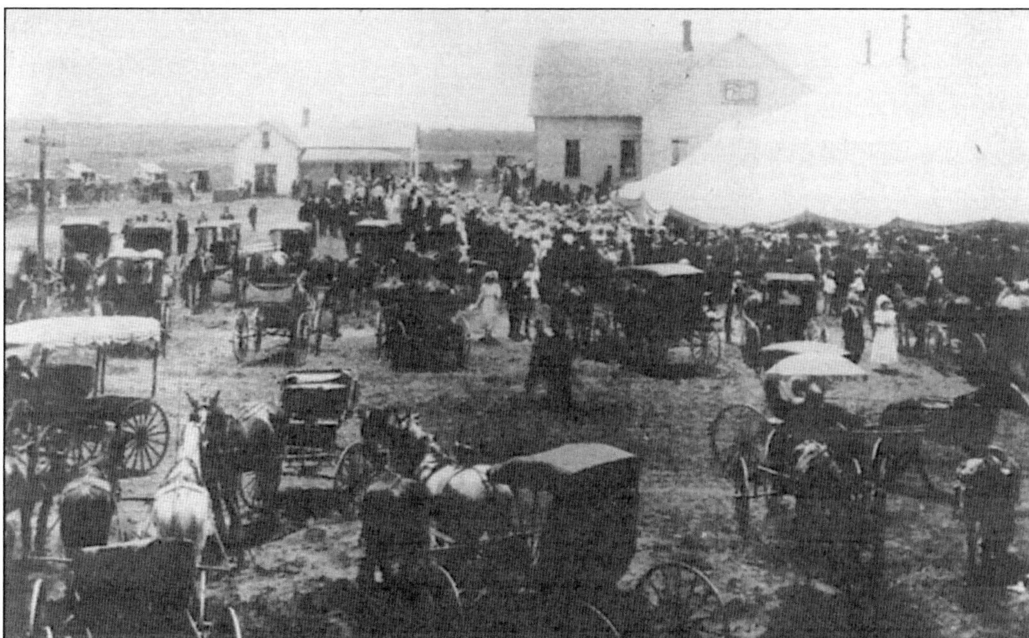

The Corn Mennonite Brethren Church hosted the Mennonite General Conference in 1898. It has often been referred to as the "Horse-and-Buggy Church Convention." Note the large tent in the photograph. Almost 1,000 attended the conference. The only transportation was by horse and buggy. (Courtesy Corn Mennonite Brethren Church.)

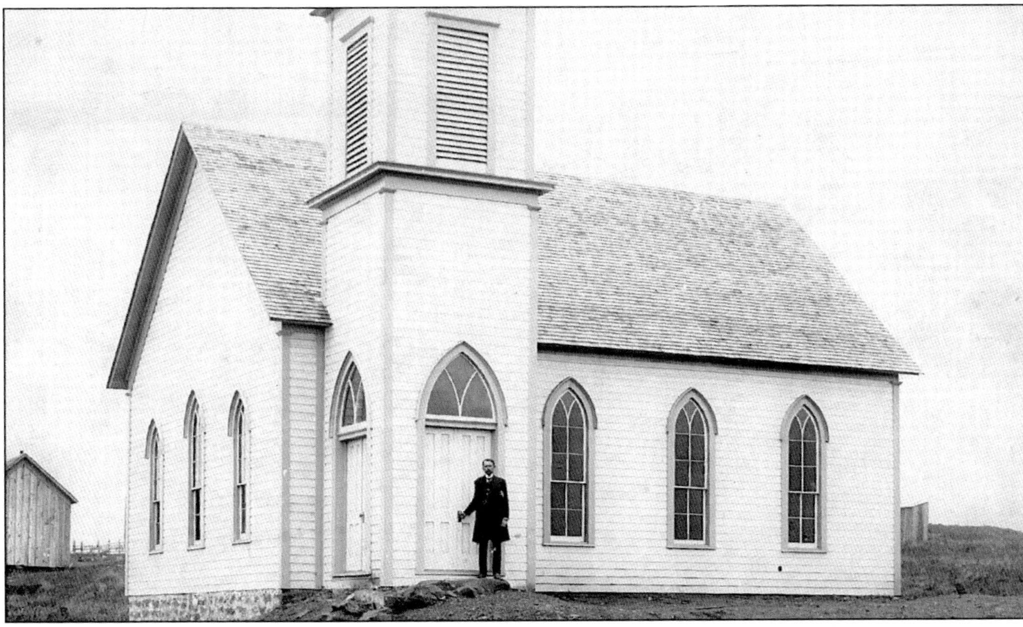

The Bible Mennonite Brethren Church was organized in 1905 at a meeting with Corn Mennonite Brethren Church. On June 16, 1906, the new building was dedicated, located on a farm seven miles northeast of Cordell. In February 1961, the Bessie Mennonite Brethren Church relocated to a beautiful new church building in Cordell. The old building and all contains were sold. Only the cemetery remains. (Courtesy Cordell Bible Mennonite Brethren Church.)

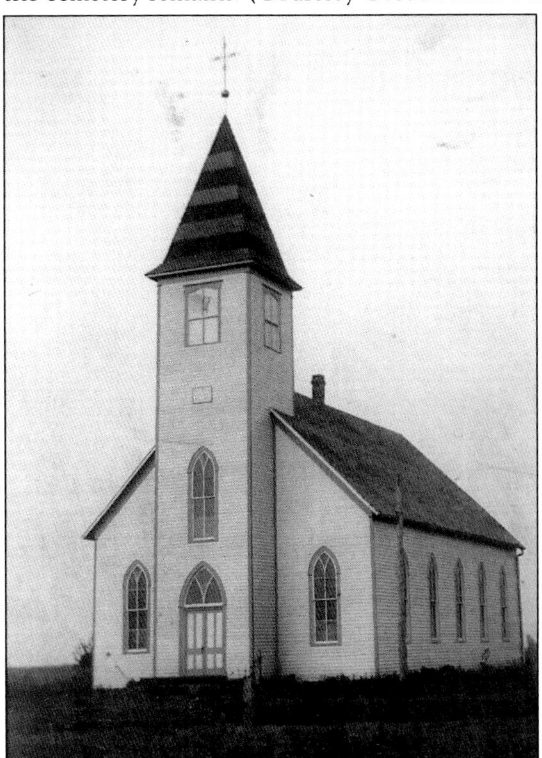

The Peace Lutheran Church at Bessie was organized on November 11, 1894. Gottlieb Goeringer wrote the church constitution in German that was adopted July 5, 1895. It was not until 1949 that the constitution was written in English. Until the 1940s, the 10:00 a.m. service was in English while the 11:00 a.m. service was in German. The first church building was completed in April 1897. Today they have a beautiful brick building. (Courtesy Paul Lenaburg.)

Four

Towns and Ghost Towns

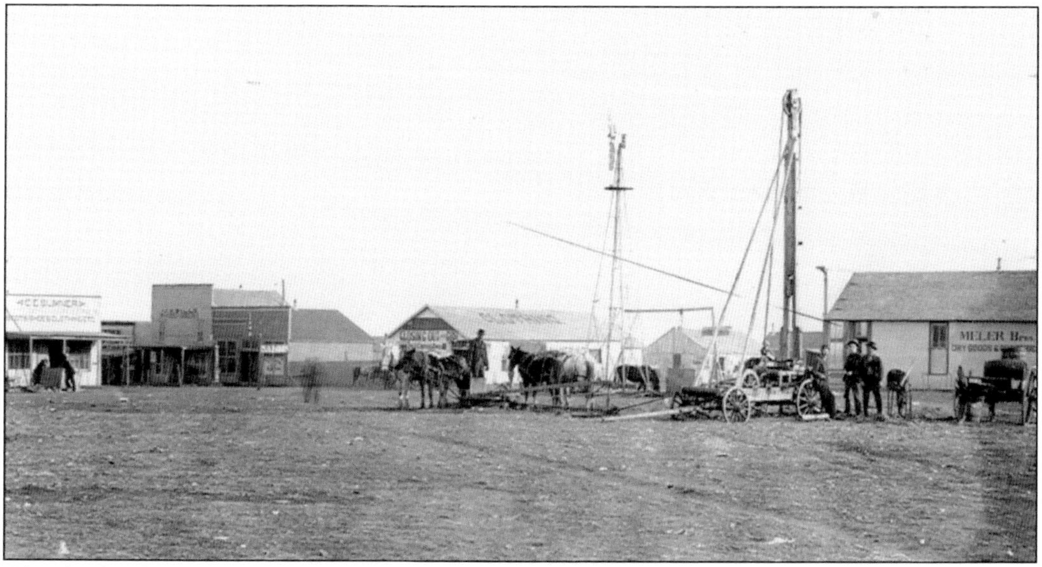

Cloud Chief, a small town with a post office established on March 1, 1892, was selected by Congress as the county seat of County H, which later became Washita County. Well water in the area was very hard and high in gypsum. Often livestock refused to drink the water, and deeper wells were drilled. This photograph is Levi Shivley and his horse-powered drilling rig in 1897, when he drilled a 250-foot-deep well in the heart of Cloud Chief. At the time the town was between 500 and 600 people and located in the southeast part of the county. People in the western part wanted the county seat moved to the center of the county. A vote was held, and the people voted 1,349 to 282 in favor of moving the county seat, which they did, illegally, however, and not without opposition and gunplay that took a bill of Congress to get corrected. (Courtesy Washita County Museum.)

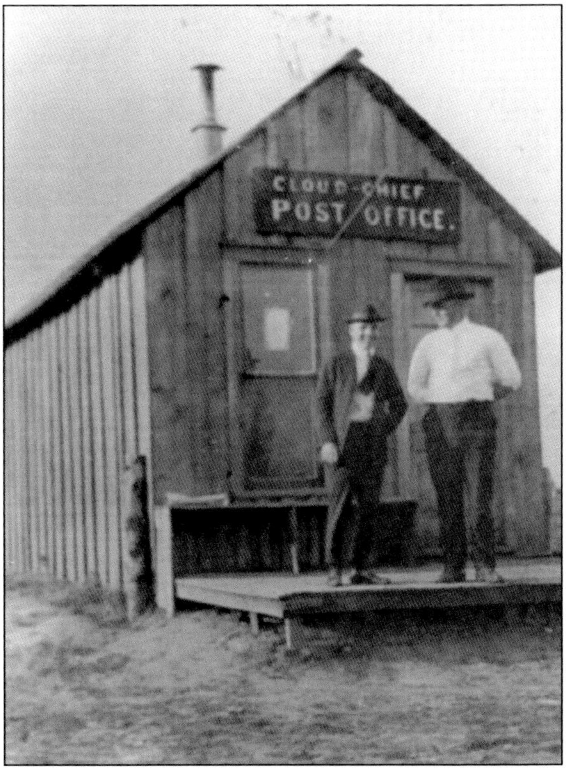

This is the Cloud Chief post office building in 1900, when the county seat was moved to Cordell. The Cloud Chief post office was established on March 1, 1892, as Tacola, the first post office in Washita County. The Cloud Chief post office was officially closed on December 30, 1964. (Courtesy Washita County Museum.)

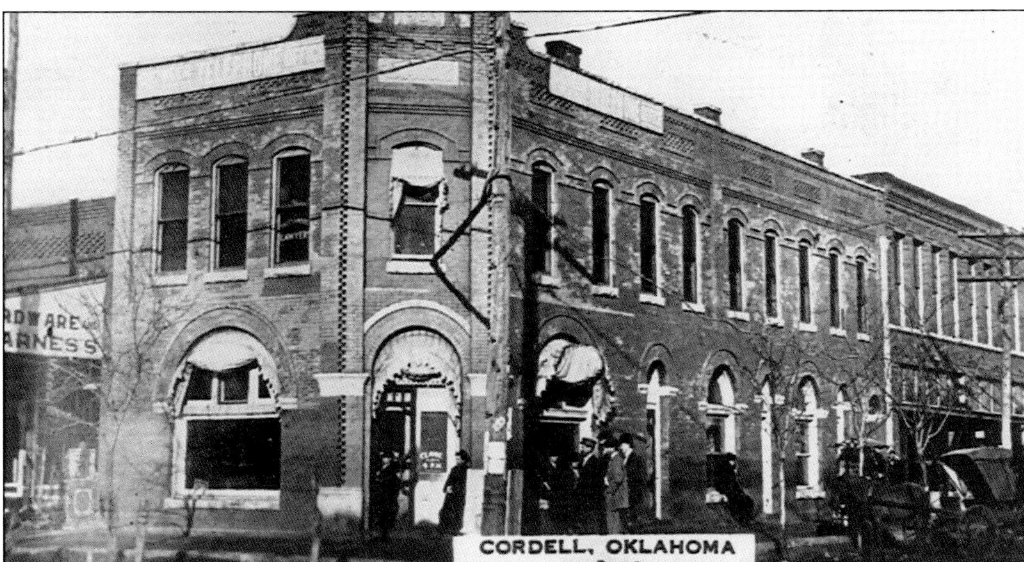

Opened in 1903, the old Cordell National Bank building was the first brick building constructed in Cordell. Prior to the railroad coming through Cordell in 1902, bricks were not available, as freight cost by wagon was prohibitive. Harve Dean and J. C. Harrel built the original building as a home for their newly organized Citizens State Bank, which involved J. M. Armfield. The building is now a financial center operated by Armfield's great-grandson Phil Kliewer. (Courtesy Washita County Museum.)

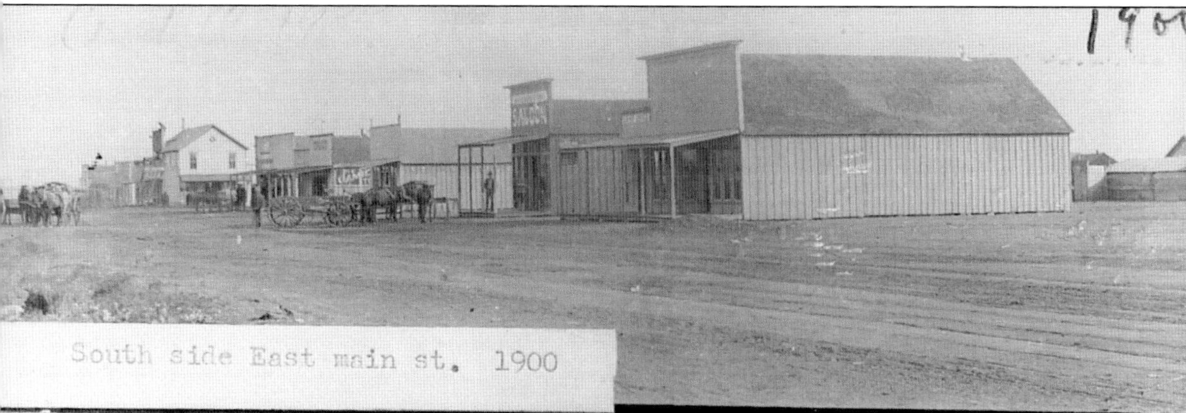

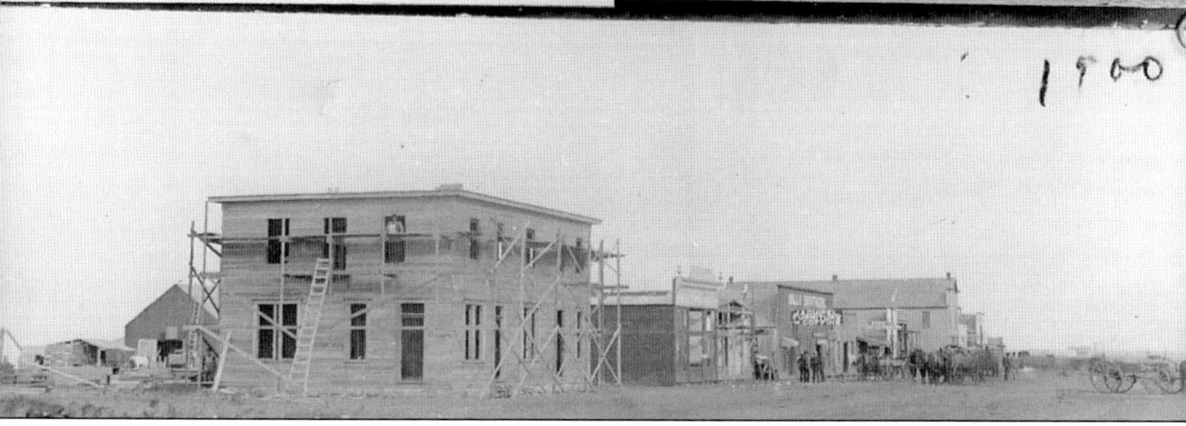

Seen here in Cordell in 1900 is a view of the 100 block of East Main Street. Between the two rows of buildings was a square block where the courthouse was to be constructed in 1902. The second building in the top picture, south side, is a saloon, as well as the fifth building. The bottom picture shows the Central Hotel under construction in the middle of the picture with people standing under a sign stating that furniture and caskets were a specialty. When the railroad came through Cordell in 1902, the depot was located three blocks west down the main street. In 1904, a water system was established, installing a 50-foot water tower that stood just to the left of the end of the block in the lower picture. A 24-foot-diameter water well was dug 40 feet deep that produced excellent water standing within 12 feet of the top of the ground. Cordell experienced a tremendous building boom from 1903 through 1908 when more than 20 brick business buildings were constructed. The town grew from approximately 400 in 1900 to a population of over 1,500 by 1910. (Courtesy Washita County Museum.)

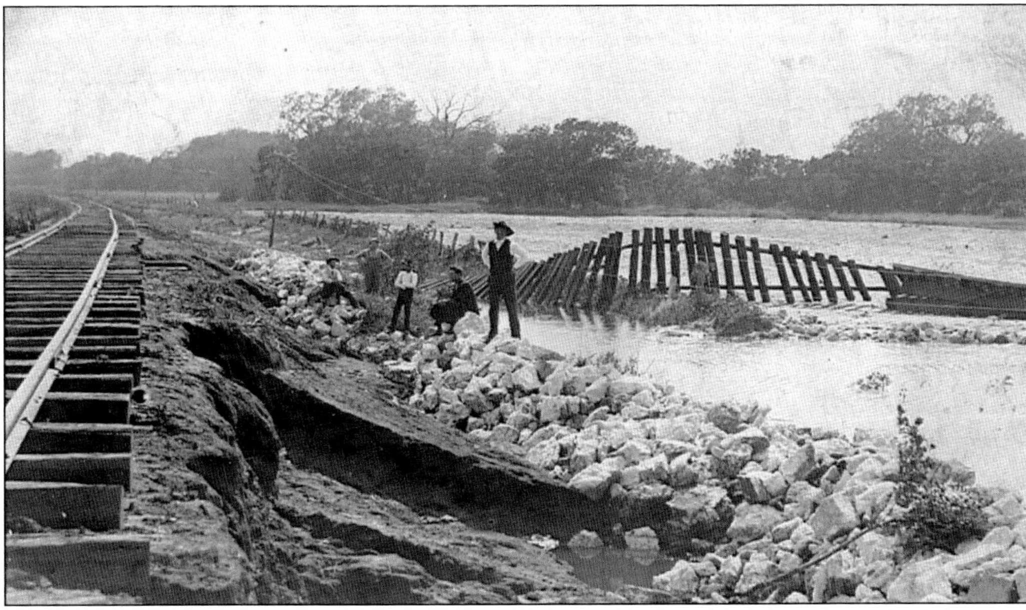

Foss was established in 1900, and by 1902, some 50 homes and business were built between the railroad and Turkey Creek. The town was struck by a devastating blow on April 2, 1902, when an eight-foot wall of water washed out about a mile of railroad track, washing away over 35 homes and businesses. Nine deaths were recorded by drowning. The young town rebuilt but moved up the hill above the railroad. (Courtesy Washita County Museum.)

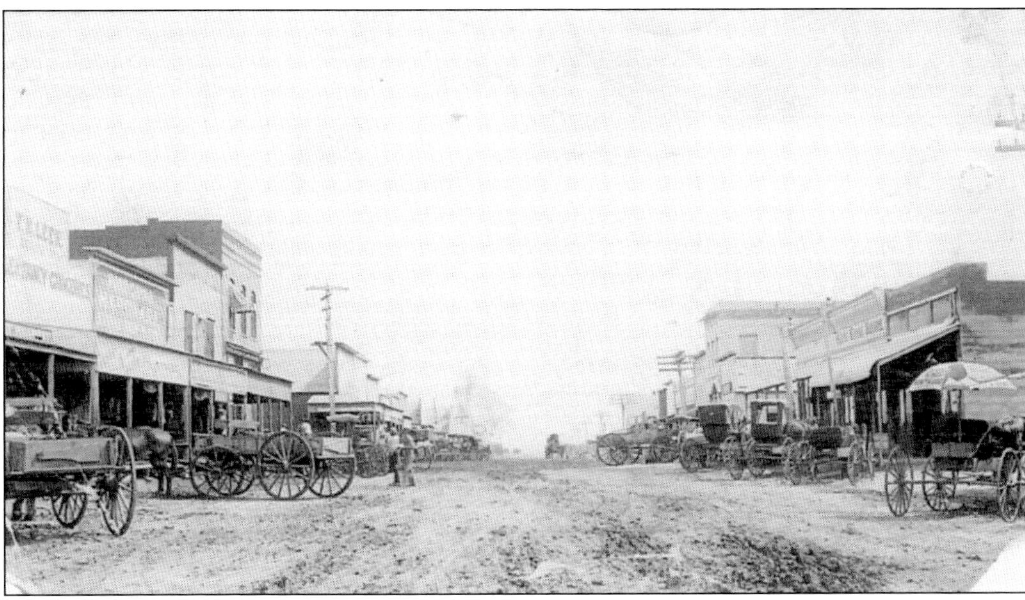

This is the main street of Rocky looking north in 1906. Rocky was established in 1897 when W. F. Shultz opened his rock-front store. Rocky actually received its name from the Shultz rock-front store. On July 12, 1898, the U.S. postal department issued approval to open the post office in Rocky. The town of Rocky became an agricultural center, and with the coming of the railroad in March 1902, Rocky experienced a tremendous growth. (Courtesy Washita County Museum.)

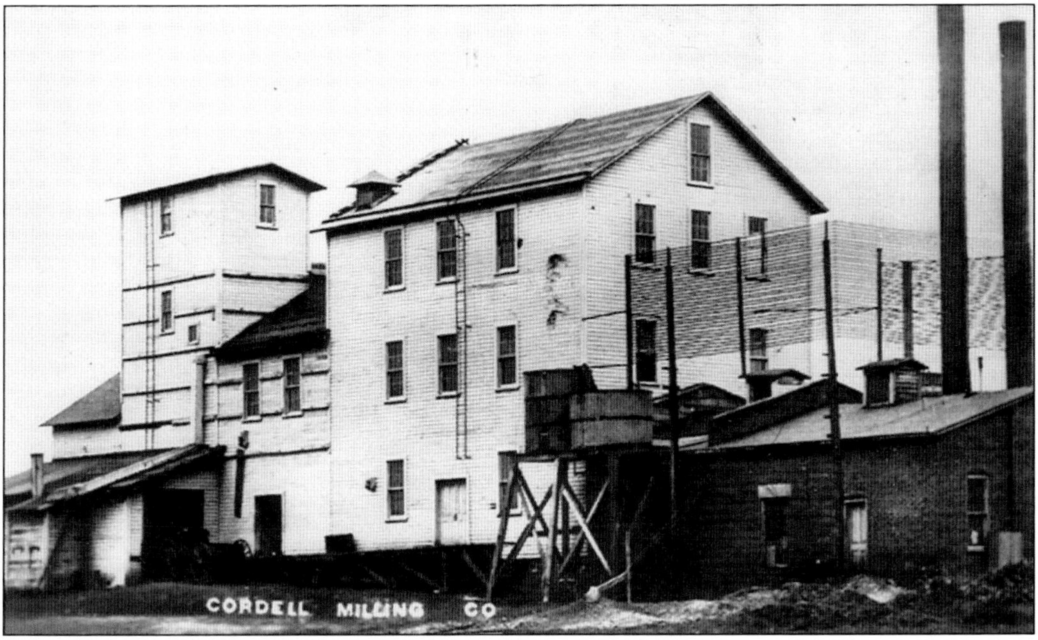

Cordell Milling Company was established in 1902 with the building of a flour mill that had a capacity of producing 250 barrels of flour per day. During World War I, the Cordell Milling Company shipped flour all over the world, operating 24 hours per day for several years. In the 1940s, during World War II, the mill was again a very important producer of food and feed. After World War II, A. J. Orr closed the Cordell Milling Company and retired. (Courtesy Washita County Museum.)

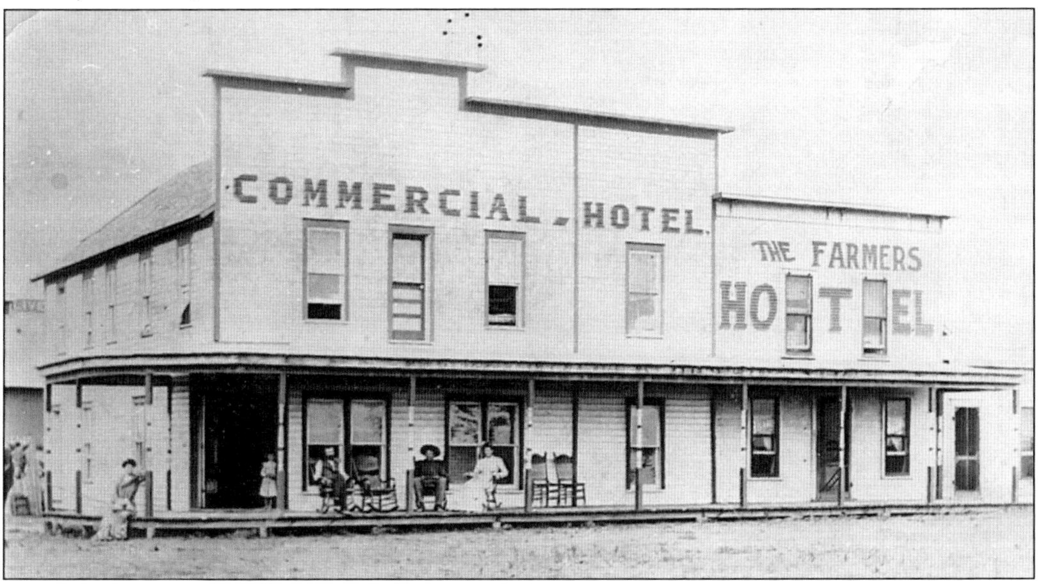

The Commercial and Farmers Hotels were built in Bessie in 1902 when the Blackwell, Enid and Southern Railroad came through town. Bessie was made a division point for the railroad with two passenger trains per day stopping for meals and two trains originating at Bessie. Both the Commercial and Farmers Hotels were destroyed by a tornado in the spring of 1905. (Courtesy Washita County Museum.)

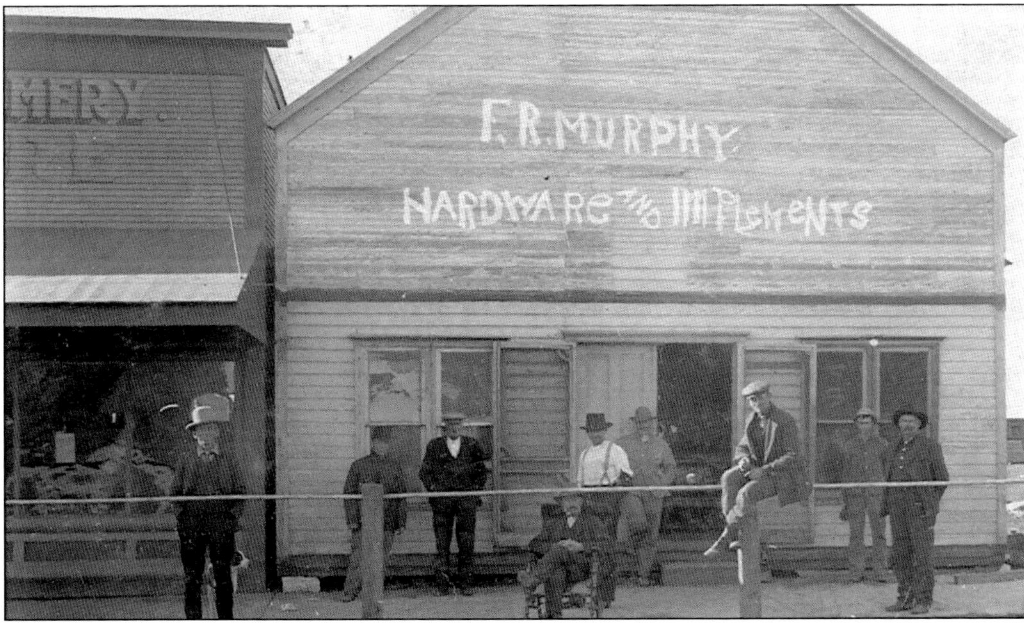

The Murphy Hardware and Implement business was destroyed in the 1902 Foss flood. The building in the photograph was constructed in 1903 up the hill on the north side of the railroad. This store was the beginning of a hardware business that was established in four Washita County communities. (Courtesy Washita County Museum.)

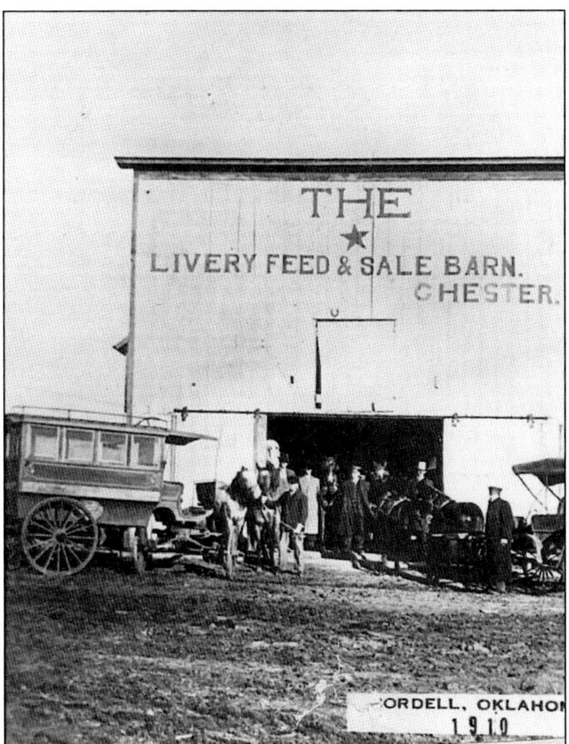

The Livery Stable and Sale Barn was established by O. D. Chedester, a veterinarian on East Main Street in 1902. Livery stables were a very necessary business during the horse-and-buggy days. Cordell supported four livery stables, sometimes they were all filled to capacity and teams had to be tied out along the creek that went through town. (Courtesy Washita County Museum.)

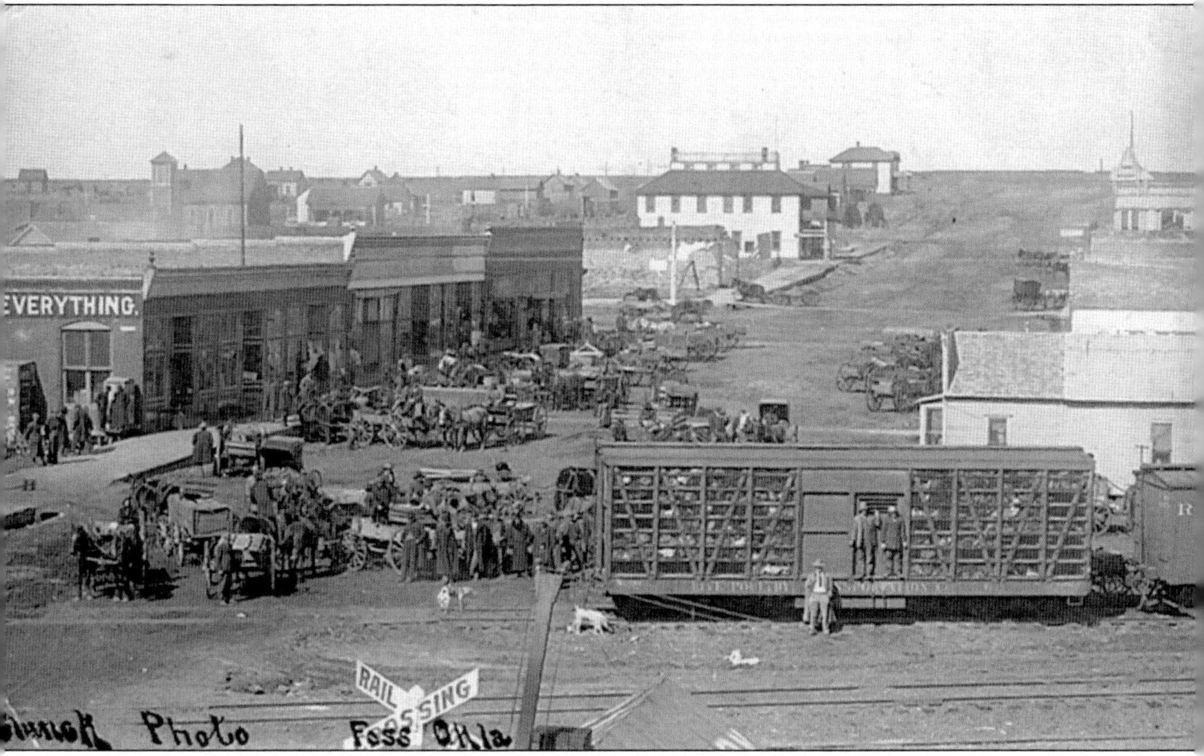

The town of Foss in 1908 was a very busy agricultural market. Their trade territory drew business from approximately 60 miles north and south and about 30 miles east and west. Every week, C. Kelley, a Foss produce dealer, would ship a carload of live chickens to New York City. After the destruction by the 1902 flood, the business district moved to the north side of the railroad out of the Turkey Creek bottomland. By 1908, Foss had three cotton gins, two grain elevators, and a flour mill with a 100-barrel-per-day capacity. Foss was also the home of two large hotels, three general merchandise stores, and a very aggressive newspaper. Foss was a shipping point for cattle and hogs by rail to Oklahoma City and Fort Worth packing plants. Today Foss is considered a ghost town with no merchants and no school, only a couple of churches and a post office. Only a few homes remain occupied. (Courtesy Washita County Museum.)

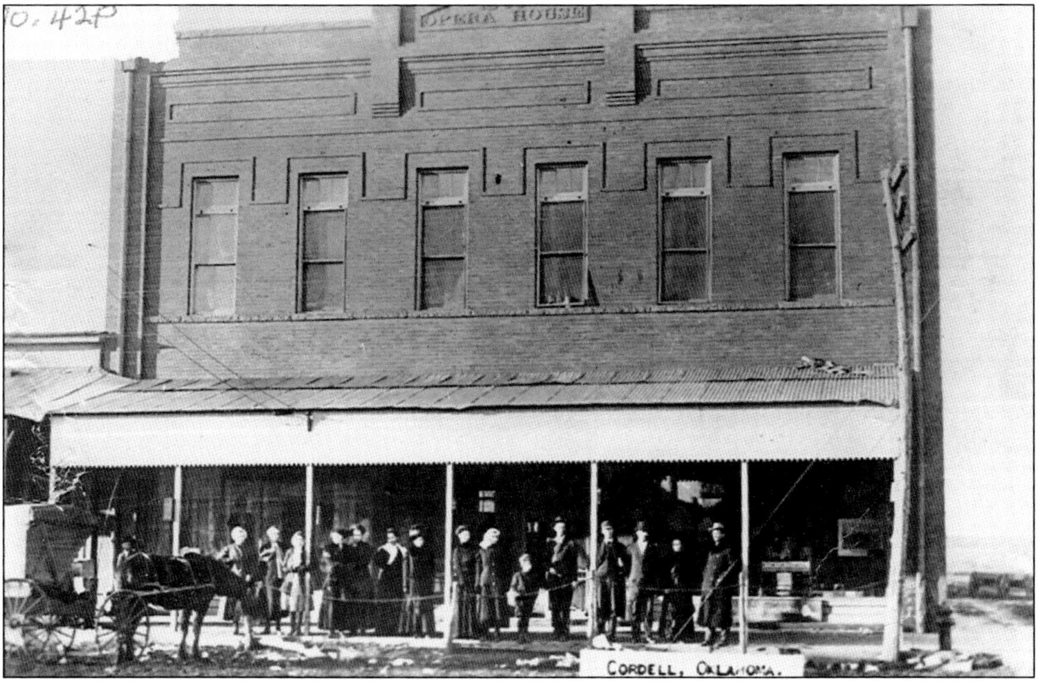

The opera house in Cordell was constructed in 1907. The Miller Brothers Dry Goods store occupied the street level while the second level was a meeting room used for traveling stage shows. From 1907 until 1926, the top flour was also used as a basketball gymnasium where Cordell High School, Cordell Christian College, and the Cordell Academy played their basketball games. For many years after 1926, the opera house's upper meeting room was the home of the Cordell Masonic lodge. (Courtesy Washita County Museum.)

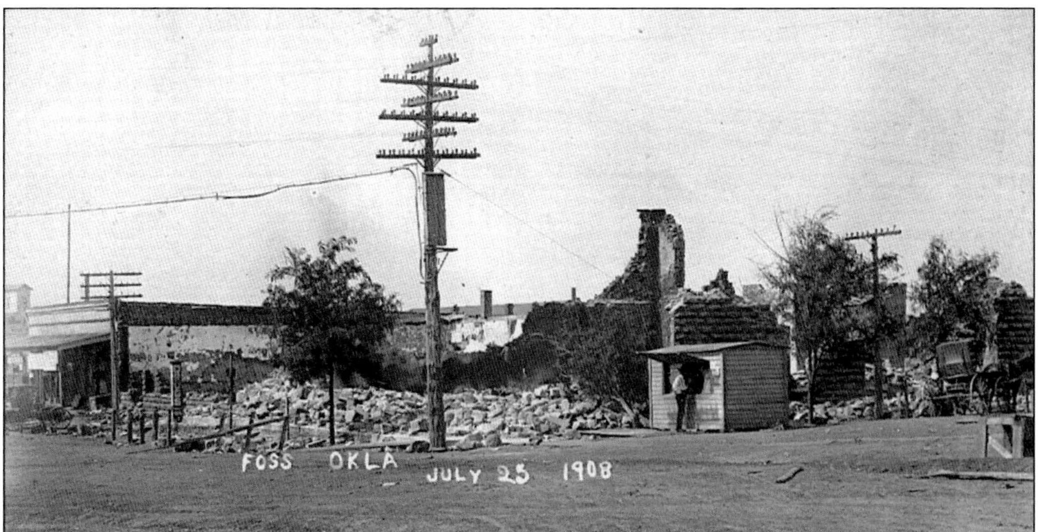

The Foss business district suffered the loss of one complete block of the businesses in July 1908. A bank, a drugstore, a hotel, a doctor's office, and other businesses were completely destroyed. The fire started deterioration in the business climate of Foss, and the once prosperous and busy community could never recover. (Courtesy Washita County Museum.)

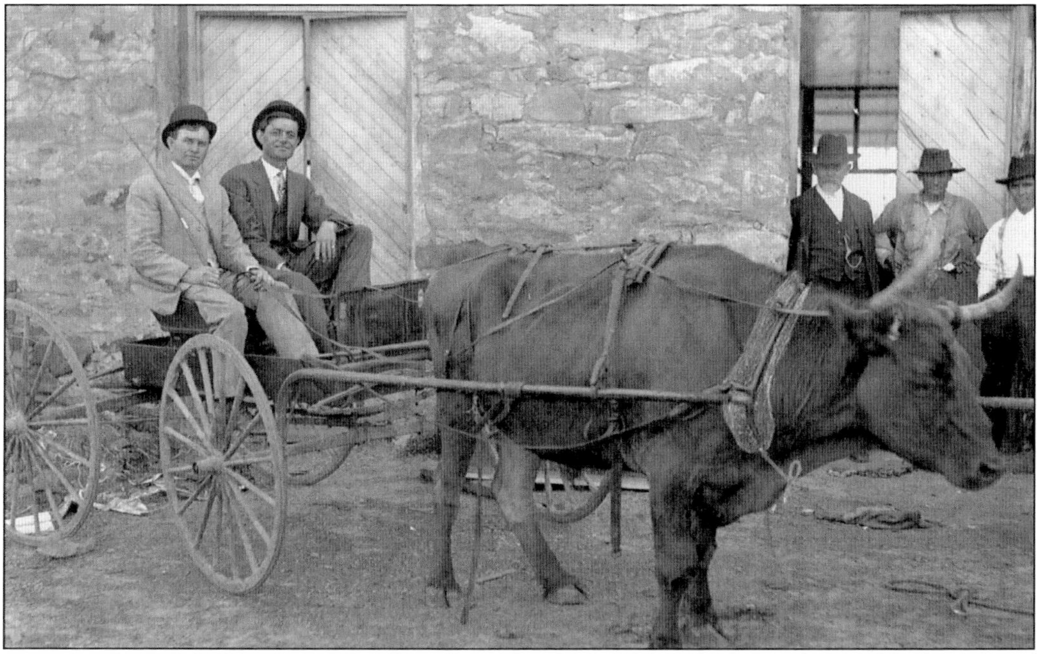

Seen here is a Saturday afternoon in 1903 in the town of Rocky. These two young farm boys were not about to lose out on a Saturday night in town. They got all dressed up in their Sunday go-to-meeting clothes, hitched their ox to the buggy, and were ready for Saturday night. (Courtesy Washita County Museum.)

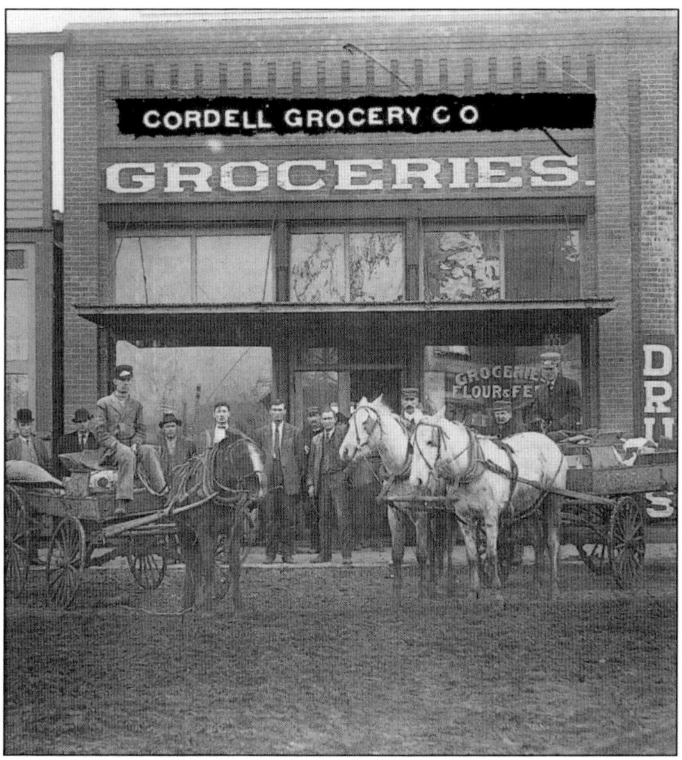

The Cordell Grocery and Feed was owned and operated by the Parman brothers in 1910. The Parman brothers took pride in their service. They had a two-horse team and heavy wagon for large deliveries, and they utilized a smaller wagon pulled by a single horse for smaller deliveries. (Courtesy Washita County Museum.)

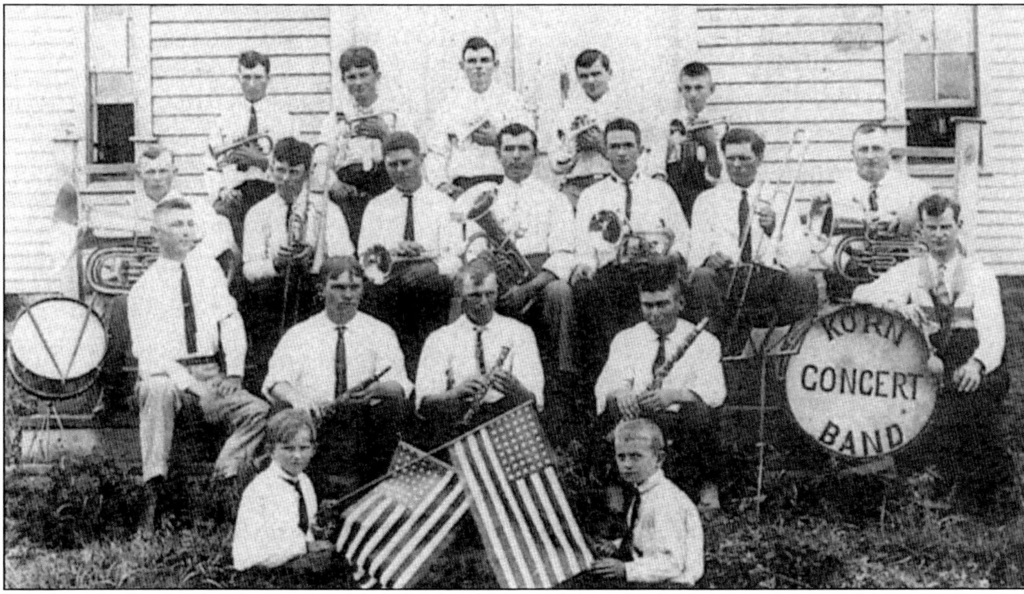

Seen here is the Korn Concert Band 100 years ago. Holding flags are Barney Ratzlaff (left) and Otto Flaming. The others are, from left to right, (first row) Sam Richert, Eill Engel, Pete Leppke, Ed Engel, and Dan Boese-drummer; (second row) H. A. Reimer, Frank Siemens, Herman Reimer, John Litke, Karl Heidebrecht, C. F. Reimer, and Henry Kroker; (third row) C. J. Funk, Abe Duerksen, A. G. Duerksen, John Thiessen, and Aron Ratzlaff. They are a proud band. (Courtesy Washita County Museum.)

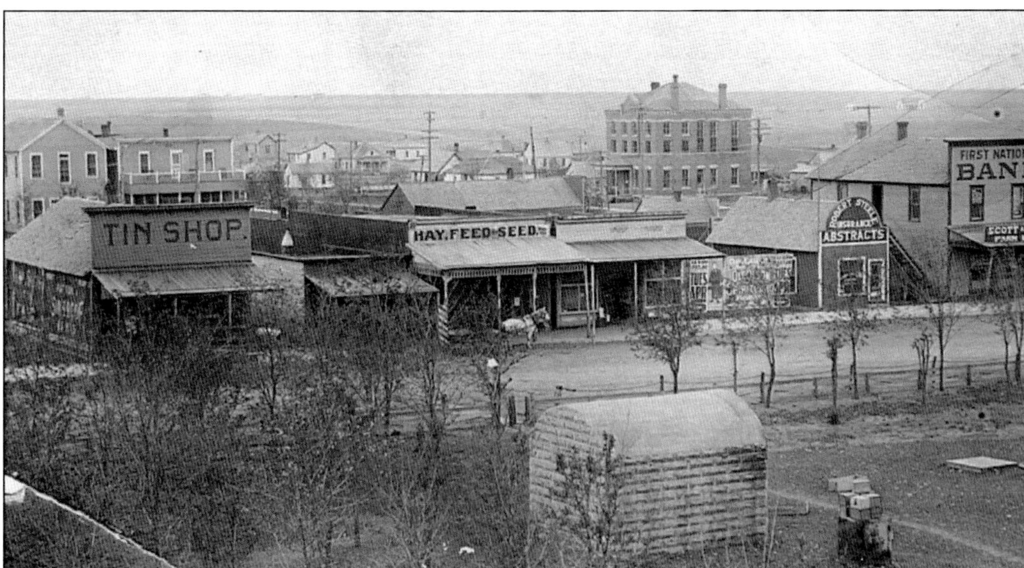

This is the north side of Main Street in Cordell in the fall of 1909 after the fire that destroyed the Washita County courthouse. The front area of the photograph shows the old jail cells, which were replaced by the large three-story jail in 1907, as seen in the background. (Courtesy Washita County Museum.)

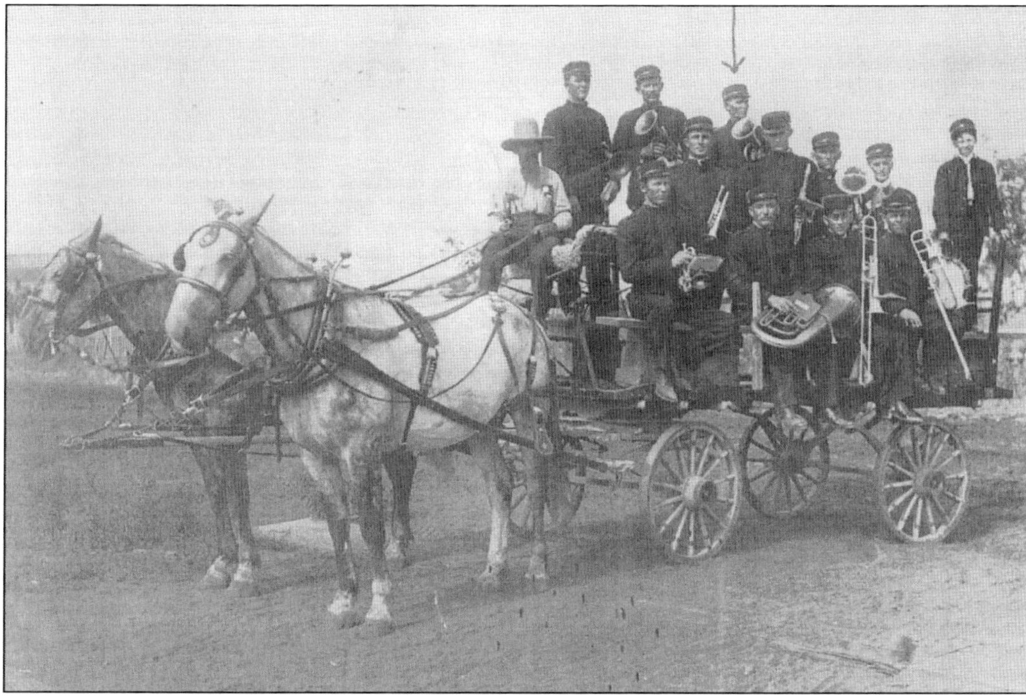

Here Sentinel town band participates in a 1903 parade. The band refused to march this hot day so transportation was furnished. C. P. Singletary, pointed out by the arrow, with the brass horn, was the bandleader. The brass horn is now a family keepsake. (Courtesy Washita County Museum.)

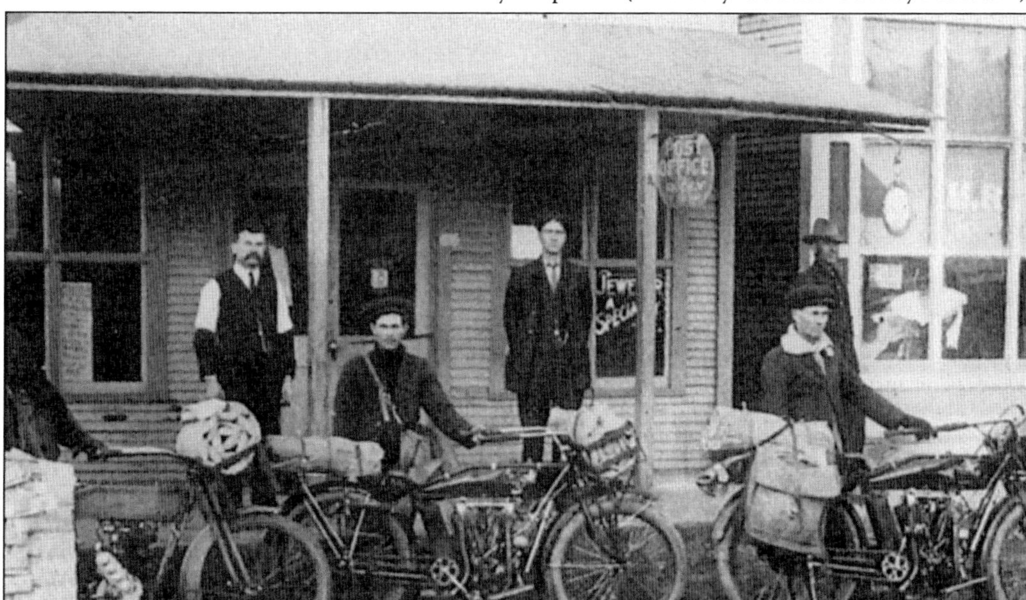

This is the Rocky post office in 1912. From left to right are Will Greenhaw, mail carrier; Lewis E. Smith, postmaster; Mack Sanders, mail carrier; C. W. "Wilburn" Squires, jeweler with "his jewelry shop located in post office"; Ira Hill, mail carrier; and Hugh Ferguson. The Rocky mail carriers changed from horse and buggy to motorcycles for mail delivery in late 1910. (Courtesy Washita County Museum.)

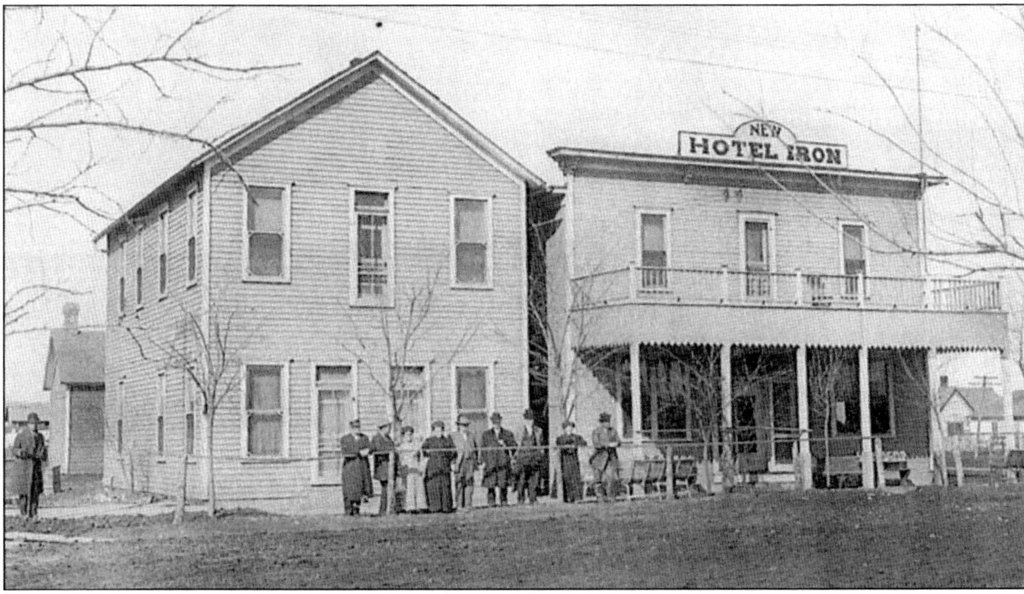

Seen here is the New Iron Hotel of Cordell. In 1892, when the town of Cloud Chief was established, the Iron Hotel moved from El Reno to Cloud Chief. In 1900, when the county seat was moved to Cordell, the Iron Hotel also moved to Cordell and was rebuilt as the New Iron Hotel. The hotel had a popular dining room, which could accommodate 200 people. It closed due to the Depression in the early 1930s. The Cordell post office was built on the hotel site in 1936. (Courtesy Washita County Museum.)

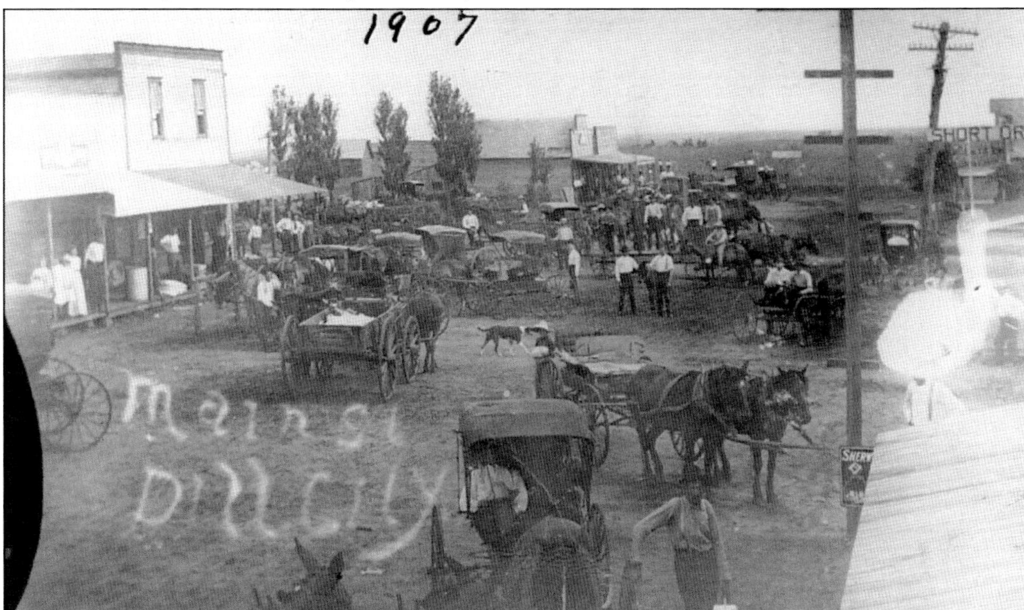

Dill City's Main Street is seen here in 1907. Dill City was established in 1902 when the North Burns post office moved to Dill City, which is located eight miles west of Cordell. When the Orient Railroad came through the town in 1907, it was quite a benefit for the little farming community, located in a sandy area, where the main crops were row crops, cotton, milo, feed grains, and forage. (Courtesy Washita County Museum.)

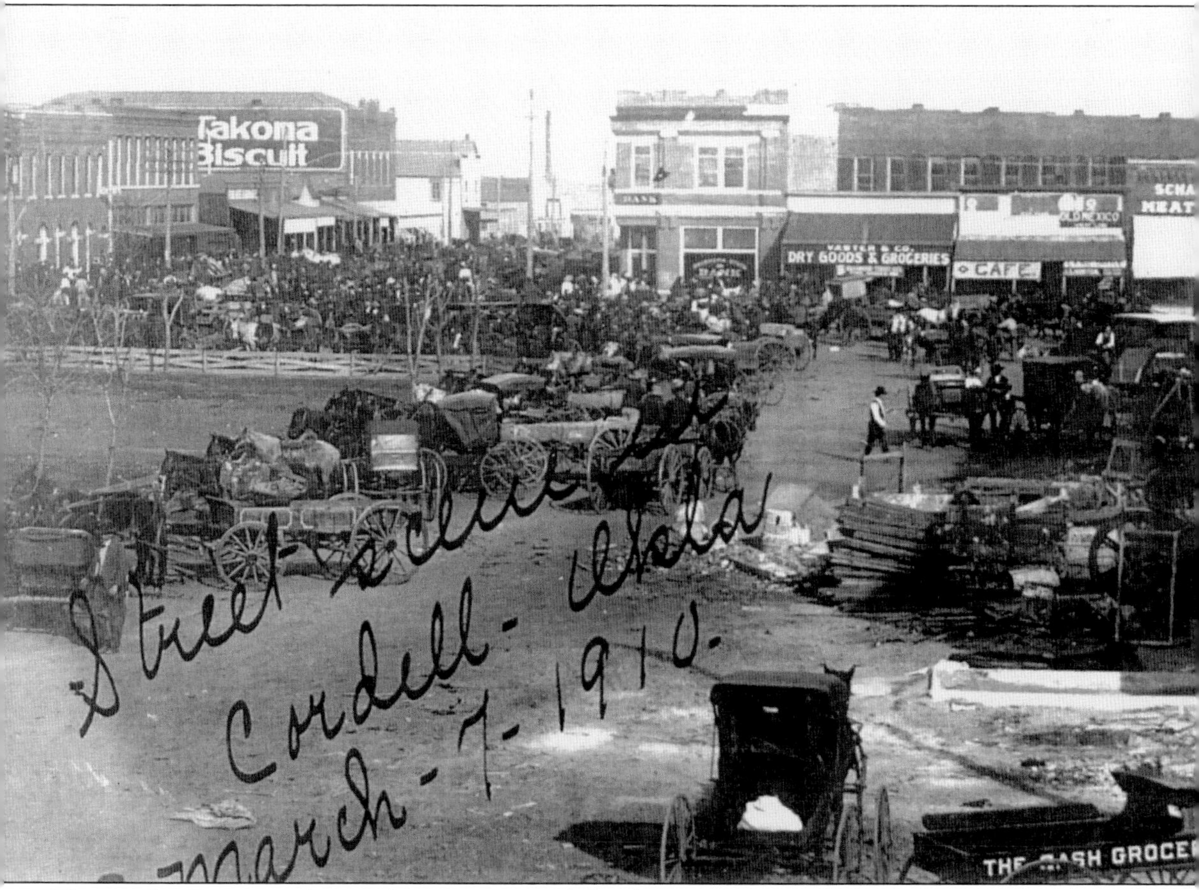

This is the First Monday Trades Day in Cordell. The Cordell Commercial Club, organized in 1902, established a special promotion, First Monday Trades Day, in the fall of 1909. Each merchant would promote specials, and a drawing would be held in the late afternoon. The commercial club employed an auctioneer who would sell farmers' excess items, charging no auction fee. Contests such as men's wood chopping, ladies wood sawing, children's recital, and spelling were held. Also during season, the best 10 ears of corn, the largest watermelon, and so on received cash prizes. The program was quite successful, as one can see from this photograph with crowds of people resulting from the First Monday Trades promotion. The First Monday promotion continued until the late 1920s, many times drawing over 5,000 people. (Courtesy Washita County Museum.)

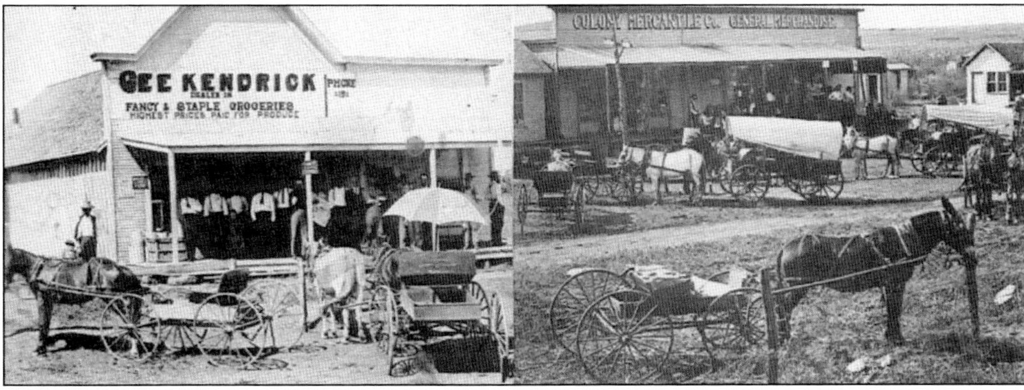

Colony, the town that had been established by John Seger and his group of Native Americans in 1889, became quite a trade center. In 1910, the two principal retail businesses were Colony Mercantile Company and the Gee Kendrick General Store. One can tell from the photographs how busy the little buzzing town was. Colony is still a proud and clean community today. (Courtesy Washita County Museum.)

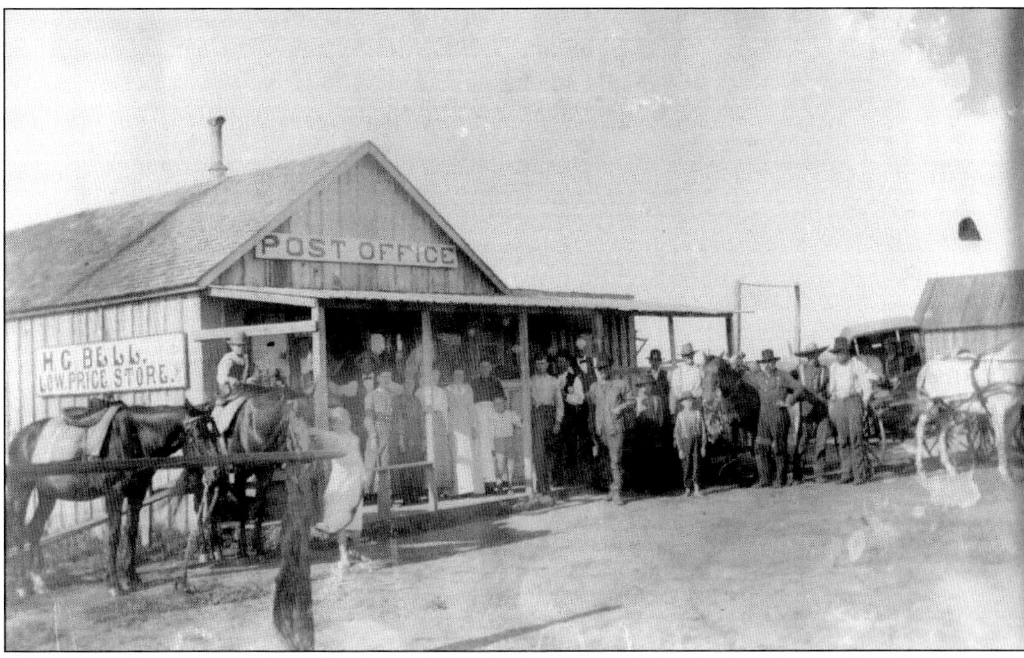

This is Cowden's new post office. Cowden, a community located 16 miles southeast of Cordell, was quite proud when its new post office was established in 1901 in the Bell General Store. One can gather from the photograph the excitement that the new post office generated. The Cowden consolidated school was a very active school and the center of a proud community. The post office closed in 1908, and the school closed in the 1940s. Only a small community center, located on the school grounds, exists today. Cowden is one of 44 ghost towns scattered over Washita County. (Courtesy Washita County Museum.)

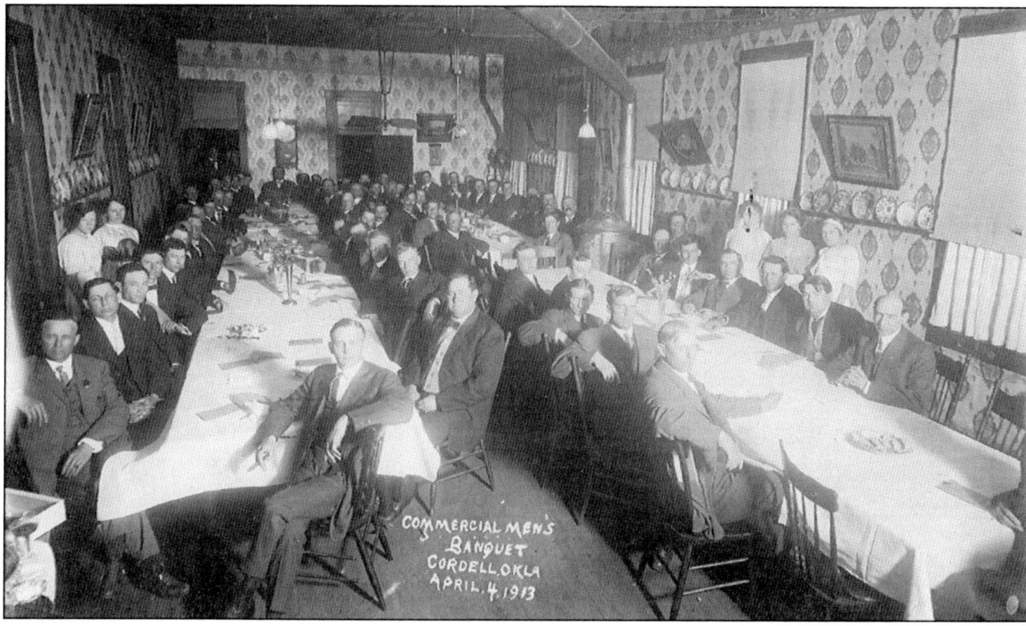

The Cordell Commercial Club banquet of April 4, 1913, was held in the dining room of the New Iron Hotel. The men of the commercial club were a very aggressive group of businessmen. It was at this meeting that a road committee was formed to establish road markers starting at Sayre, directing traffic through Cordell, and on east to Oklahoma City. As a result of that committee, Highway 41 was established, which is now U.S. 152. (Courtesy Washita County Museum.)

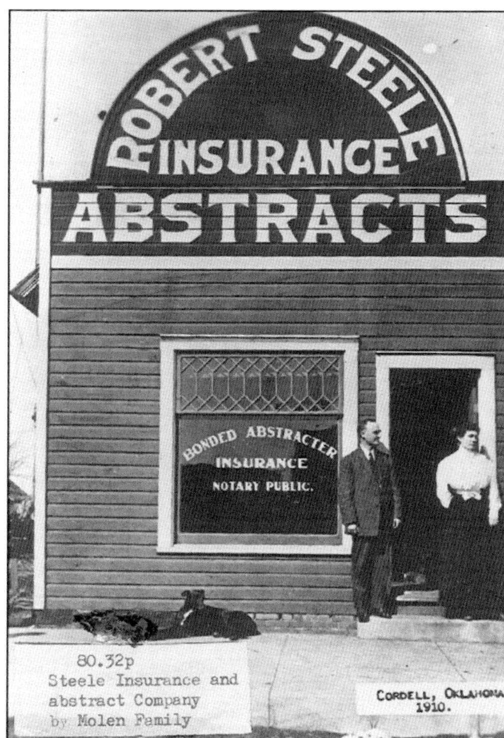

In 1903, Robert Steele constructed this building located at 125 East Main Street. Steele is standing in front of the building with his wife, Kate. He was the first elected mayor of Cordell. The building in the photograph was replaced in 1929 with a brick building, which stands on the site today. (Courtesy Molen family.)

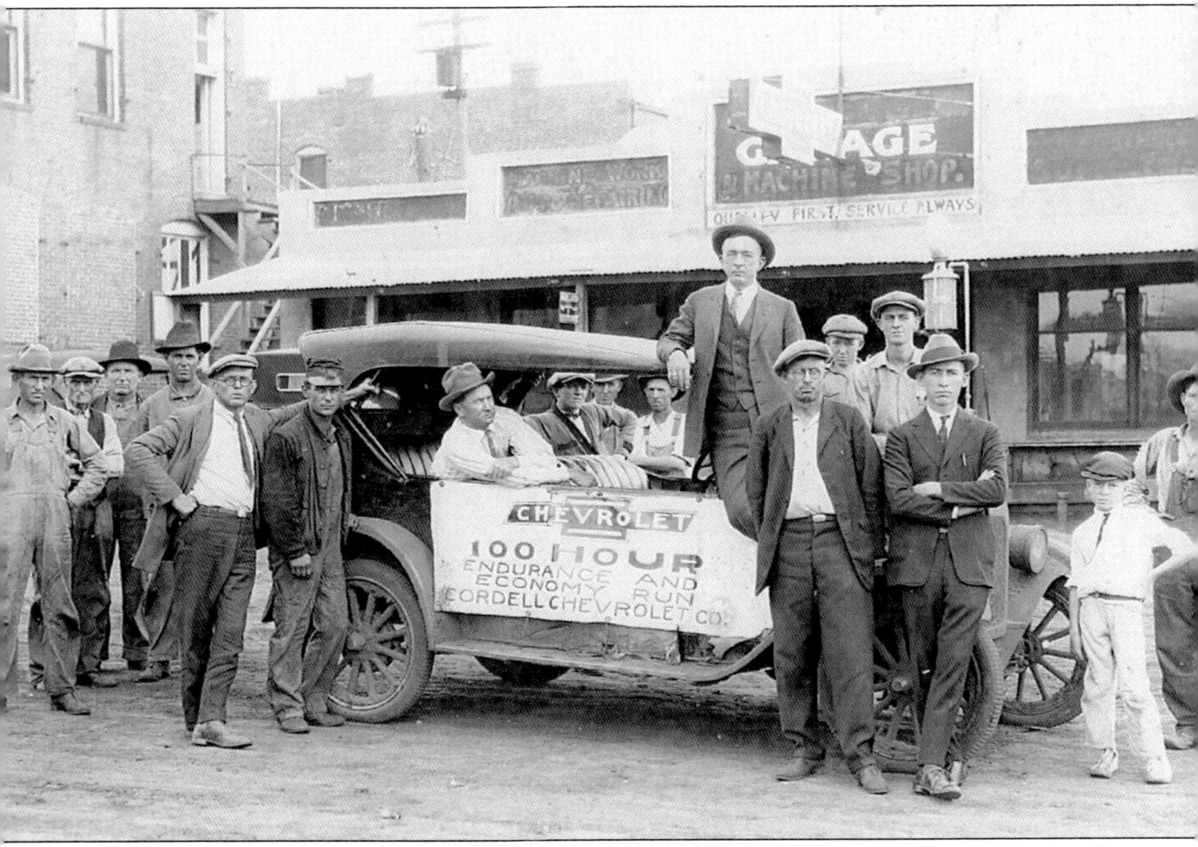

The 1913 Chevrolet automobile drew quite a crowd of curious admires as it was parked in front of the Ed Smith Chevrolet Company located at 215 East Main Street in Cordell. The gentleman with the white shirt leaning against the back of the car is Joe Reis, the company salesman; standing in front of Reis is Herman Horn, a mechanic; the gentleman sitting in the backseat is Edgar Jennings, company manager; standing on the fender is company owner Ed Smith; standing on the ground in front of Smith is Burt Walker, a mechanic; the gentleman leaning on the front fender is Roy Morris, a salesman. This 1913 deluxe Chevrolet touring automobile was priced at $418 delivered. In the five years between 1908 and 1913, automobile dealers in Cordell became numerous. In 1913, there were nine automobile dealers in Cordell, each with a different make car. In 1912, the City of Cordell passed an ordinance that 10 miles per hour was the maximum speed limit, whether it was horse or automobile. (Courtesy Washita County Museum.)

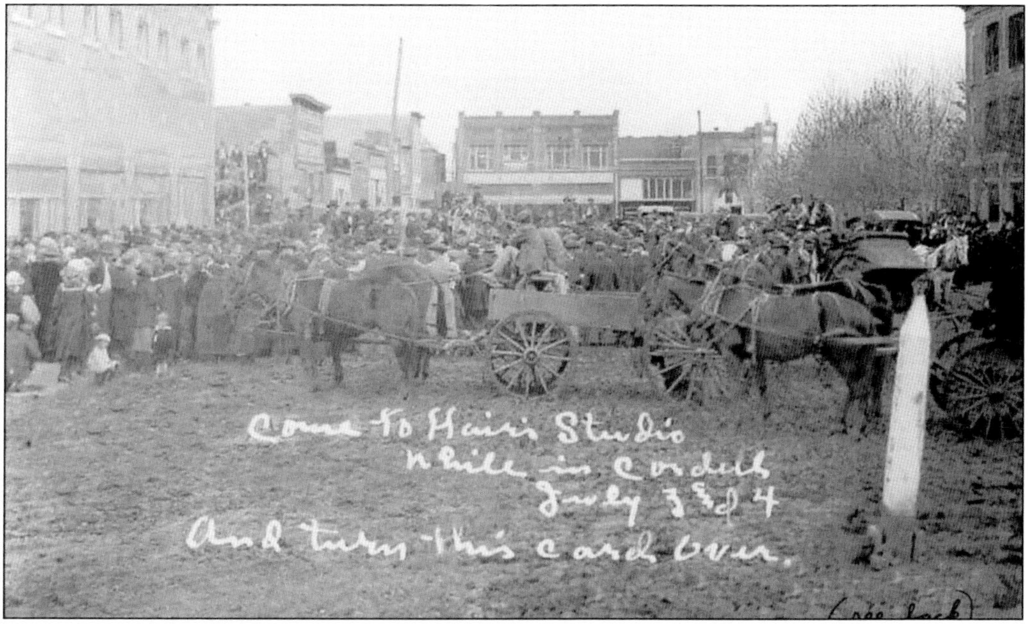

The July 3 and 4 trade day promotion in 1913 caused quite a parking problem on the north side of the square in Cordell. After a two-inch rain, the people came to town for trade day. The board sidewalks gave some help; however, the crowd did not let the mud affect their enthusiasm. (Courtesy Washita County Museum.)

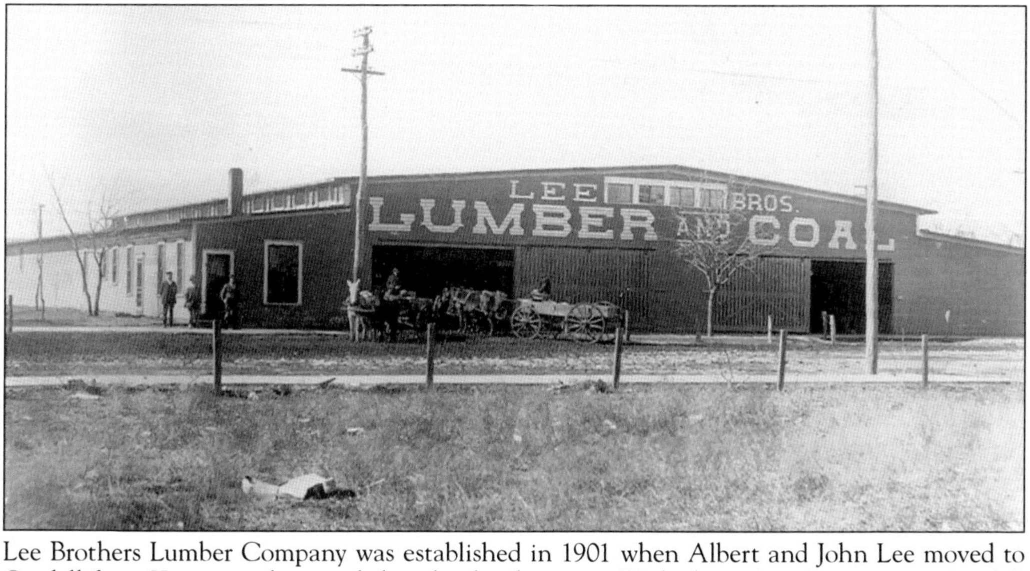

Lee Brothers Lumber Company was established in 1901 when Albert and John Lee moved to Cordell from Kansas and opened their lumber business. With the railroad arriving in Cordell in February 1902, the Lee brothers expanded, developing the largest lumberyard in the county. It was through their efforts that 400 trees were planted in 1904 and Lee Park was established. Today several of those trees can be seen along the streets and in the park of Cordell. (Courtesy Washita County Museum.)

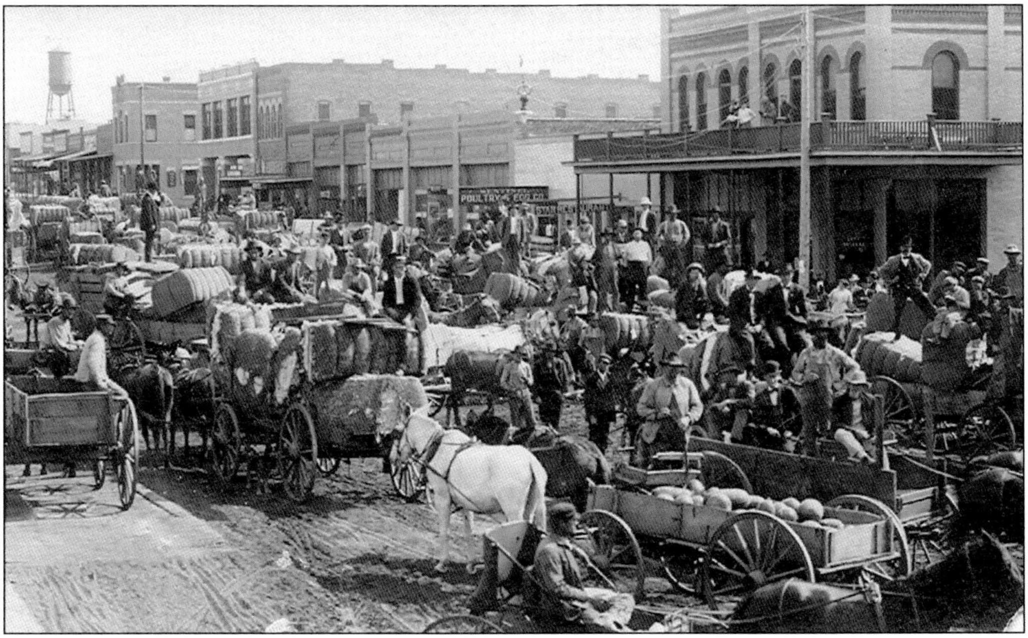

This is a street scene in the early fall of 1911 in Sentinel. The Wright Hotel, the building with the overhang, was built in 1910. Cotton buyers were at the hotel, and many farmers brought in their early bales of cotton to try to sell to get operating money to pay bills. Sentinel has the oldest farmers co-op in Washita County. The co-op cotton gin started operating in 1905. (Courtesy Washita County Museum.)

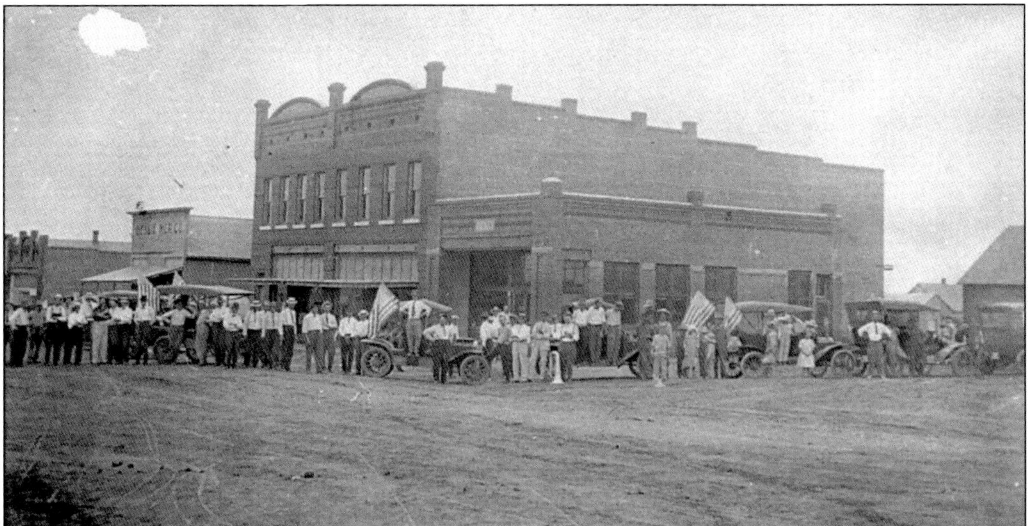

The Cordell Commercial Club organized a booster club that visited communities throughout the county, hoping to create an increase in business and good relations for Cordell businessmen. This photograph was taken in 1918 when the Cordell Boosters visited the town of Bessie. (Courtesy Washita County Museum.)

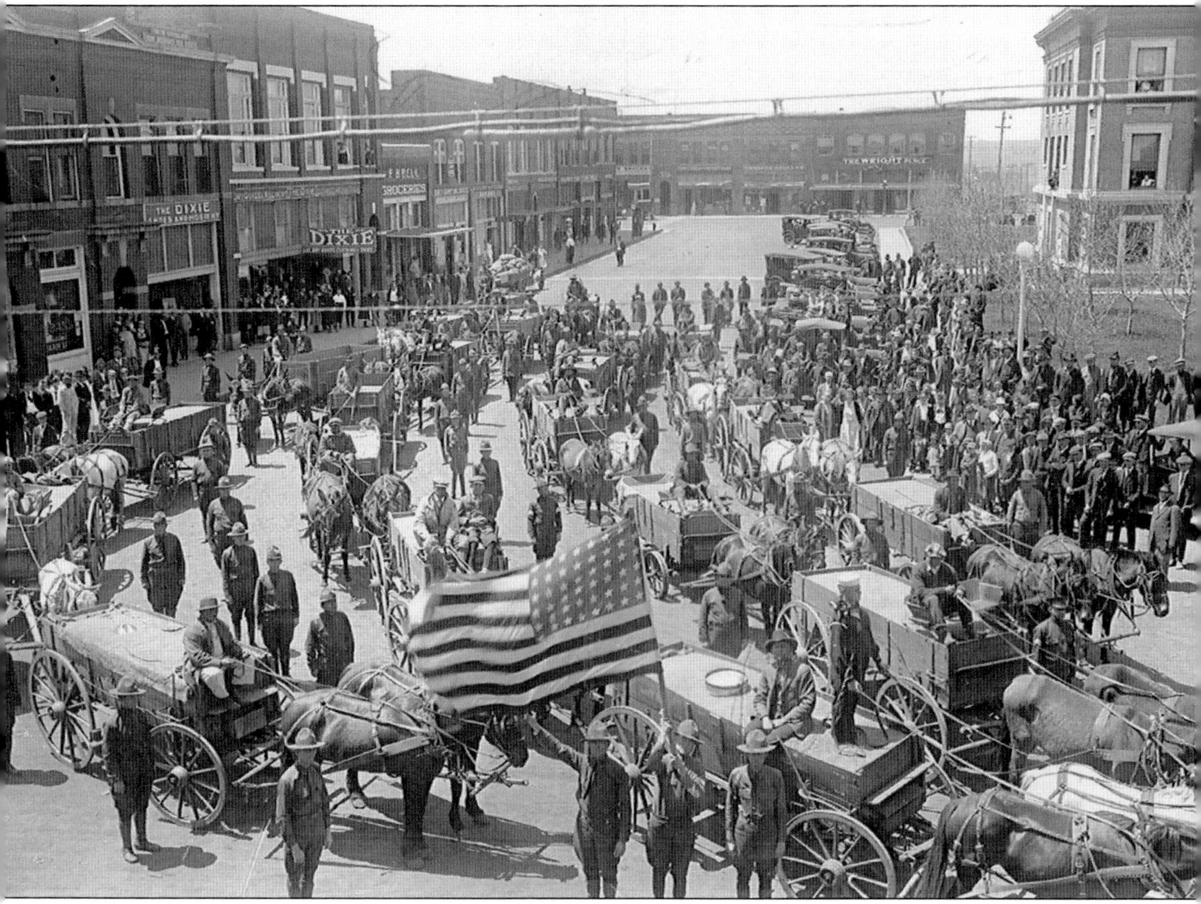

During World War I those who were not in the service organized the home guard. Many of the farmers in Washita County refused to sell their wheat in 1918 because they felt it was making a contribution to the war effort. Several of the farmers had a very strong religious conviction in opposition to the war. Flour became scarce as flour mills ran short on milling wheat. In March 1918, the Cordell Milling Company had no wheat available to make flour. It was common knowledge throughout the county that several farmers had bins full of last year's wheat crop. Most every weekend, members of the home guard would volunteer their services by hauling in the wheat. With a court order and police or army protection, the guard would load and haul the wheat to the flour mill. The wheat was sold, and the farmer-owner would receive the check for the grain. This March 1918 weekend, the home guard loaded 62 wagonloads, 3,120 bushels, of wheat from a farmer living seven miles northwest of Cordell. The guard paraded around the courthouse square on the way to the flour mill located three blocks west on the railroad. (Courtesy Washita County Museum.)

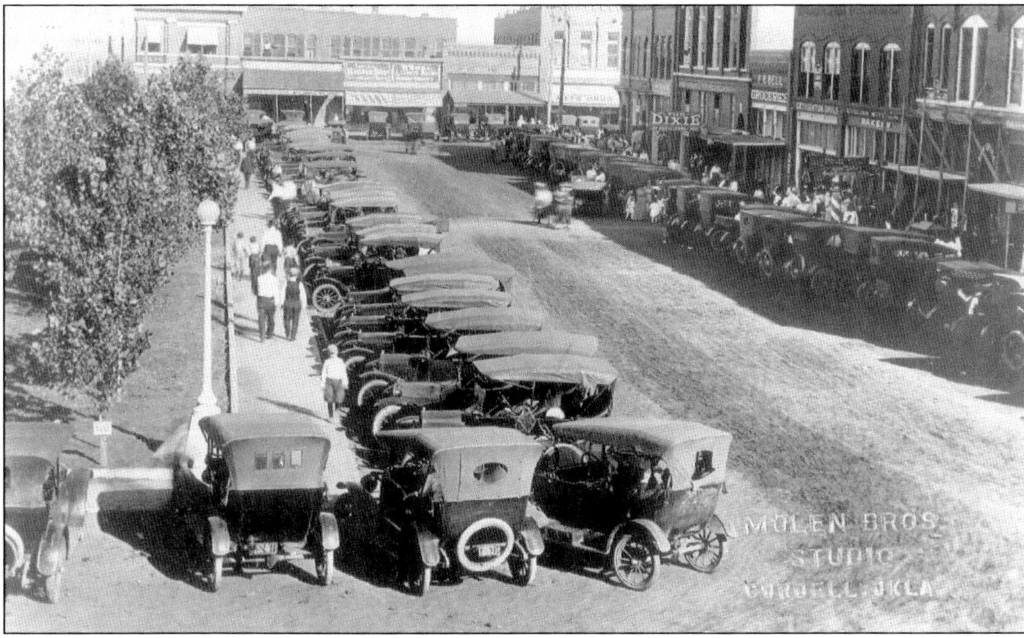

This is the day that the boys left for World War I. The town was full of people and cars the day that the group of men from Washita County reported for service. There was hardly a parking place in town as the men reported for training. They were sent to Fort Sill at Lawton to train for army duty. (Courtesy Washita County Museum.)

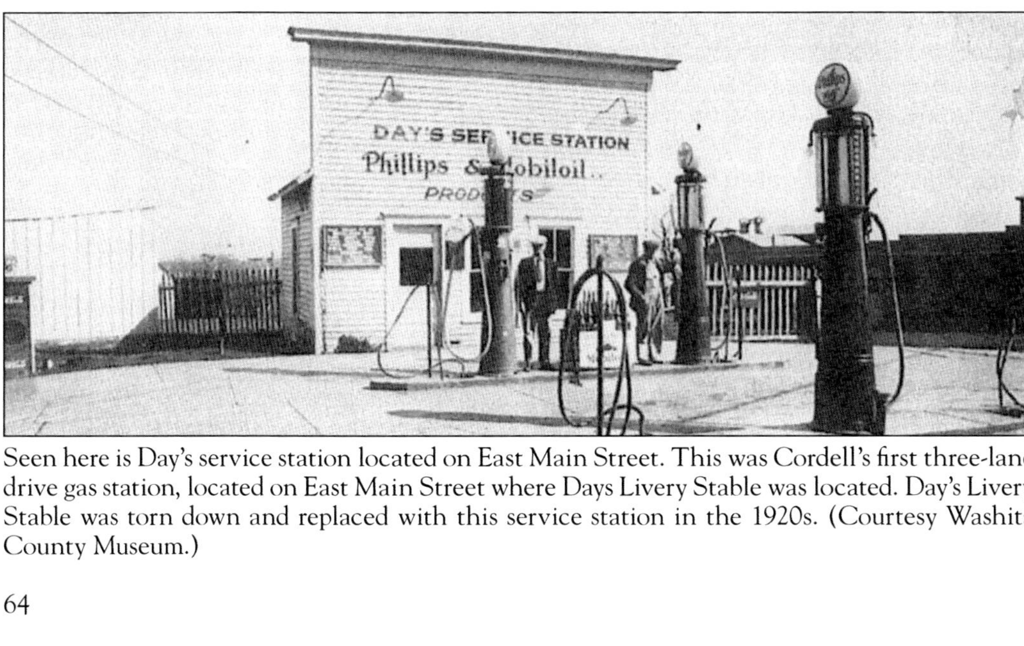

Seen here is Day's service station located on East Main Street. This was Cordell's first three-lane drive gas station, located on East Main Street where Days Livery Stable was located. Day's Livery Stable was torn down and replaced with this service station in the 1920s. (Courtesy Washita County Museum.)

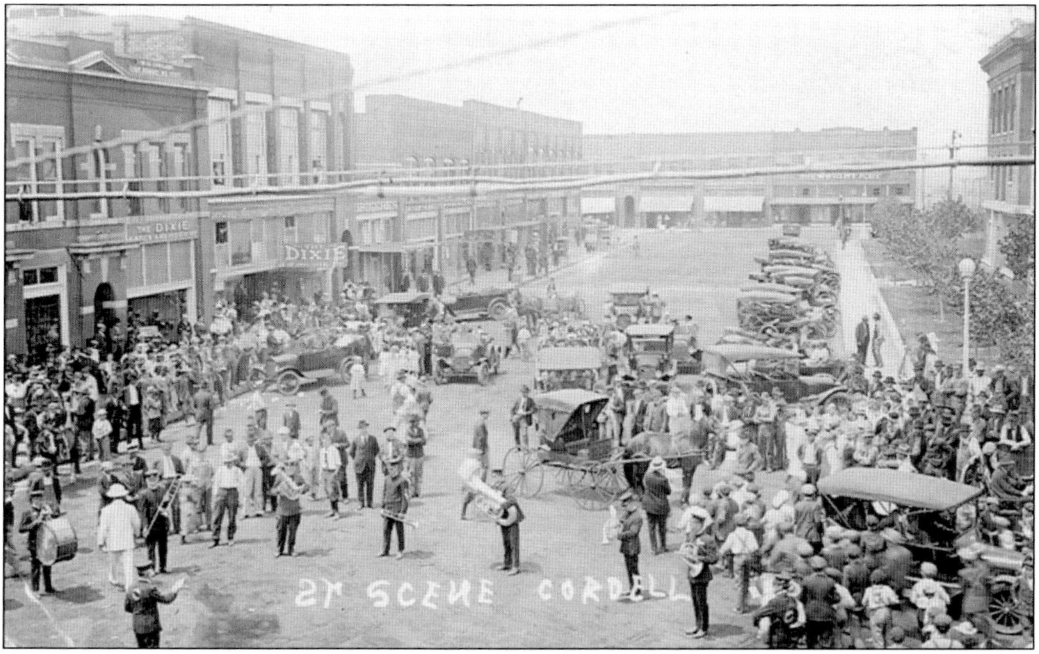

A street scene in Cordell in 1912 is seen here. The town band is in a circle giving a performance. Notice the mixture of automobiles and horse and buggies parked around the square. The streets are still dirt, but curbs and sidewalks have been installed. (Courtesy Washita County Museum.)

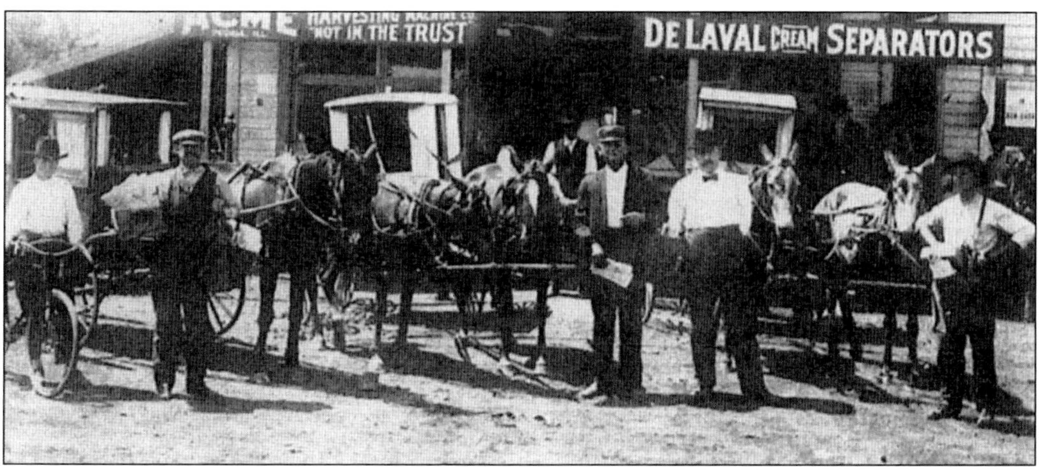

In 1912, the Cloud Chief rural mail carriers were still using horses and buggies to deliver the mail. Euel Sheets, with bicycle, is on the left. The next man is a Mr. Keykendell, then S. J. Jordan, the others are not identified. (Courtesy Washita County Museum.)

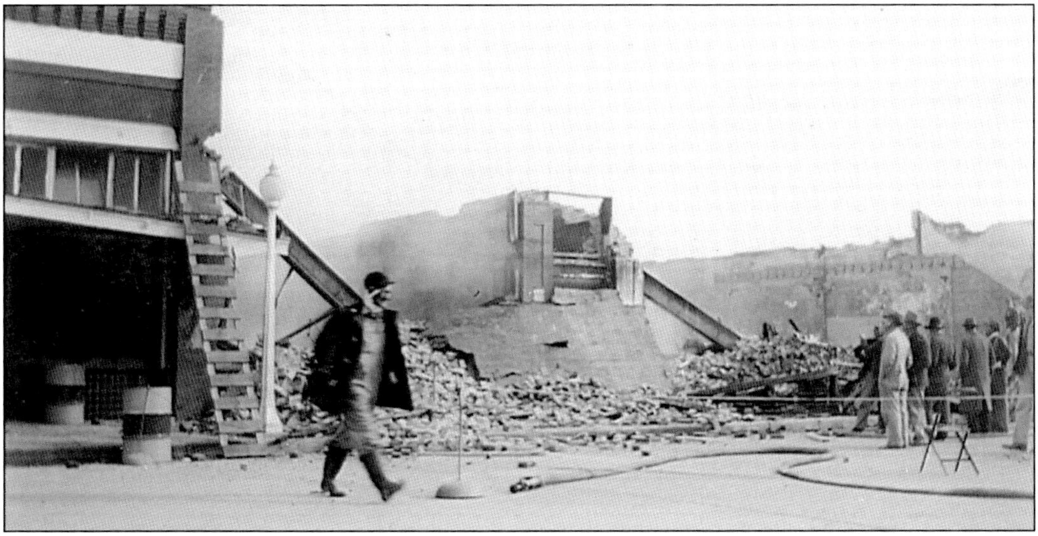

In January 1942, a fire destroyed four buildings in Cordell, the Aachte Implement agency, the Aachte three-story hardware, the A-muse-u Theatre, and Ira B. Taylor Drug Store, and heavily damaged a café. (Courtesy Washita County Museum.)

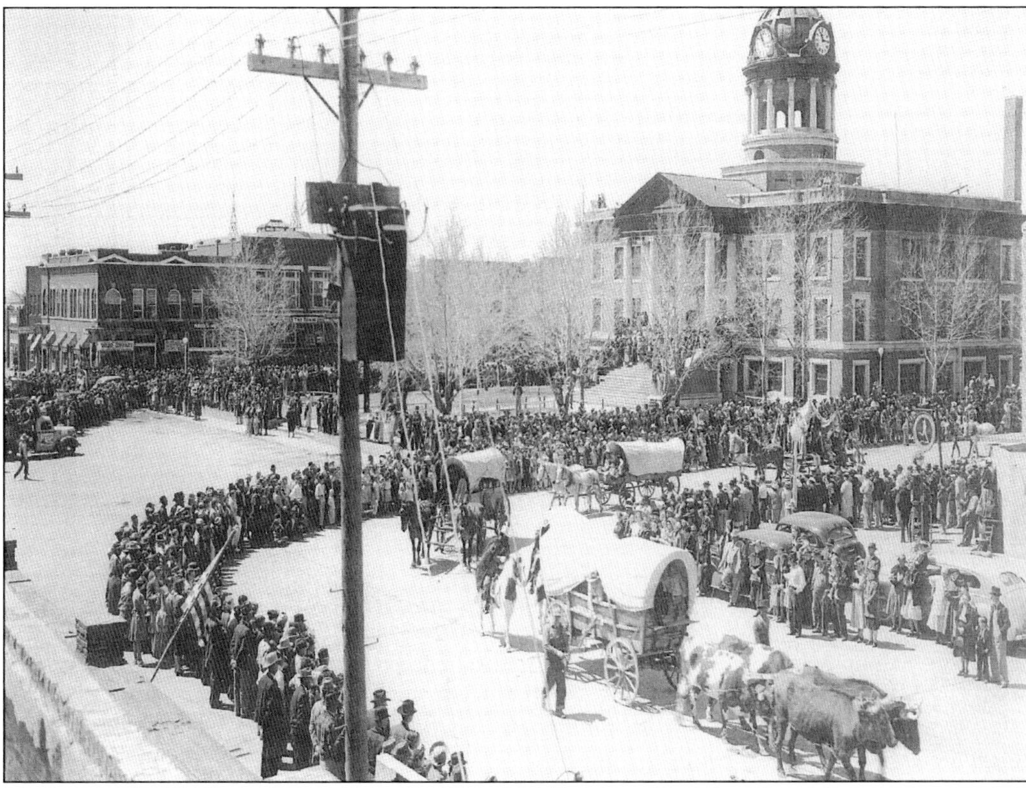

A 1940 pioneer celebration parade was held in Cordell commemorating the 48th anniversary of the opening of the Cheyenne-Arapaho reservation for homesteading. Between 4,000 and 5,000 people were in attendance at the pioneer days parade, which was approximately two miles long and took about 1 hour and 45 minutes to pass by the review stand. (Courtesy Marjorie Taylor.)

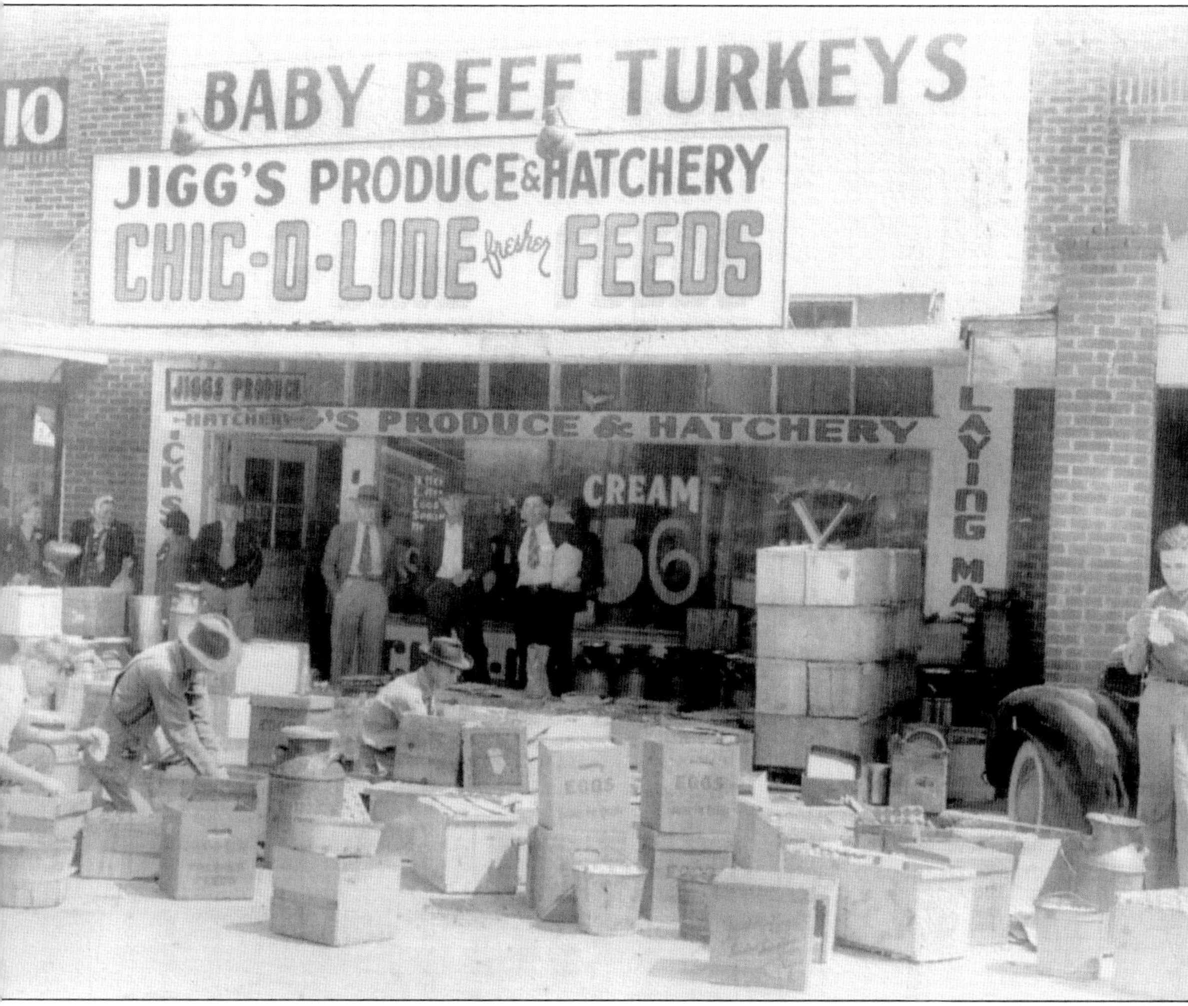

Cream stations and produces, such as Jiggs Produce, were very popular during the Depression and dust bowl days. Employees in front on the left, from left to right, are Jimmy Keller, Claude Mathis, R. B. Ainsworth, and Aubry Drumgoole. It was income from sale of cream and eggs that let many families plant a crop and survive during the 1930s. Cordell had 17 businesses where farmers could sell their cream and eggs at that time. Cordell had three chicken hatcheries and three creameries, which churned butter and shipped out by truckloads. Grocery stores would pay an extra 2¢ per dozen for eggs when they were traded for groceries. It was cream and egg money that kept many of the people from going hungry. (Courtesy Jiggs Botchlett Estate.)

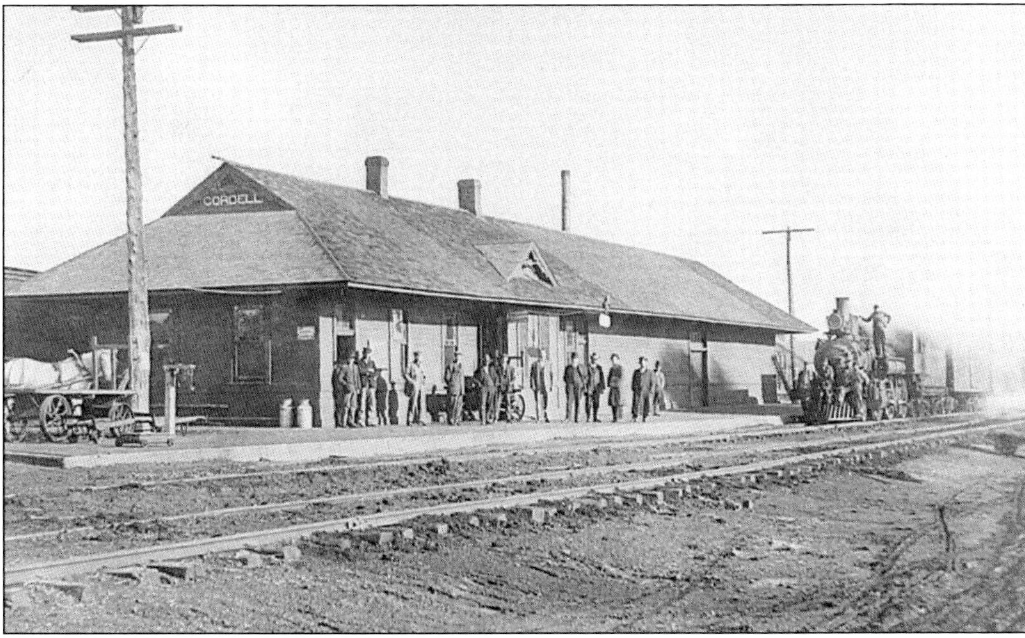

The arrival of a railroad gave towns a big boost to developing business. The railroad came through Cordell in 1902. Flour mills, grain elevators, cotton gins, and stockyards were built along the railroad track. A large overhead water tower was a necessity for the steam engines. (Courtesy Washita County Museum.)

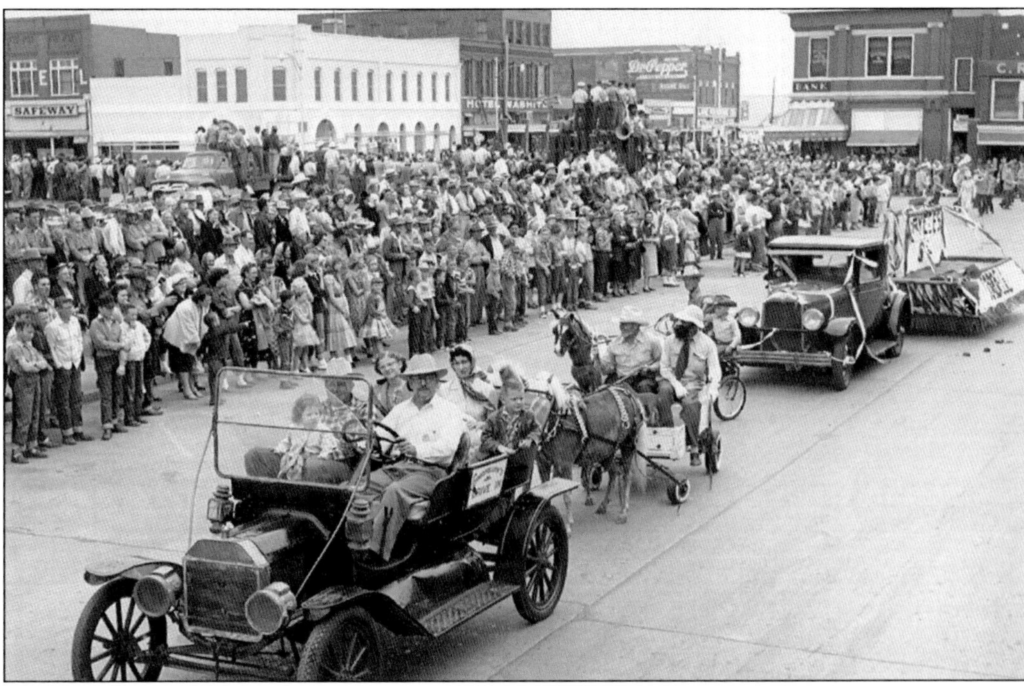

The 50th pioneer anniversary parade celebrating the establishment of Washita County brought several thousand people to Cordell in 1942. A beautiful day and a large parade and many pioneer celebration activities were enjoyed by all. (Courtesy Washita County.)

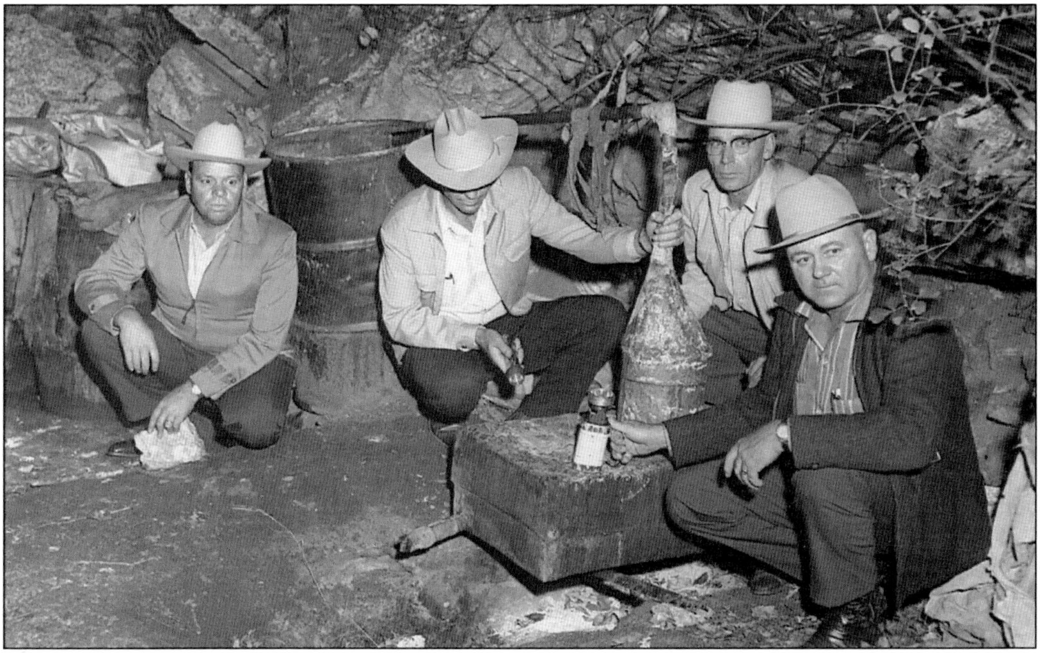

From left to right, Washita County officers Cleo Meeks, deputy sheriff; Skip Hines, sheriff; Dave Dobbs, deputy; and Custer County deputy Ted Hubbard are shown with this canyon run liquor distilling equipment, found 17 miles northeast of Cordell in Washita County. The still had a capacity of 10 gallons of whiskey per day. (Courtesy Washita County Museum.)

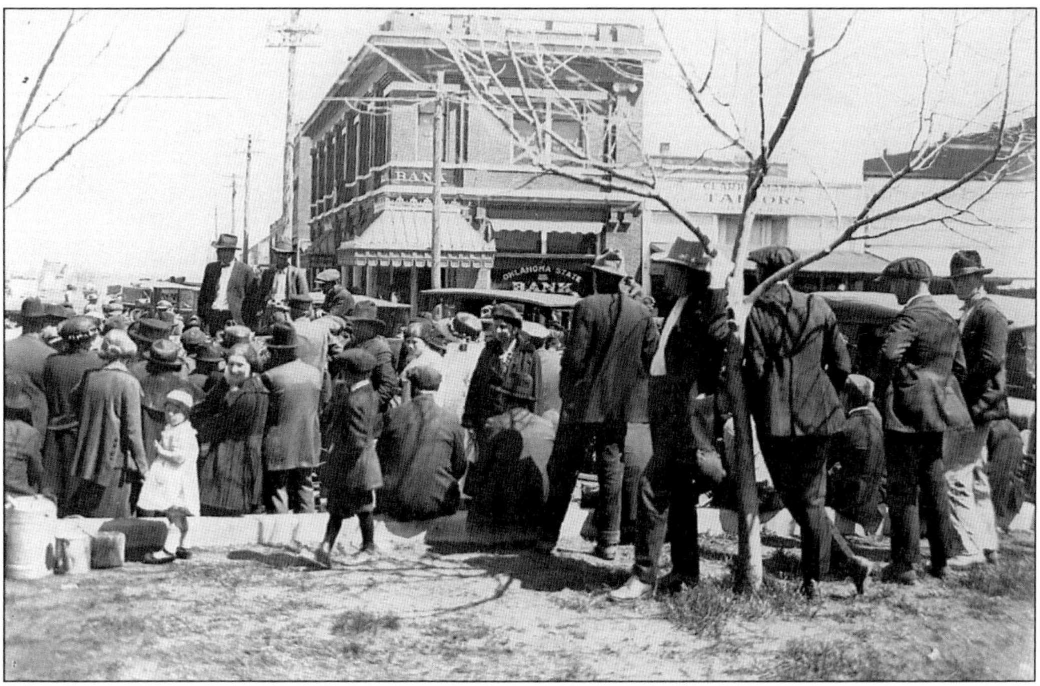

A street sale on the corner of the courthouse square would draw a crowd of people. The auctioneer is standing on a platform in the center of the crowd selling a farm for a man who is going to serve in World War I. (Courtesy Washita County Museum.)

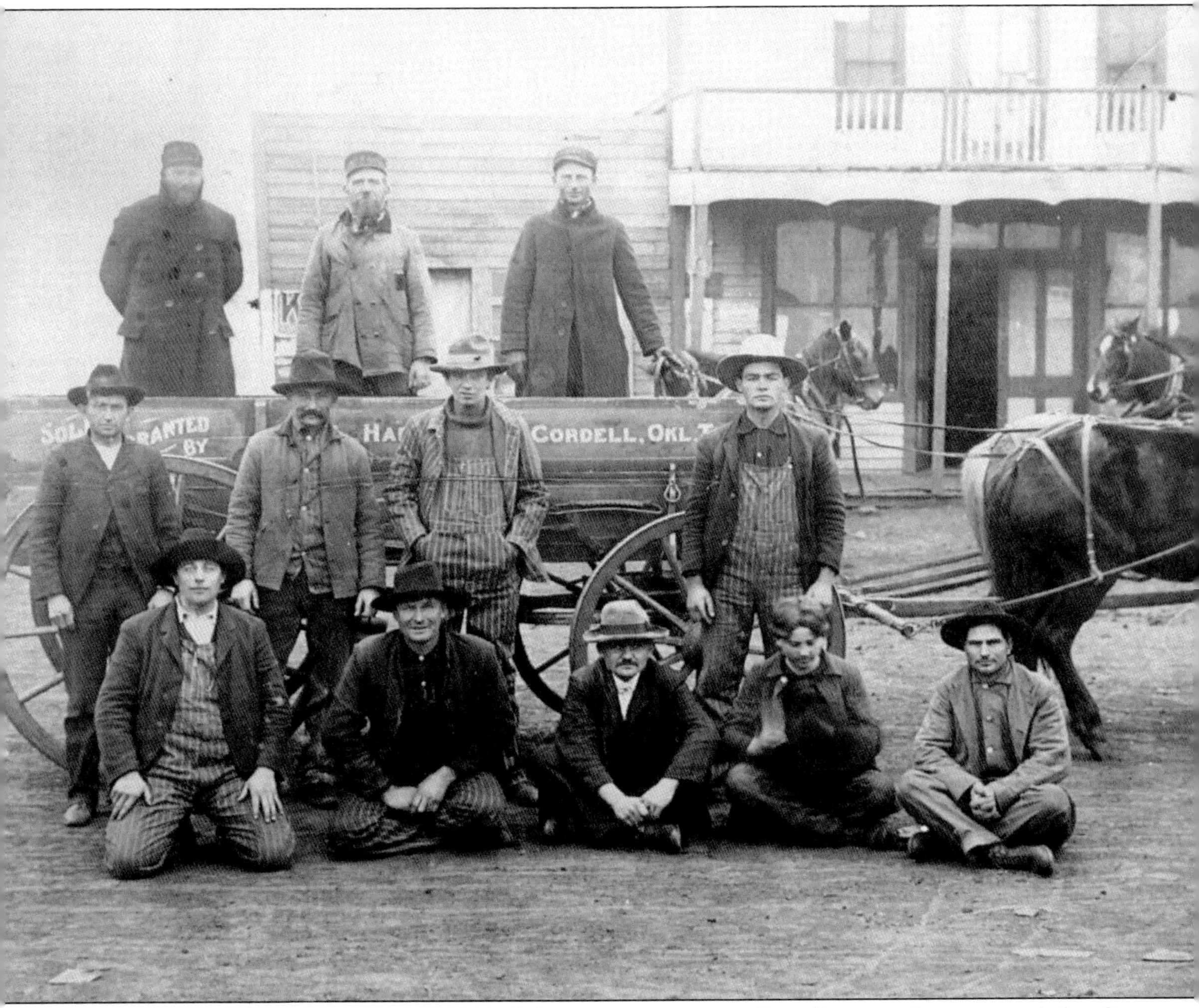

Shelly, a thriving town in 1901, used the water wagon in this photograph to control the dust from the dirt streets. Members of the Shelly wagon crew who volunteered their help for the project are, from left to right, (first row) Fred Jacobs, J. J. Regier, George Harder, George Huebert, and John Schmidt; (second row) John Ratzlaff, A. H. Harder, D. C. Heidebrecht, and C. H. Harder; (third row, in wagon) Peter Duerksen, A. K. Hamm, and Jake Dyck. The railroad did not come through Shelley, which was founded in 1889, soon died, and is only a ghost town today. (Courtesy George Hamm.)

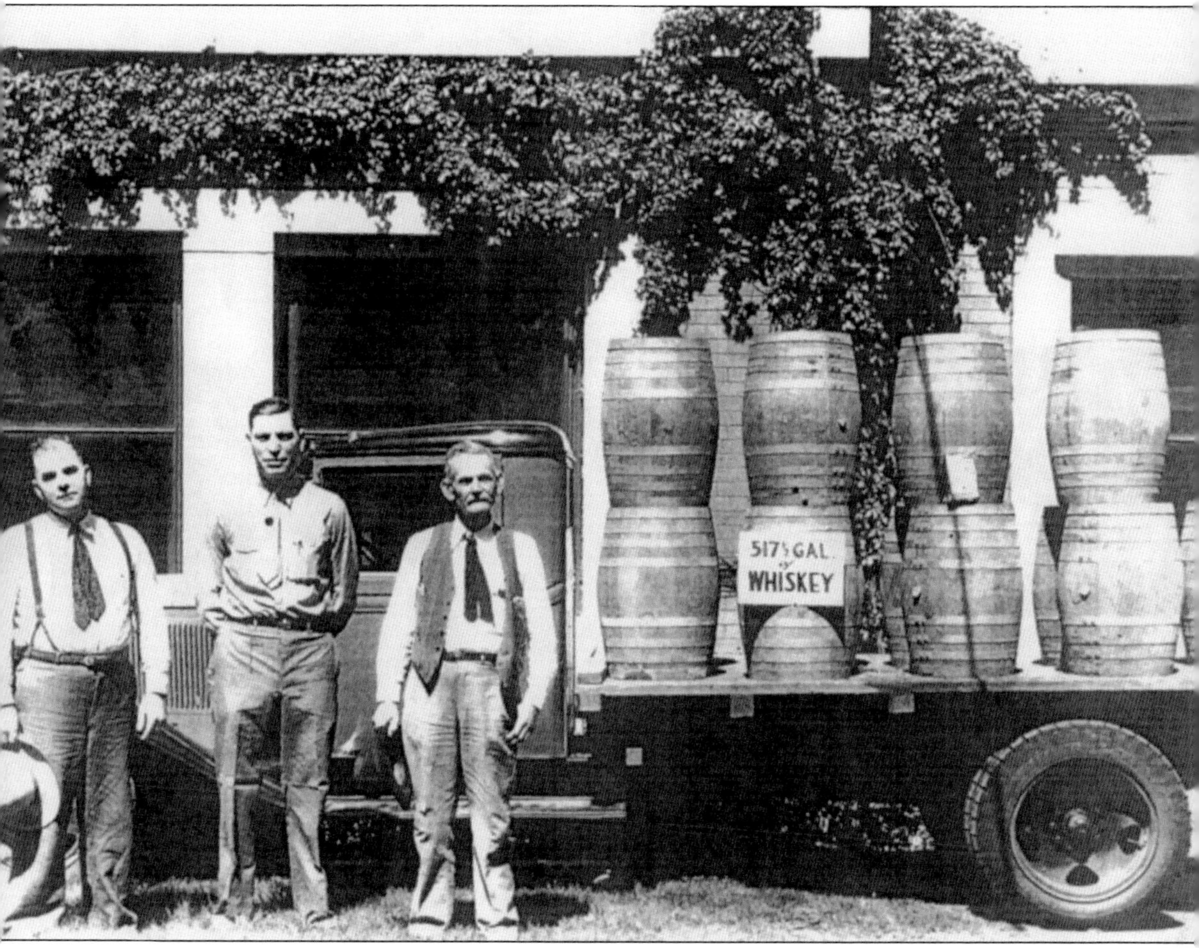

Harve Dean was sheriff of Washita County in the 1930s. This photograph shows the county sheriff department in action. On the left is undersheriff Ed Walker, in the center is deputy Perry Sullins, and on the right is Harve Dean, Washita County sheriff. In 1934, the sheriff's department made a raid on a farm south of Canute, confiscating a whiskey still and over 517 gallons of whiskey. Dean and his deputies drew quite a crowd of curious onlookers as 517.5 gallons of whiskey were poured into a sewer manhole. Also, the deputies from the sheriff's department completely destroyed the whiskey still with sledgehammers and axes as the crowd watched on that fall afternoon in 1934. (Courtesy Washita County Museum.)

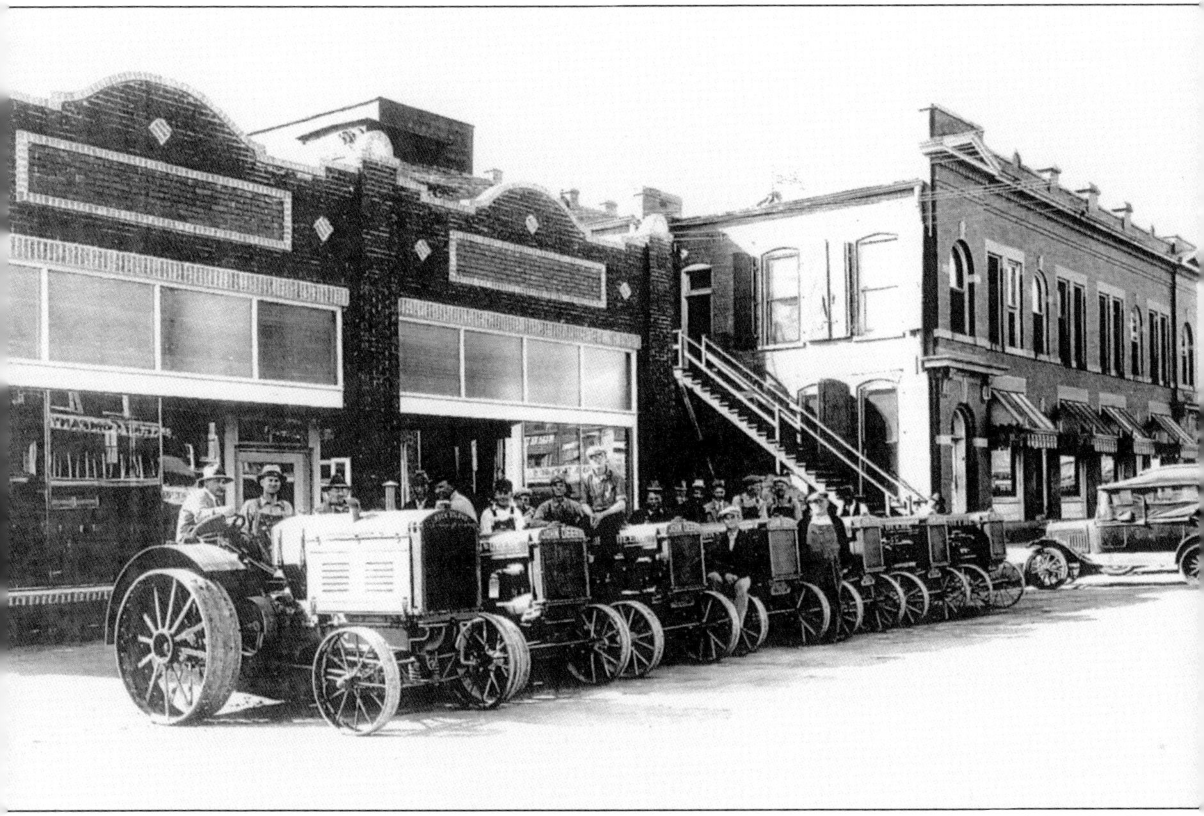

This photograph was taken in 1929. The lineup of tractors on display is in front of the Grady Smith Implement Agency, located at 120 South Market Street in Cordell, where the First National Bank is located today. The first tractor on the left is a Rock Island, and the other six are John Deere Model D tractors. With the financial crash of 1929, which started the Great Depression, the Rock Island tractor company ceased tractor manufacturing. The Rock Island tractor was priced at $750 when this photograph was taken. In the fall of 1930, Claude Boothe purchased the Rock Island tractor for just half price of $375, of course wheat fell to 25¢ per bushel and cotton to 3¢ per pound, and times were really tough for the next few years. (Courtesy Walter Miller.)

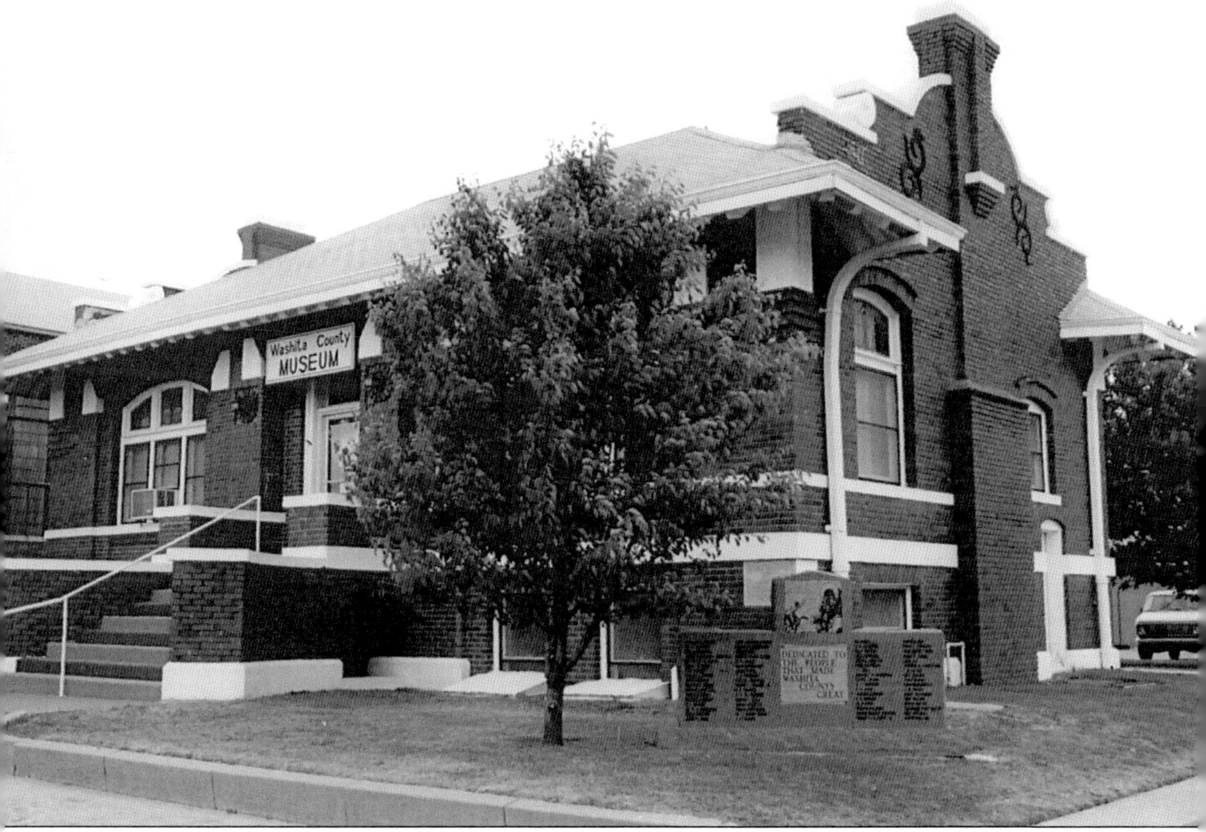

The Washita County Museum, located at 115 East First Street in Cordell, is housed in the old Carnegie library building. The Carnegie library building was constructed in 1911 when Andrew Carnegie gave a $9,000 gift to the City of Cordell to build a library building with an agreement from the city to fund the operational cost of the library. The Andrew Carnegie Foundation financed 25 library buildings in Oklahoma. The building is now on the National Register of Historic Places. With the building of a new library in 1981, the Washita County Historical Society established its museum in the old Carnegie library building. The Washita County Museum has over 10,000 items of Washita County history on display. It is the goal of the Washita County Historical Society "to preserve the past for those of the future." (Courtesy Washita County Museum.)

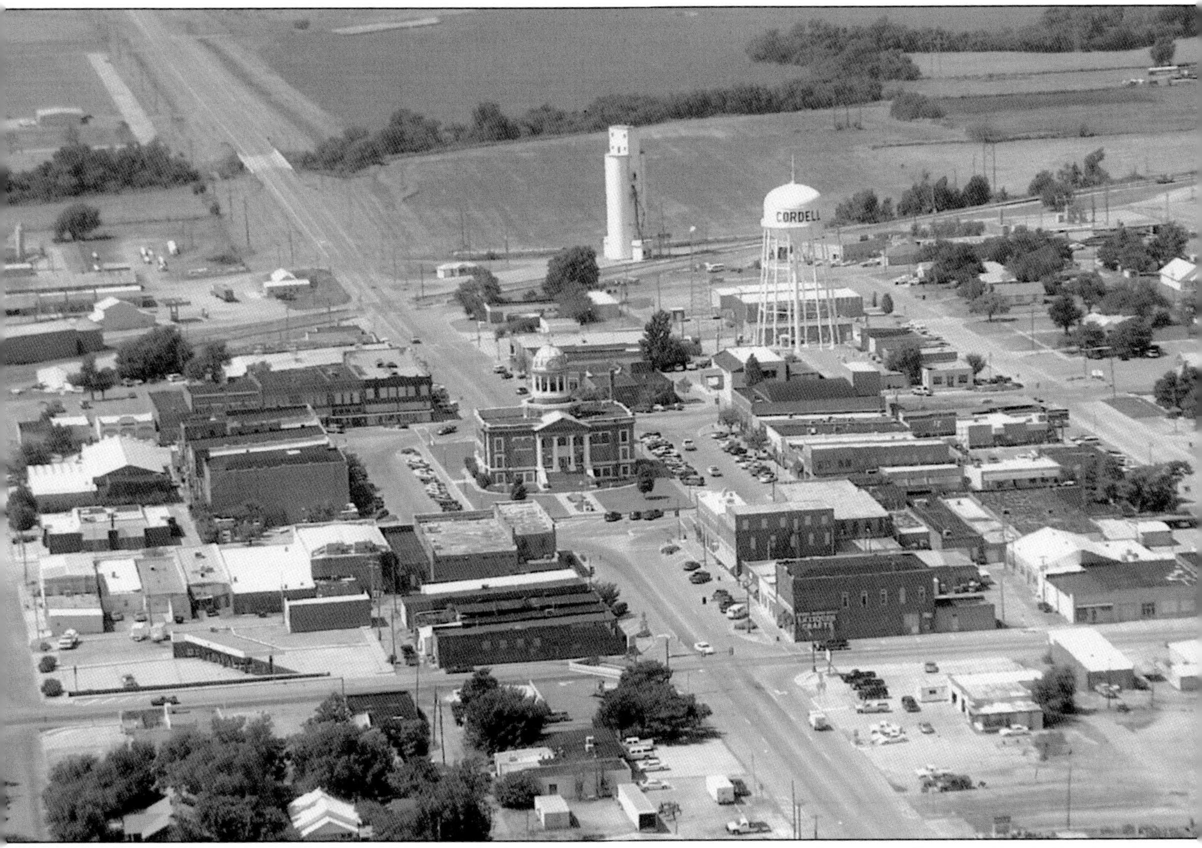

Seen here is a view from the air of the main business district of the city of New Cordell, which was established in 1897. The county seat was established at New Cordell in August 1900, when the citizens of Washita County voted to relocate the county seat from Cloud Chief. The courthouse, which today sits in the exact center of Washita County, was built in 1911. (Courtesy Alex Damon Photography.)

Five

AGRICULTURAL CROPS

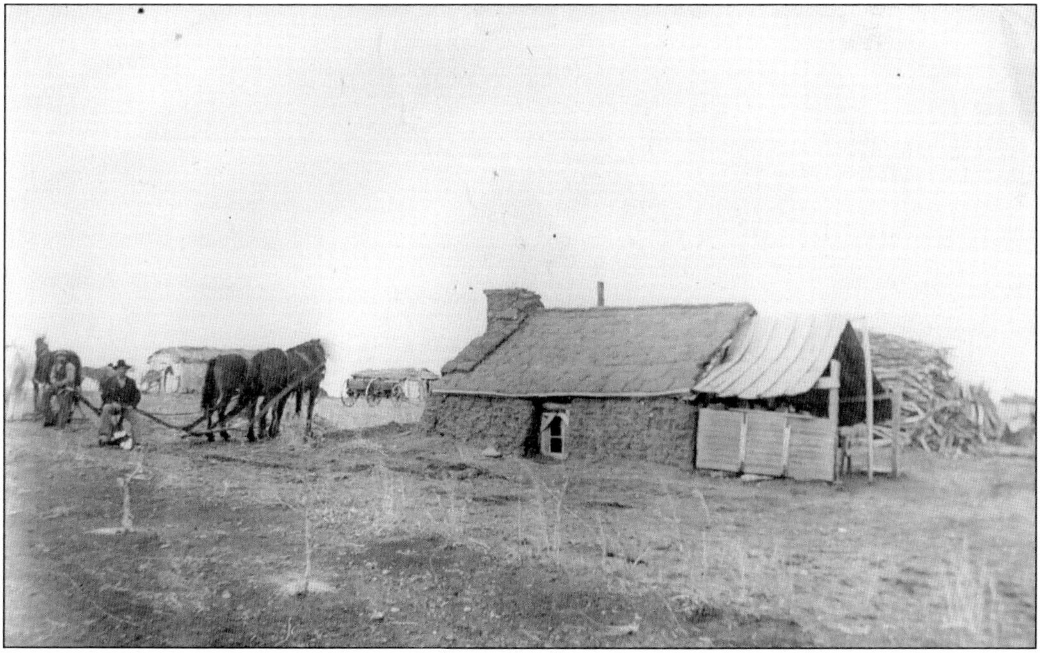

After staking and recording their homestead, the homesteaders had three years to prove their claim and receive a patent to obtain a deed. The homesteader must live on his homestead at least six months of each year. He must construct a residence and make improvements by fencing and planting a crop. Most of the pioneers who filed on a homestead constructed a dugout or half-dugout for living quarters. This photograph of the half-dugout on the Stewart homestead, located 10 miles east of Cordell, was taken in 1893. The half-dugout was constructed with sod blocks taken from their homestead. The Stewart home was one of the larger and nicer homes in the community. They had added a protected porch area were they could enjoy the summer breeze. With no trees in the area, they quite frequently slept outside or under the porch during the warm summer nights. (Courtesy Washita County Museum.)

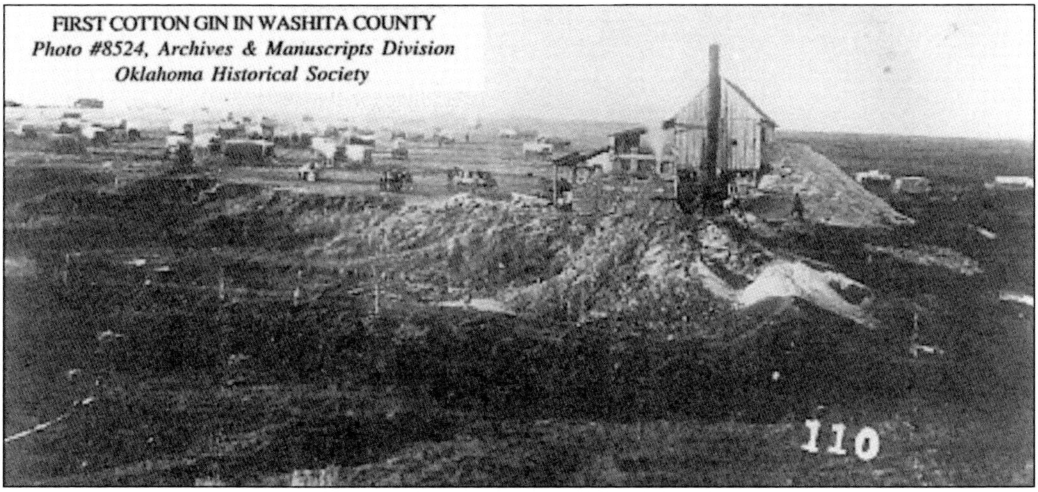

The first cotton gin in Washita County was built in 1896, located in the south part of Cloud Chief on Oak Creek. Cotton was one of the major crops in Washita County at one time, when there were 47 cotton gins operating. Today only two cotton gins are still in operation, one at Dill City and the other at Burns Flat. (Courtesy Oklahoma Historical Society.)

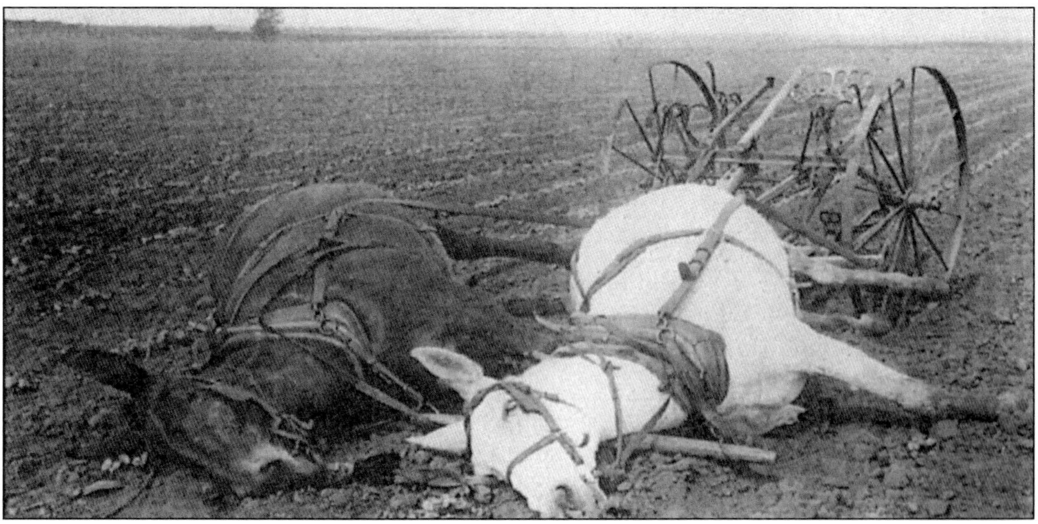

This is an early-day miracle. Louis Sasseen was cultivating cotton when old Pete and Kate were struck and killed by lightning in June 1911. Sasseen, who lived 12 miles northwest of Cordell, was only shook up and soon good as ever. But he had to get a new team. (Courtesy Washita County Museum.)

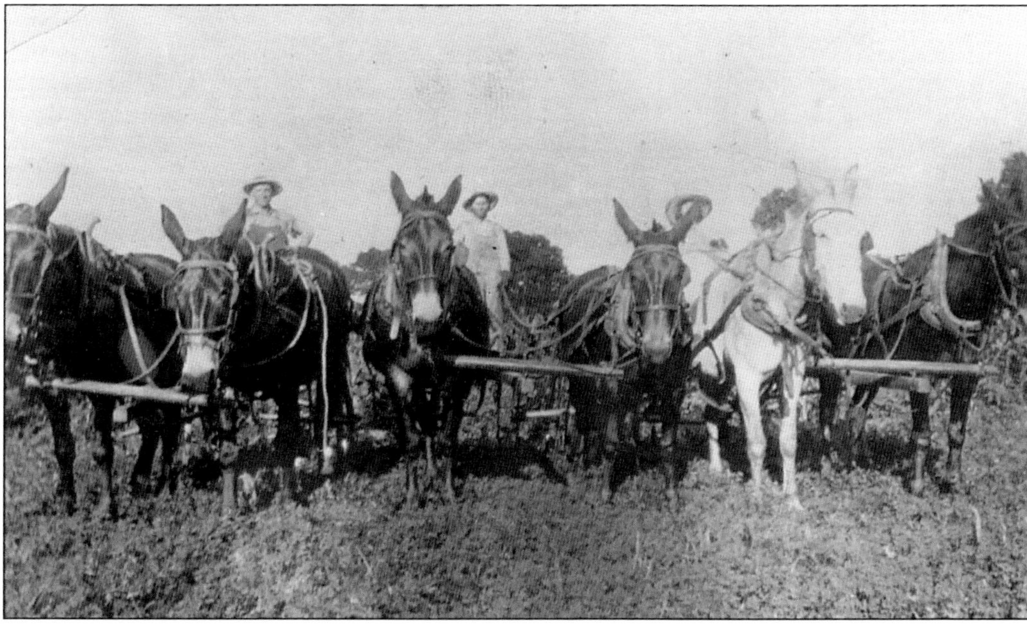

Horse and mule power was the most important source of farm power for the pioneers, as shown in the photograph with the three mule teams working their farm ground. (Courtesy Washita County Museum.)

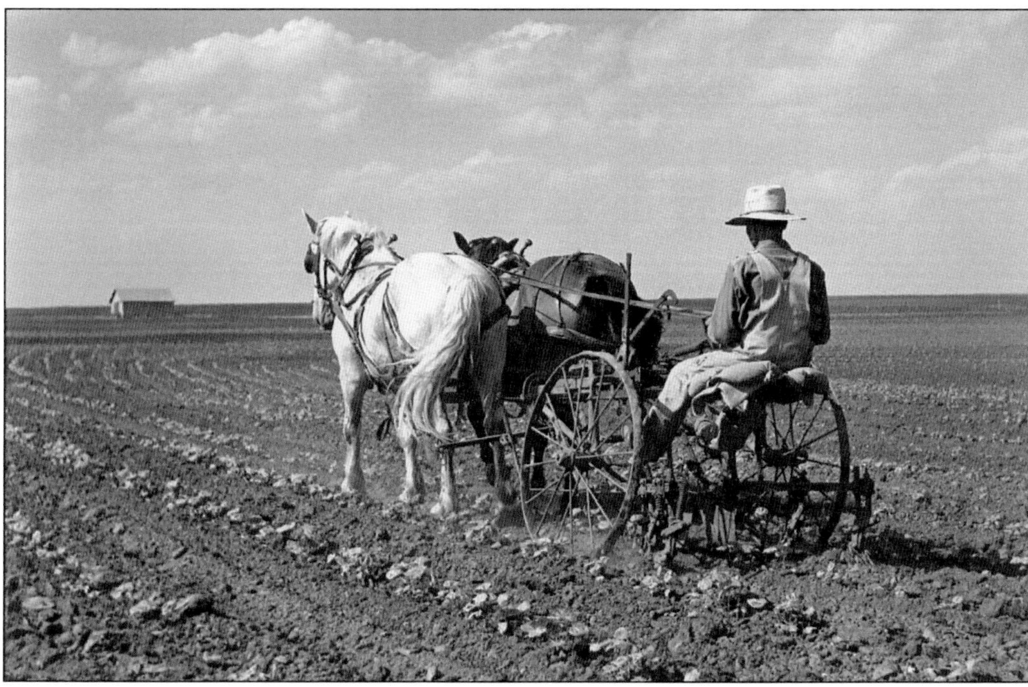

Plowing cotton one row at a time, C. H. Kaiser of Bessie is cultivating his cotton in 1951. With a one-row cultivator and a team of horses, if one covered 10 to 12 acres it was a good day's work. (Courtesy Bob Taylor.)

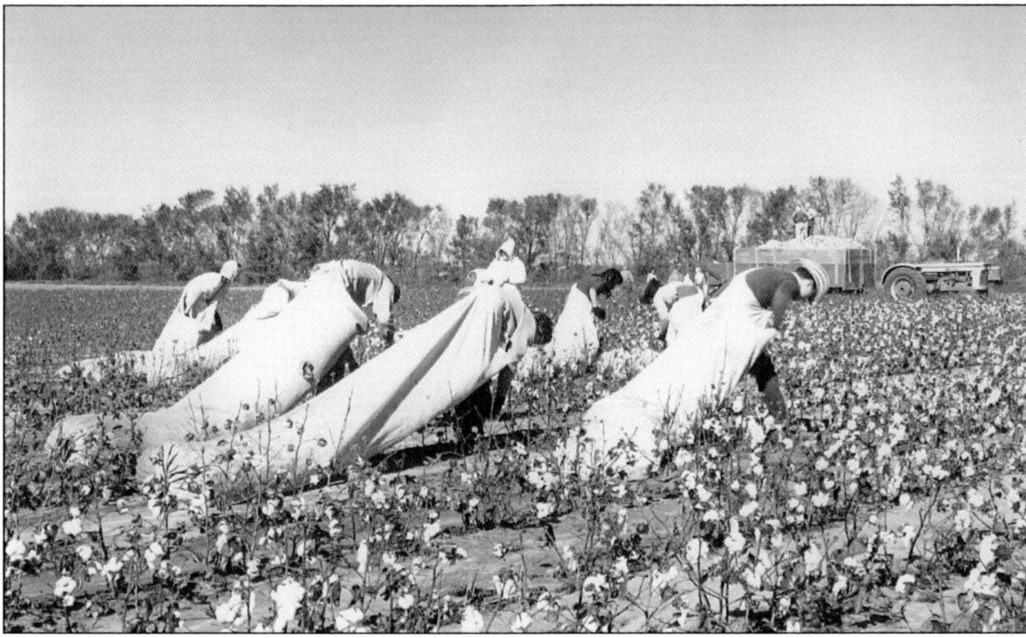

Pulling cotton is done here by hand in the Dill City area in 1960. Note the shelter belt at the end of the field established in the 1930s to control wind erosion. Pulling cotton is pulling burr, lent, and seed, while picking cotton is much more tedious, picking only the lent and seed from the burr. (Courtesy Bob Taylor.)

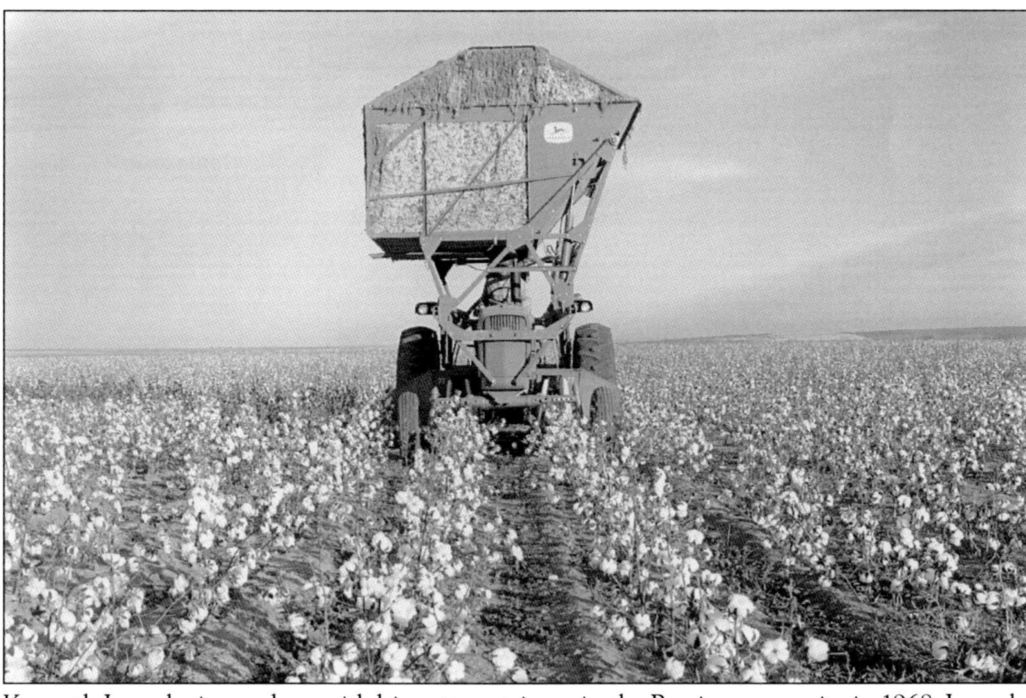

Kenneth Javorsky is seen here with his cotton stripper in the Bessie community in 1968. Javorsky could harvest more cotton in a day's time than 20 cotton pullers could harvest by hand in a week. (Courtesy Bob Taylor.)

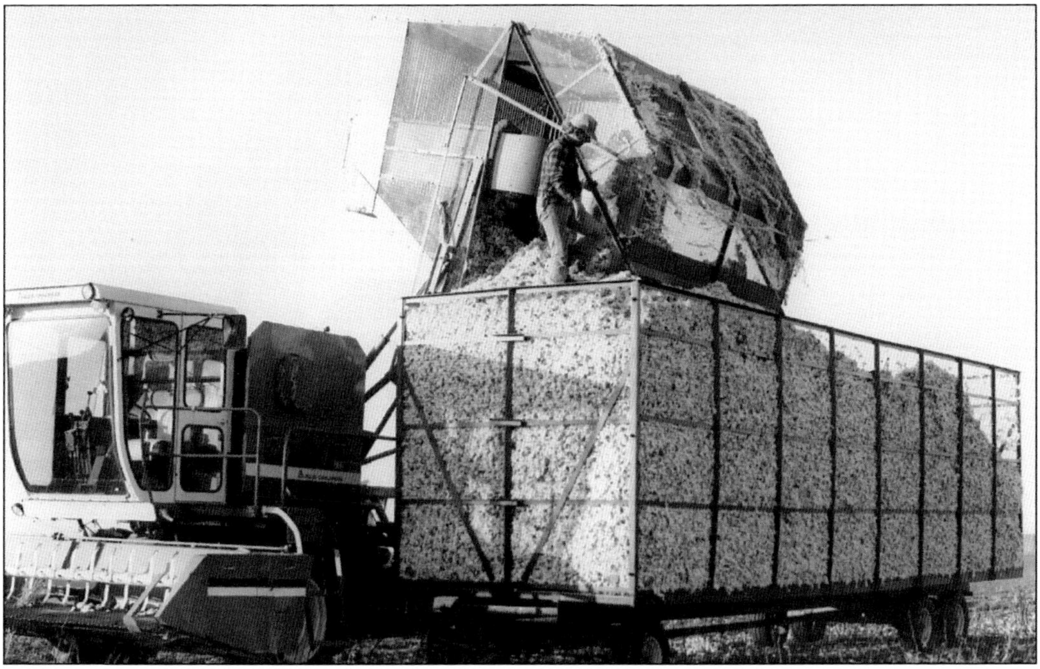

Allen Diffendaffer is harvesting cotton in the Rocky area in 1975. The new improved broadcast cotton stripper with a burr extractor could fill a six-bale cotton trailer with good cotton in an hour's time. (Courtesy Bob Taylor.)

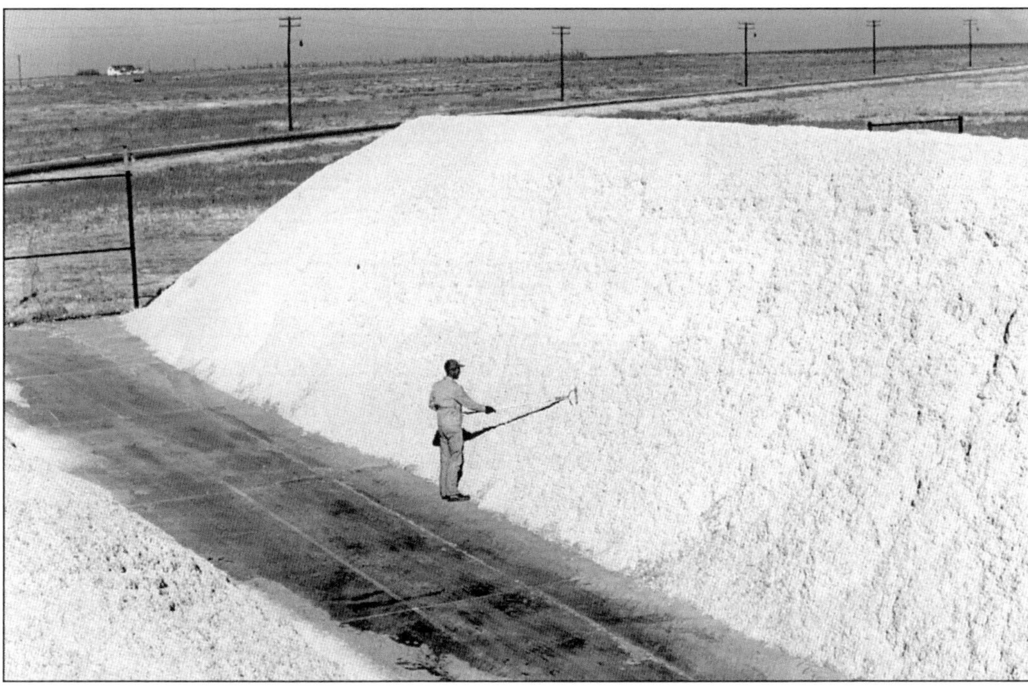

The 1950 cotton crop was a whopper. Cottonseed oil mills were unable to receive all of the seed from the bumper crop. Several hundred tons of cottonseed were stacked outside at the Burns Flat Air Base. (Courtesy Bob Taylor.)

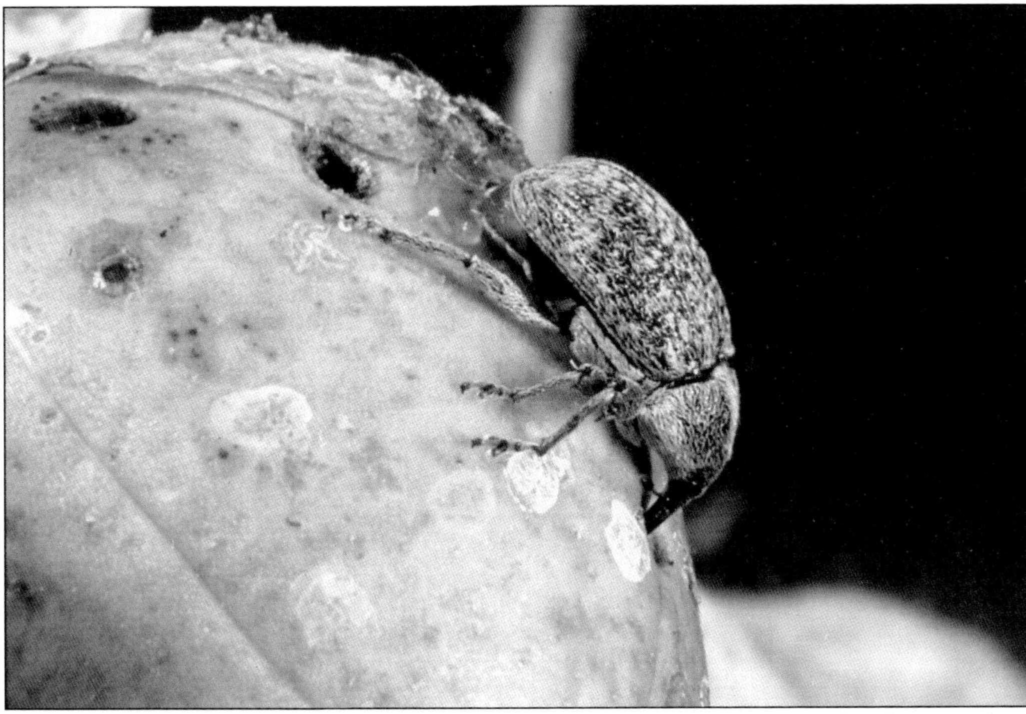

A boll weevil is at work here. This is a very unusual picture of a boll weevil as he is working on a cotton boll. This little fellow is what put many cotton producers out of cotton production. (Courtesy Bob Taylor.)

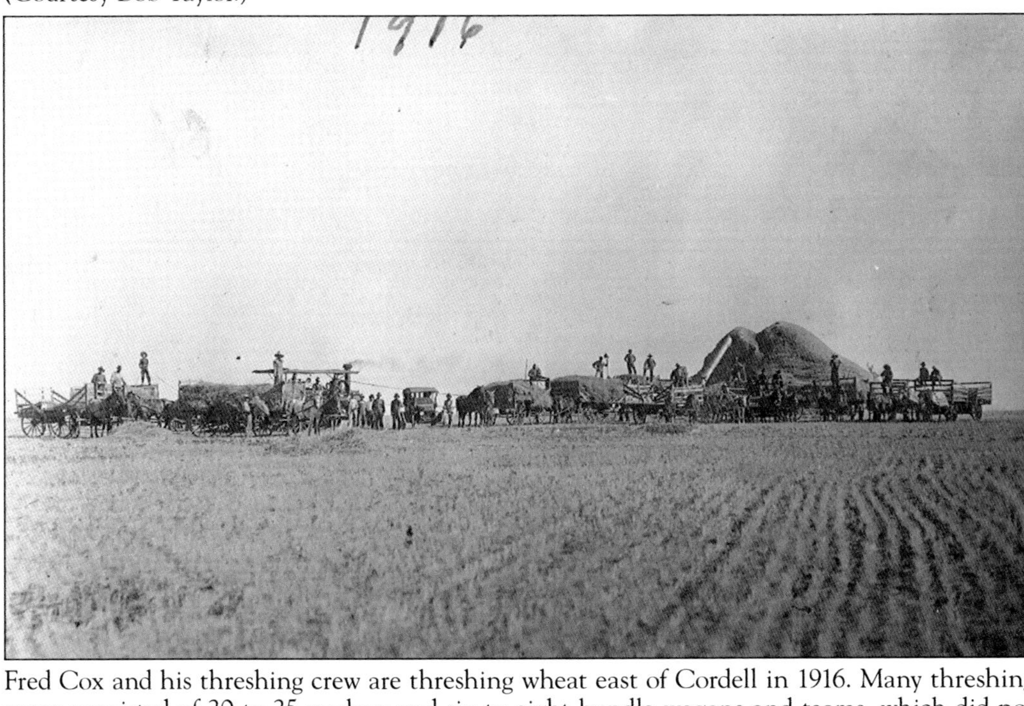

Fred Cox and his threshing crew are threshing wheat east of Cordell in 1916. Many threshing crews consisted of 20 to 25 workers and six to eight bundle wagons and teams, which did not include hauling away the threshed grain. (Courtesy Washita County Museum.)

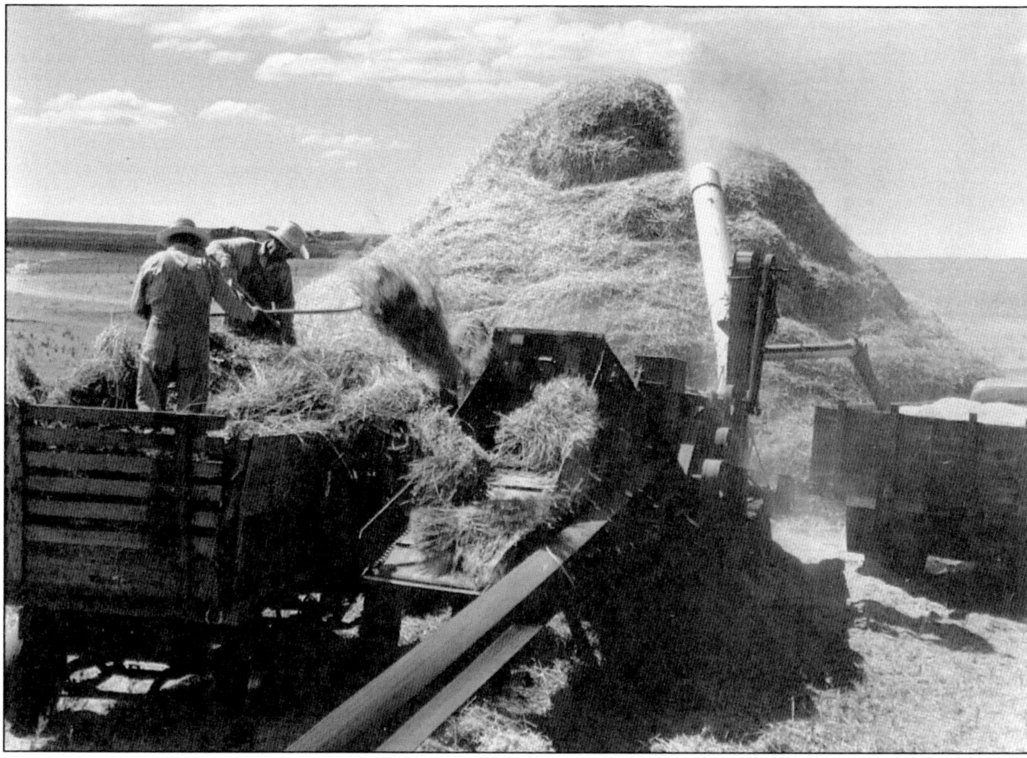

Here is a close-up photograph of the threshing machine, hands feeding bundles to the machine, straw stack, and grain truck. Herman Horn is threshing wheat in 1950 on the Walt Green farm one mile southwest of Cordell. (Courtesy Bob Taylor.)

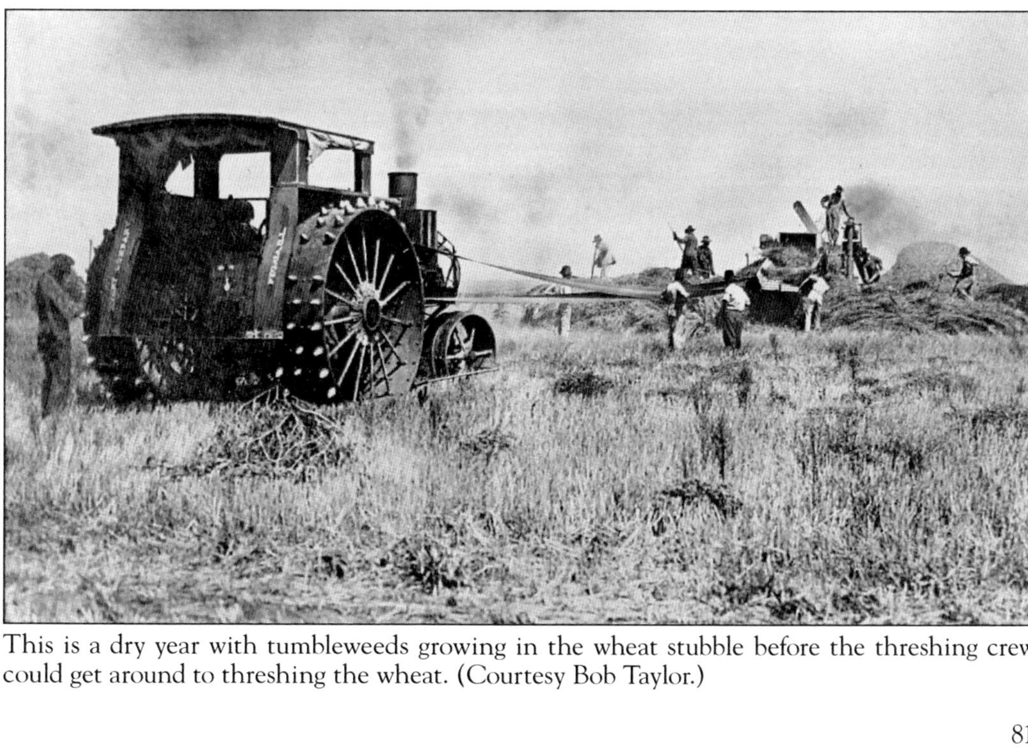

This is a dry year with tumbleweeds growing in the wheat stubble before the threshing crew could get around to threshing the wheat. (Courtesy Bob Taylor.)

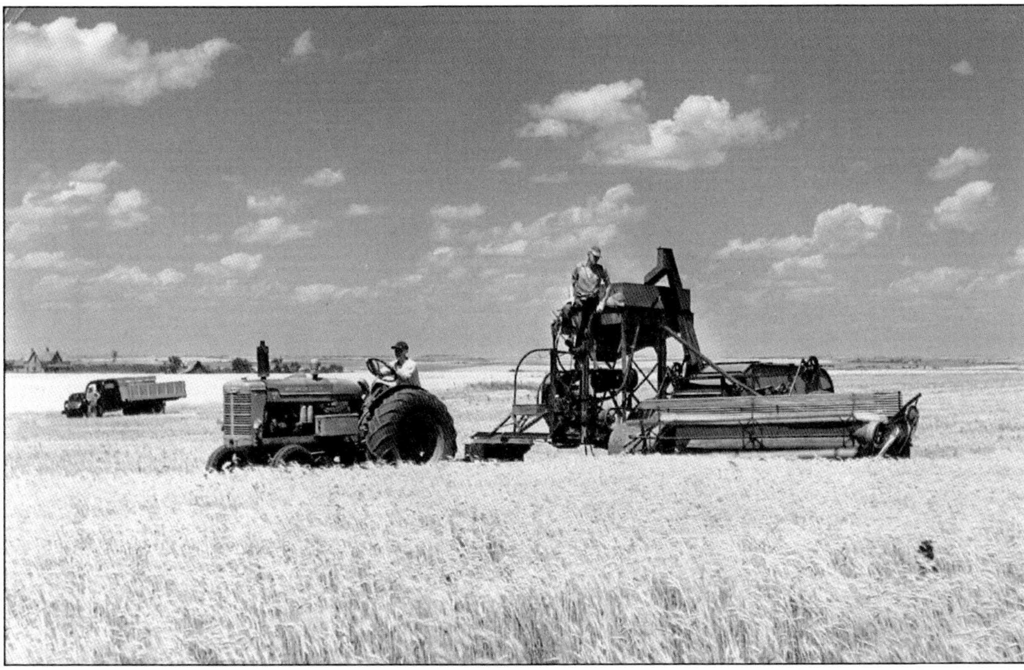

Noble Groves is seen here cutting wheat in 1950 with a 12-foot pull-type gleaner combine on his farm, three miles east of Cordell. (Courtesy Bob Taylor.)

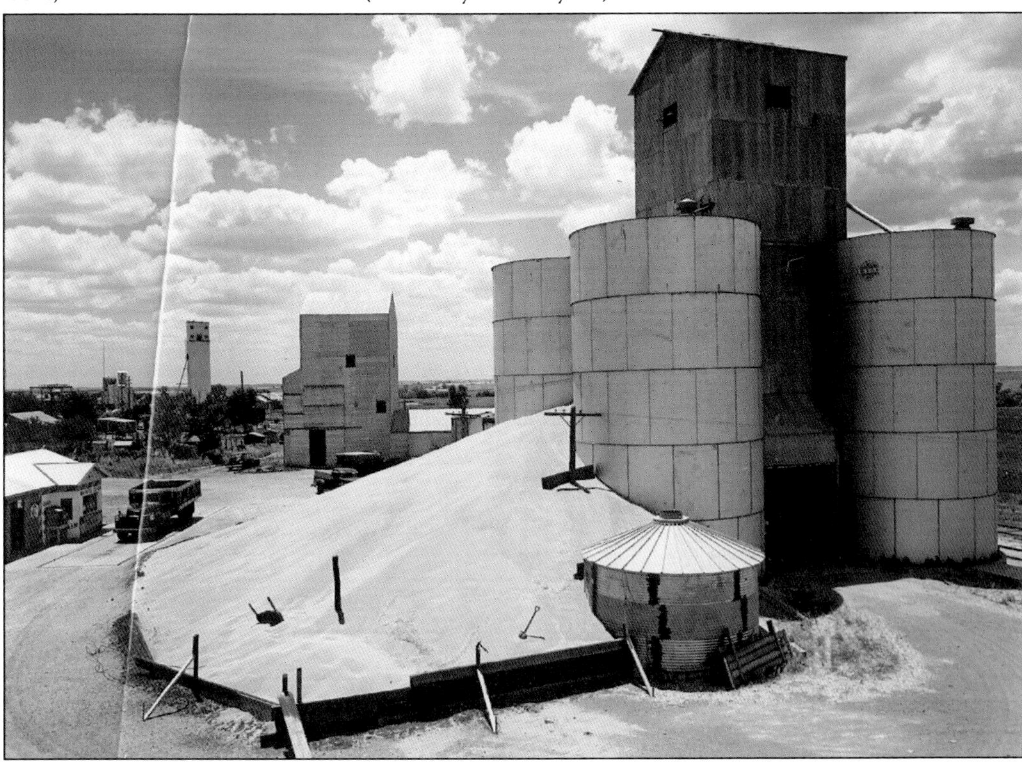

A bumper wheat crop in 1954 combined with a railcar shortage caused the Farmers Co-op Elevator at Cordell to pile wheat on the ground. (Courtesy Bob Taylor.)

Trucks are lined up at the Bessie Farmers Co-op elevator in 1960. They are waiting in line to be unloaded so they can go back to the field and bring in another load of wheat. Many times the combine bins are full of wheat and waiting for the trucks to return so they can unload and return to harvesting. (Courtesy Bob Taylor.)

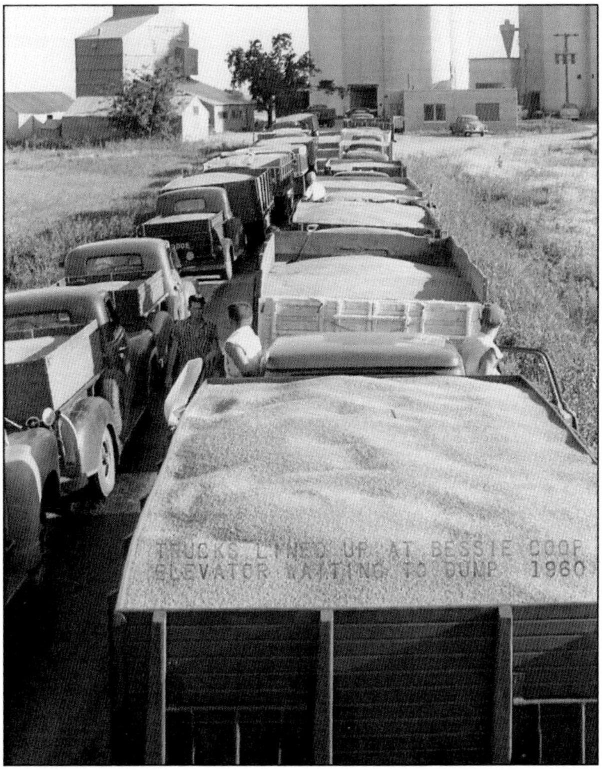

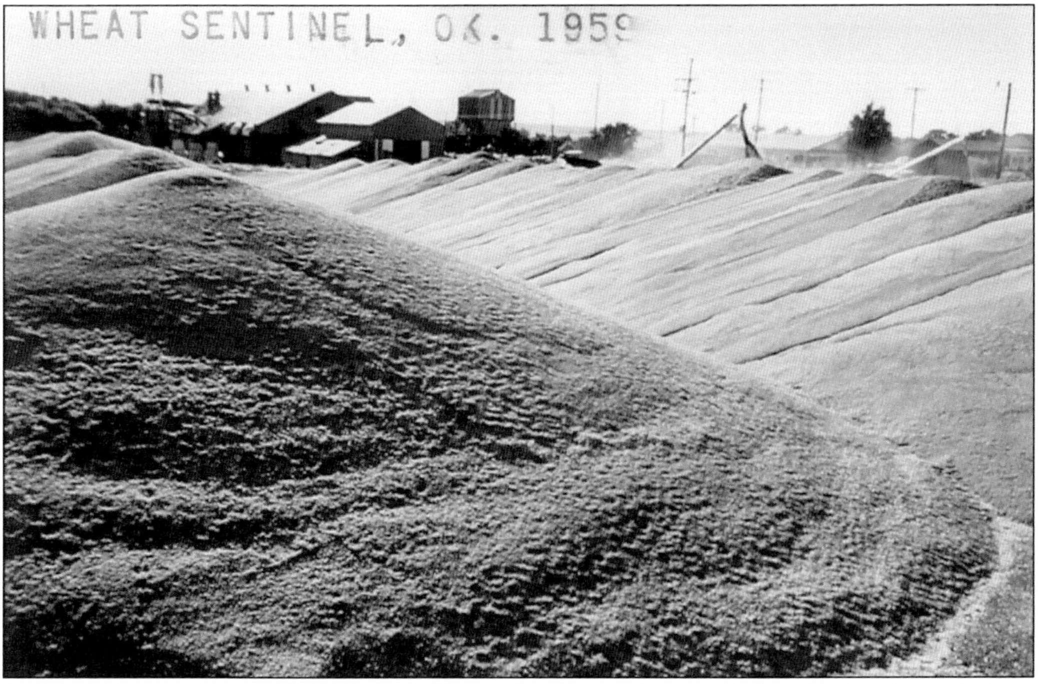

Sentinel Farmers Co-op elevator in 1959 was forced to pile several thousand bushels of wheat on the ground at harvest due to an excellent wheat crop and a railcar shortage. (Courtesy Bob Taylor.)

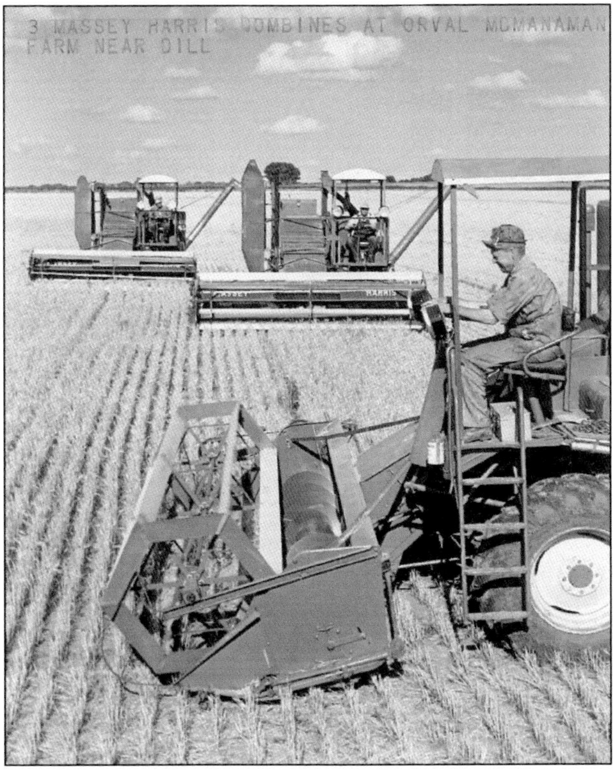

Getting wheat harvest over in a hurry in the late 1960s, Orval McManaman of Dill City was able to harvest his wheat crop in a single day when he had three Massey Harris combines cutting his wheat crop. (Courtesy Bob Taylor.)

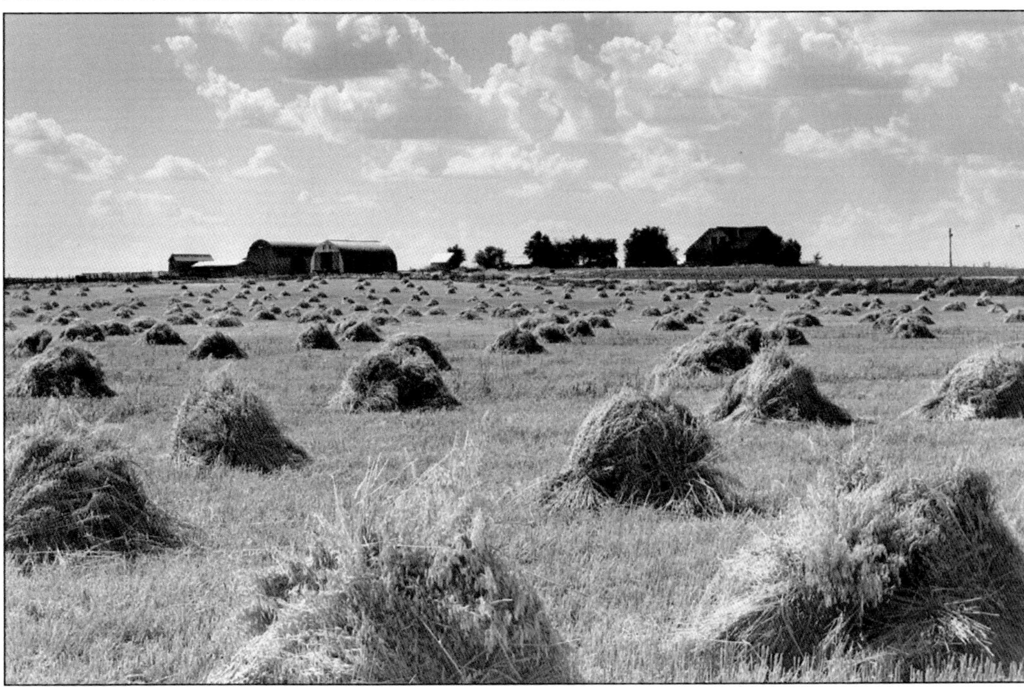

Shocks of oats are seen here waiting for the thresher. In 1954, Arthur Dick, who lives a mile south of Bessie, bundled and shocked his oats and waited for a threshing machine. Very few threshing machines were still operating in Washita County in 1954. (Courtesy Bob Taylor.)

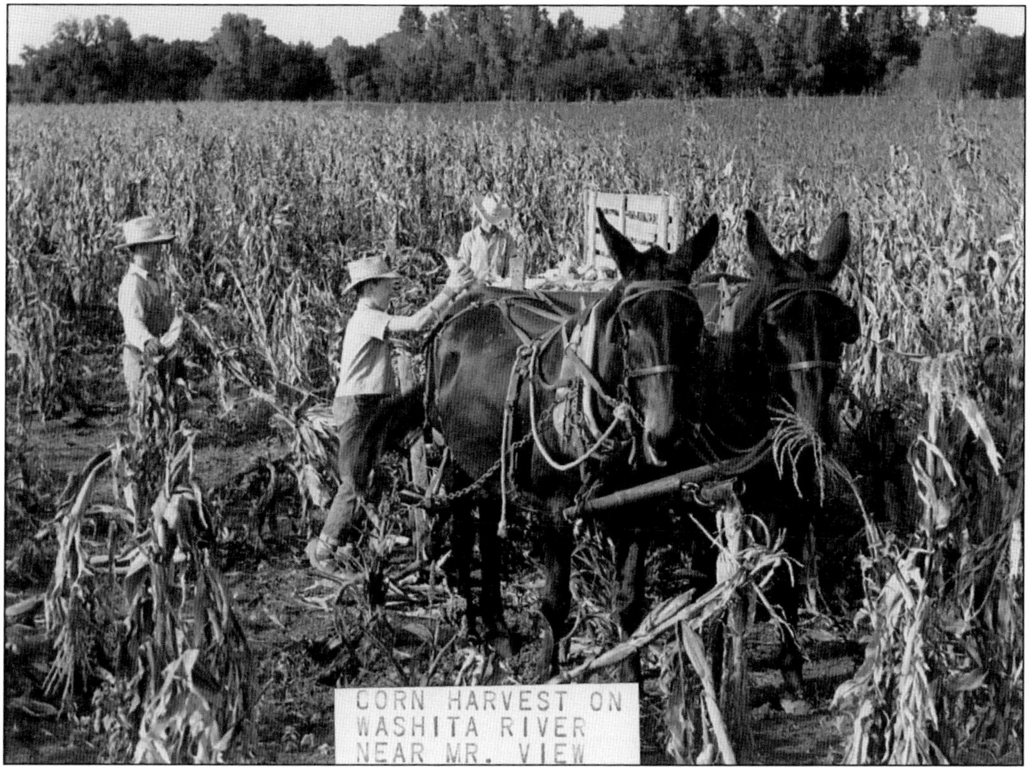

Here corn is being harvested by hand on the Washita River, north of Mountain View in the south part of Washita County. (Courtesy Bob Taylor.)

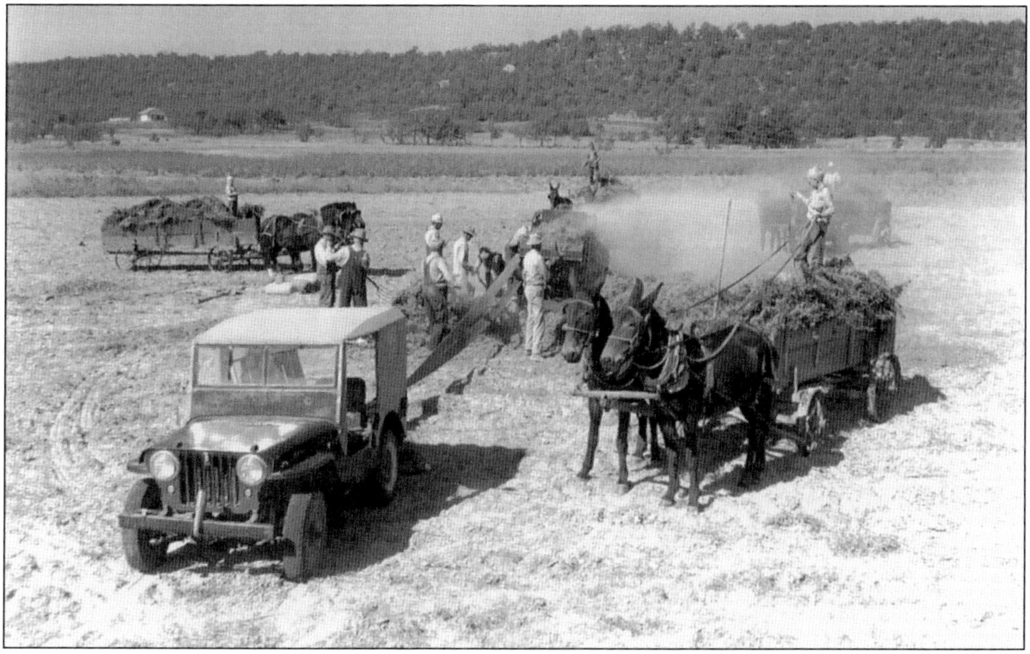

This image is of threshing peanuts in 1951. Note the Jeep being used for the power to run the peanut thresher. (Courtesy Bob Taylor.)

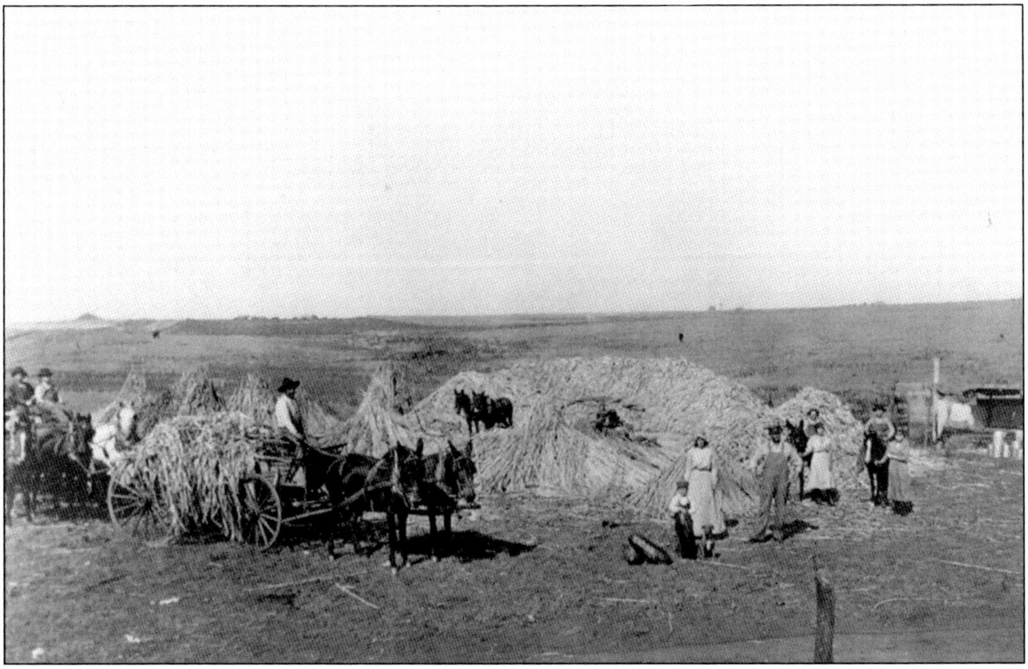

This is a sorghum cane press operation in 1912 on the Lee Morris farm, located six miles east of Rocky. The cane press extracts the juice from the cane to make sorghum molasses. Notice the press is powered by a team of mules. (Courtesy Orval Morris family.)

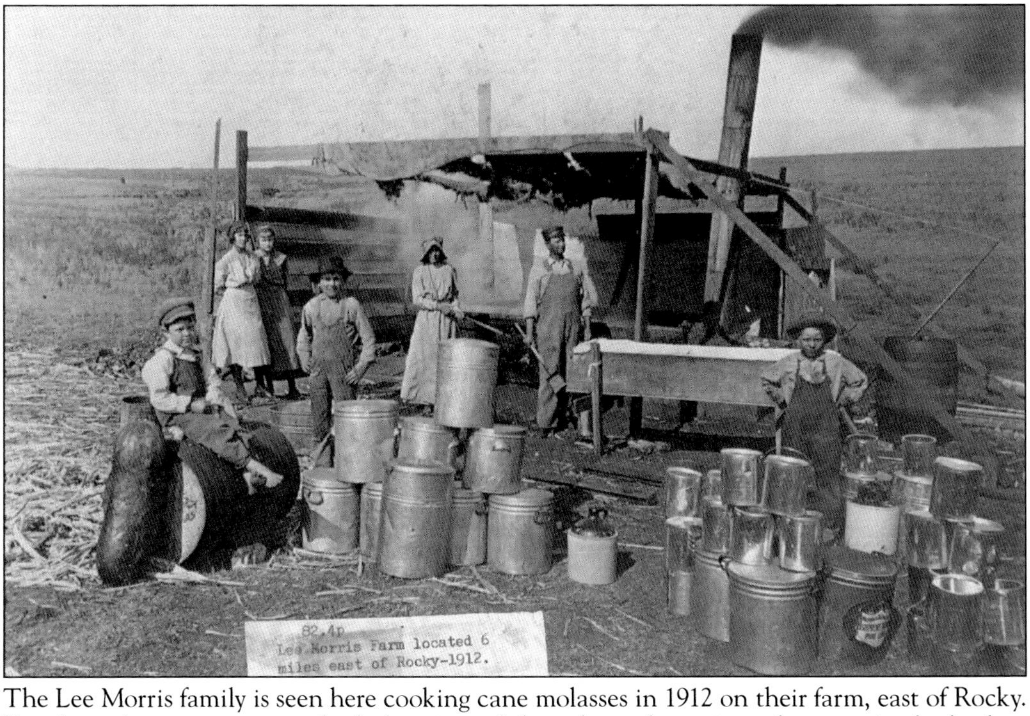

The Lee Morris family is seen here cooking cane molasses in 1912 on their farm, east of Rocky. First heat the cane juice to a boil, skim it, and then the molasses is ready to put in the bucket. (Courtesy Orval Morris family.)

Wilma Taylor is gathering eggs on the Doyle Sluder poultry farm near Dill City. Chickens were lifesavers for many Washita County farmers during the dust bowl days and the Depression of the 1930s. (Courtesy Bob Taylor.)

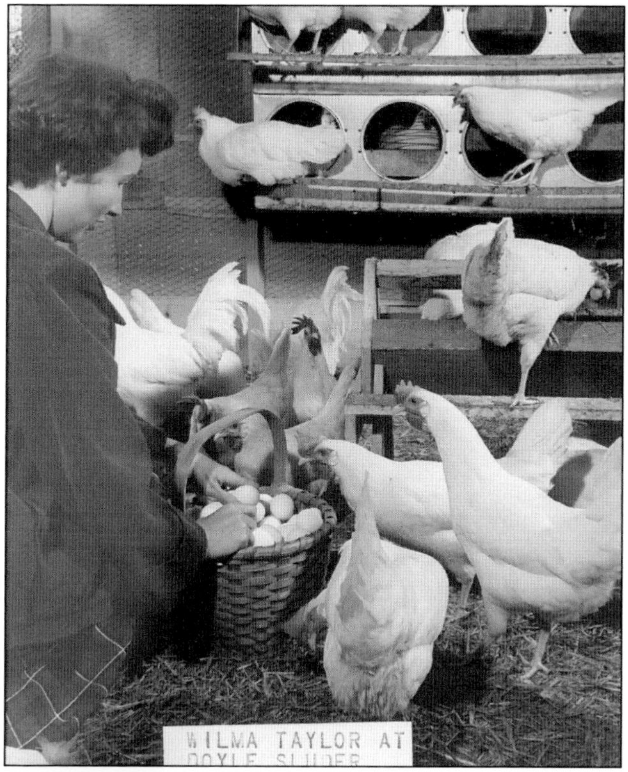

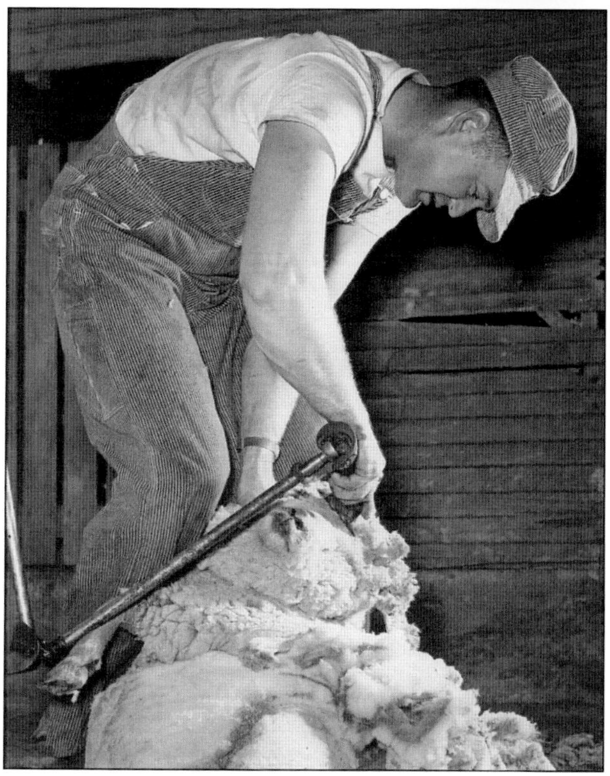

Shearing sheep during the 1950s is seen here. Dale Woods, who lives near Rocky, is shearing the sheep. Woods was about six-feet-eight-inches tall and had to stoop over a long way to shear sheep, but it was an annual spring job that had to be done. (Courtesy Bob Taylor.)

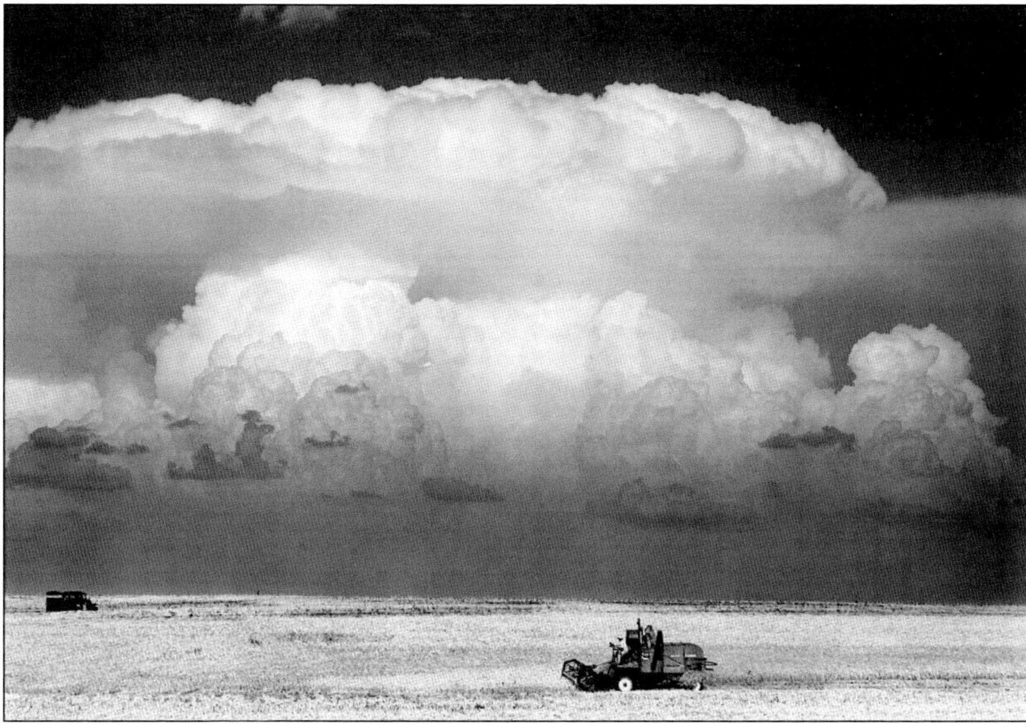

With wheat ready to cut and storm clouds coming, one would try to speed up and cut as much grain as possible. A hail storm at harvest can destroy a whole year's work. (Courtesy Bob Taylor.)

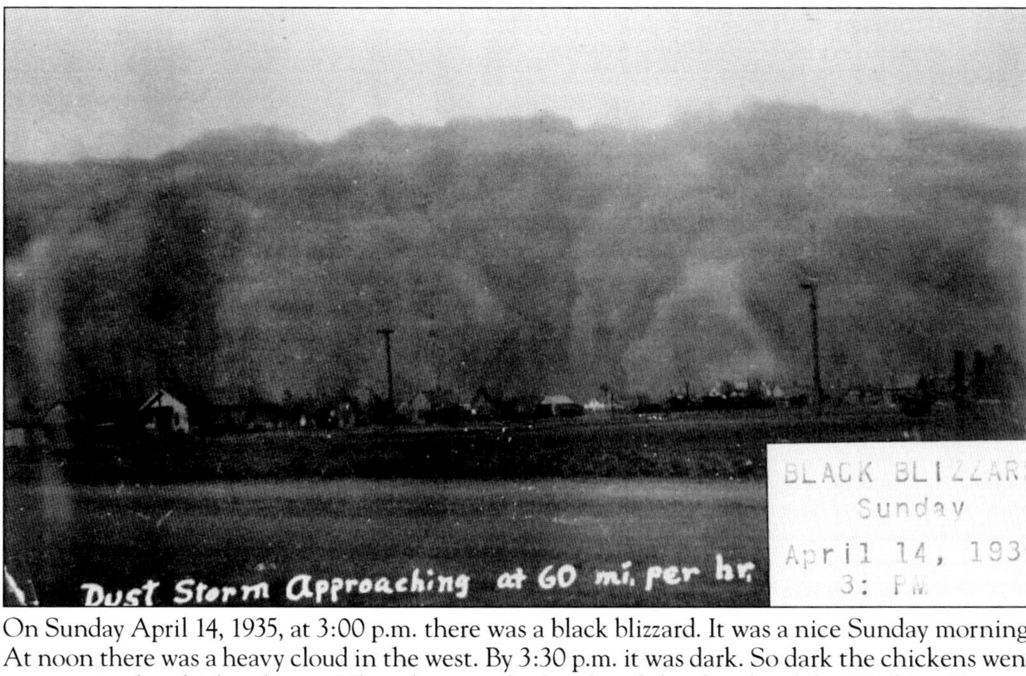

On Sunday April 14, 1935, at 3:00 p.m. there was a black blizzard. It was a nice Sunday morning. At noon there was a heavy cloud in the west. By 3:30 p.m. it was dark. So dark the chickens went to roost in the chicken house. That day was the height of the dust bowl for Washita County. (Courtesy Washita County Museum.)

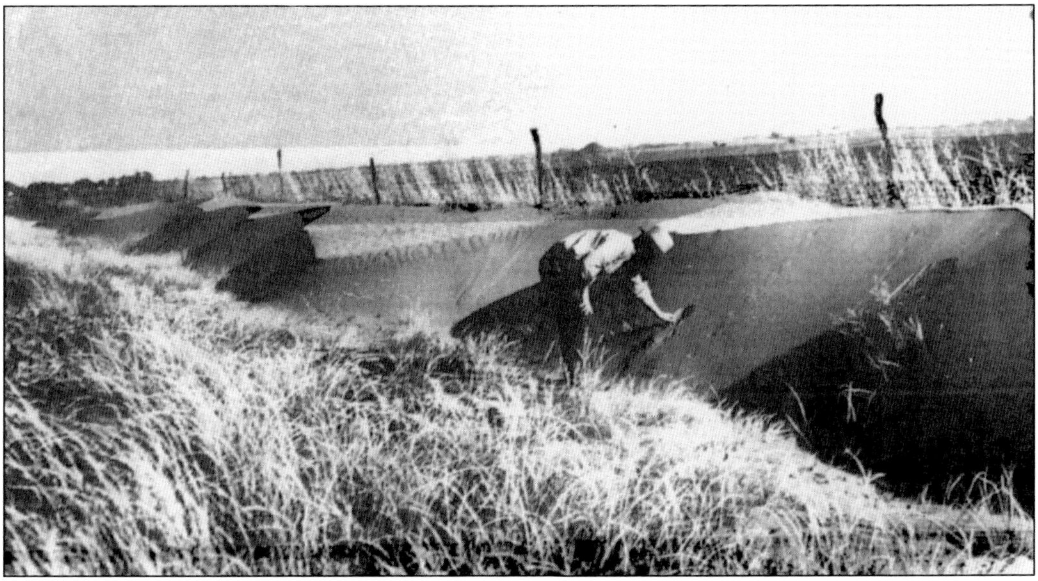

Sand has drifted into fence rows in 1936 near Sentinel. It was very difficult to control the dry soil and keep it from blowing. Many fences, especially if weeds were growing in the fence row, were completely buried under sand drifts during the dust bowl of the 1930s. (Courtesy Washita County Soil Conservation District.)

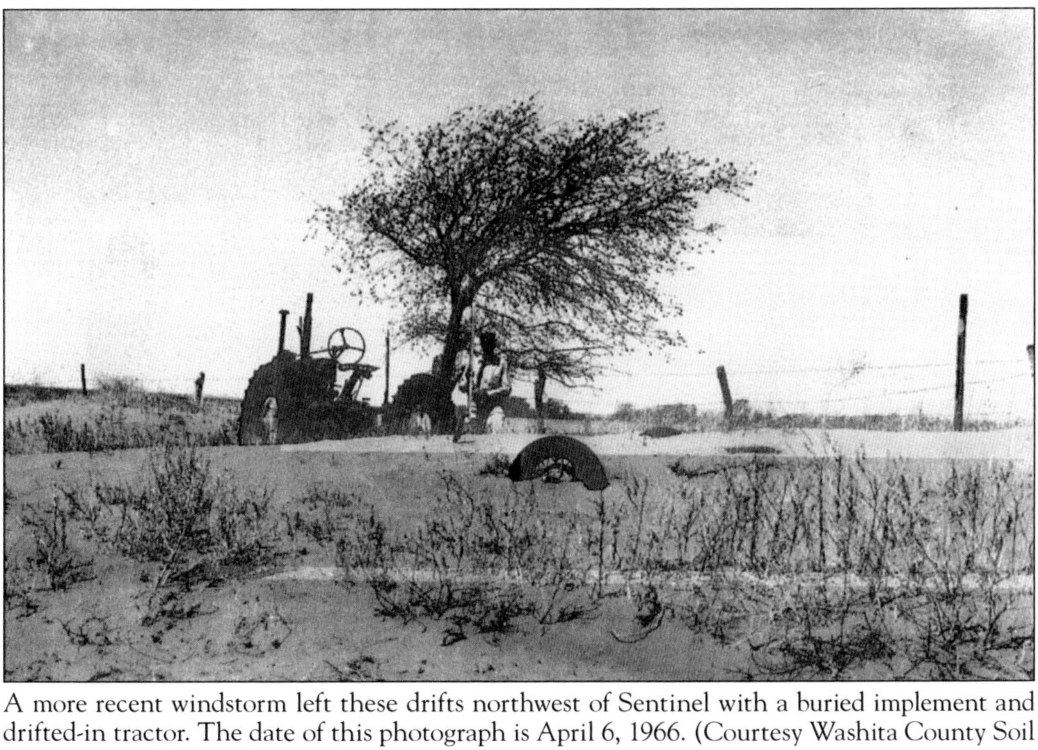

A more recent windstorm left these drifts northwest of Sentinel with a buried implement and drifted-in tractor. The date of this photograph is April 6, 1966. (Courtesy Washita County Soil Conservation District.)

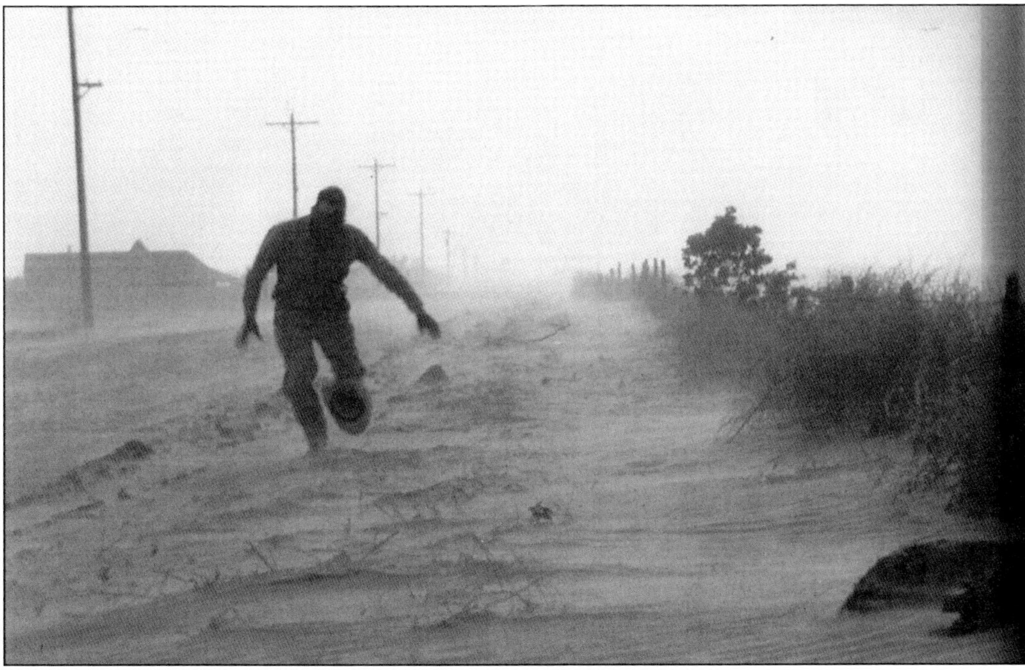

A dust storm in Washita County in the early 1950s is seen here. One does wonder if the man ever caught his hat, odds are that he did not. (Courtesy Washita County Soil Conservation District.)

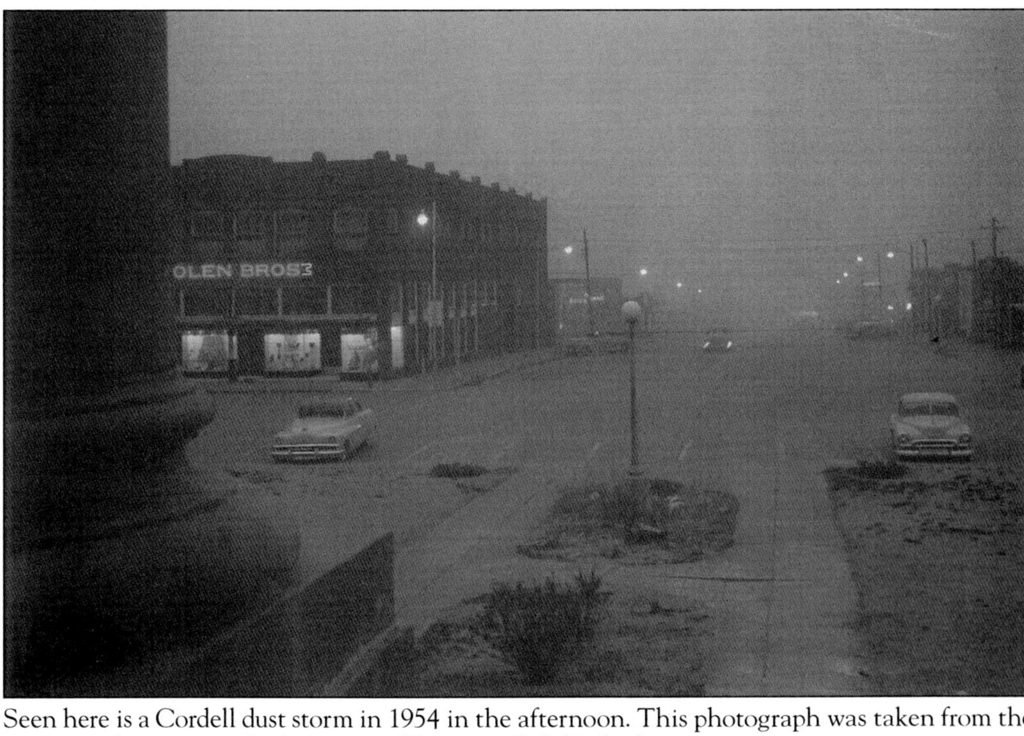

Seen here is a Cordell dust storm in 1954 in the afternoon. This photograph was taken from the west courthouse steps, looking west. (Courtesy Bob Taylor.)

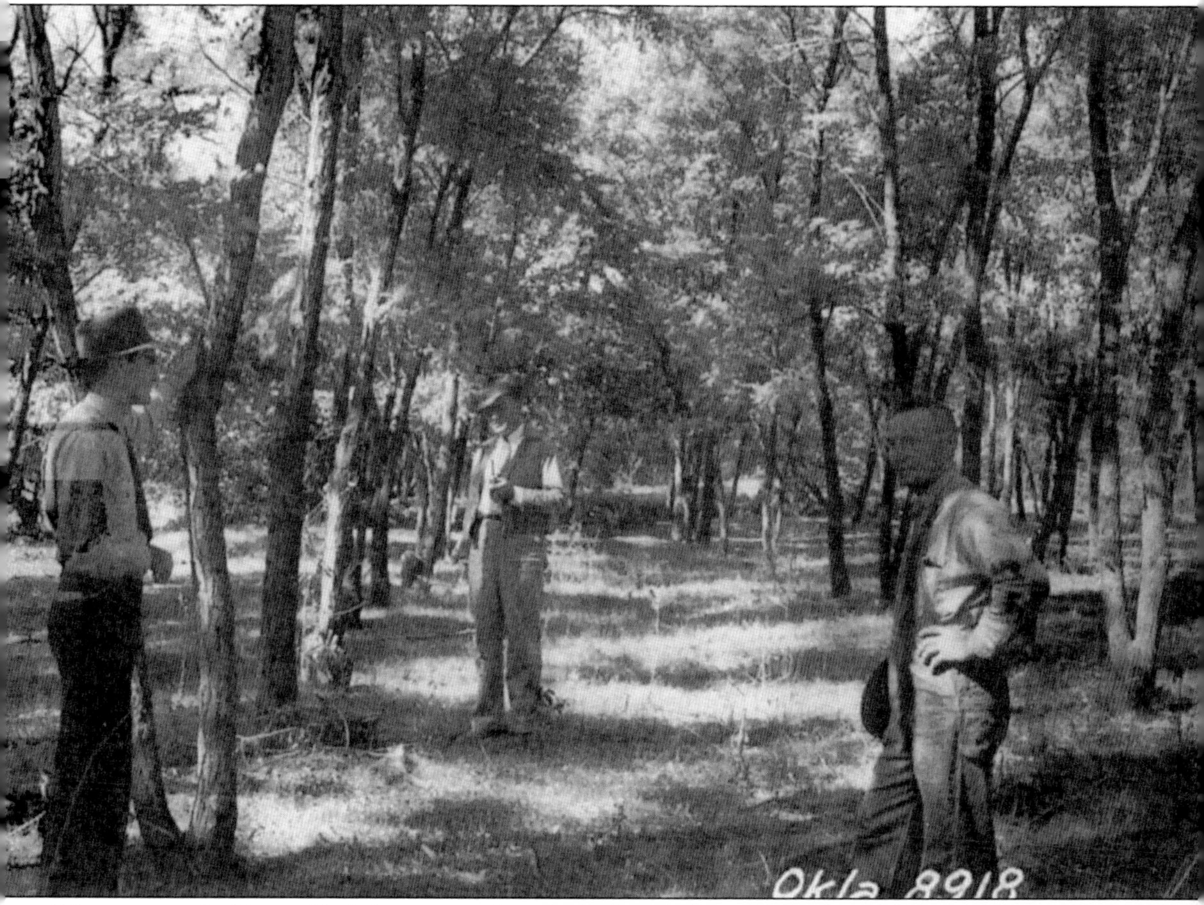

This is part of a 10-acre black locust post lot, planted in 1935 by the Civilian Conservation Corps (CCC) when it was establishing shelter belts. The photograph was made on October 18, 1944. On the left is Ray Murrell, work unit conservationist; Myrl Gray, county extension agent; and Tom Lucas, land owner. Lucas started cutting posts in 1941, and one acre yielded 1,500 posts. The black locust plot is located nine miles northwest of Sentinel. A CCC camp was established at Sentinel in 1935. The camp included 200 young men and a staff of 22 conservation and army personnel. The young men did conservation work and planted many miles of shelter belts, which helped control soil erosion from wind.

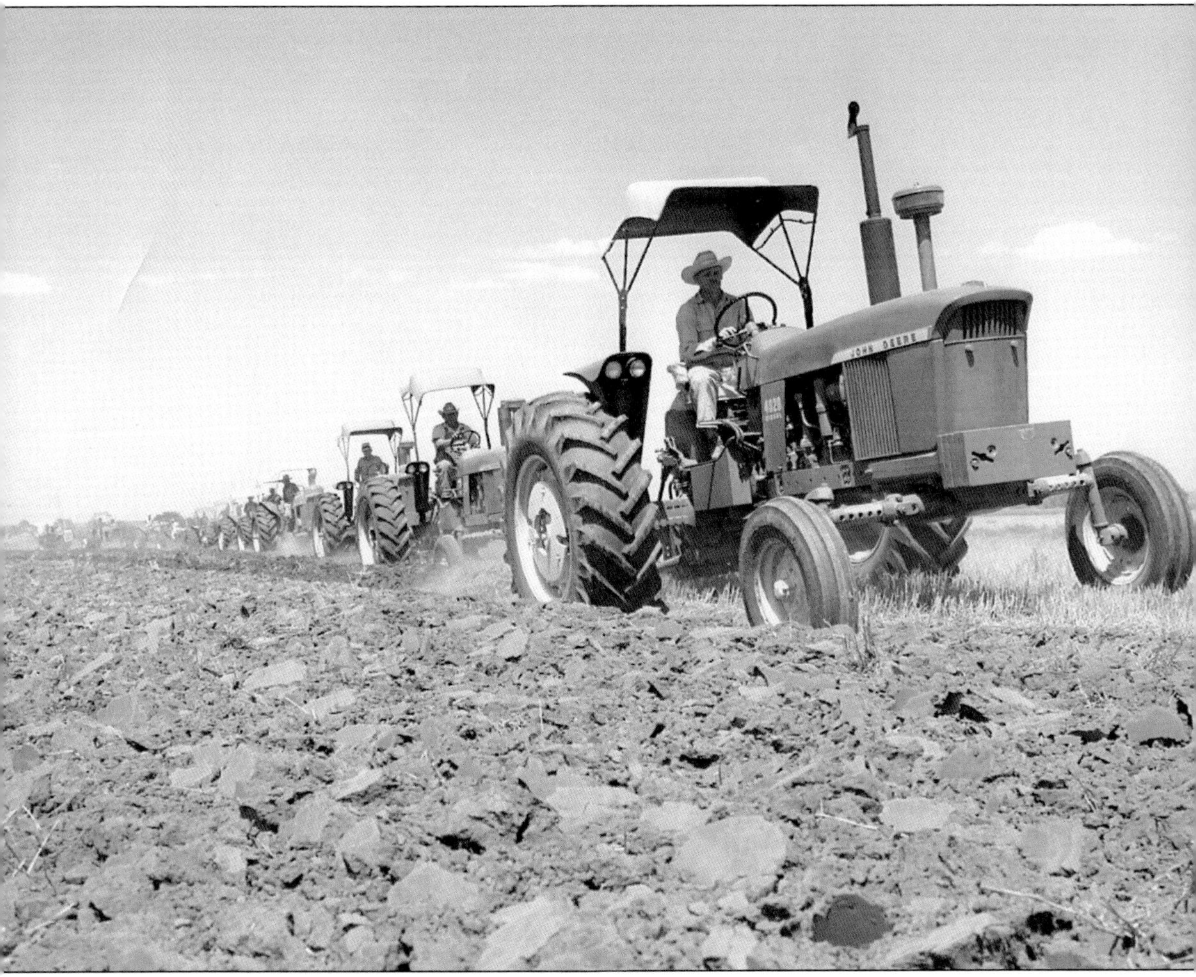

In 1964, farmer John Bonham was very sick. Bonham was too ill to do any farming, and his wheat stubble ground had not been worked. The pioneer spirit of helping a neighbor in need showed up when 17 neighbors brought their tractors and plows and worked all his wheat land in one day. It was this kind of spirit by its founders that made Washita County so great, and the spirit still remains in the county today. (Courtesy Bob Taylor.)

Six

The People

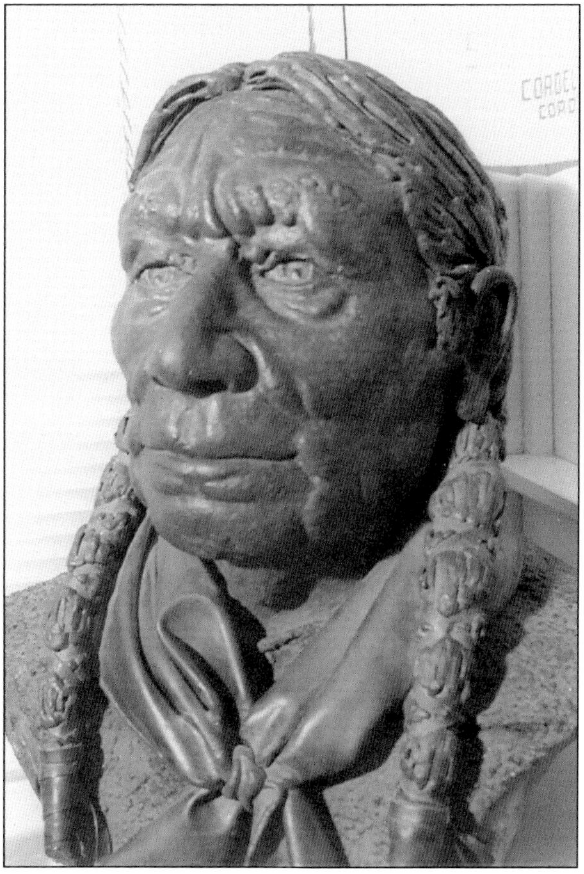

Cloud Chief, a Cheyenne Indian chief, was a popular Cheyenne who emerged as a leader during the negotiations to dissolve the Cheyenne-Arapaho Reservation. Cheyenne chiefs were difficult to deal with; however, Cloud Chief spoke English and was a man of his word. Cloud Chief had represented his tribe in working with the federal government's Indian Service. Pres. Benjamin Harrison awarded him a silver medal, which he wore with pride. After negotiations resumed, Cloud Chief asserted his intent to sign the agreement, and in doing so the other Native Americans followed suit. Securing allotments and peaceful settlements was much easier because of Cloud Chief; however, he was not a pushover for the Indian Service. As a reward for his leadership, the U.S. government gave him and his family the first four land allotment numbers in the Cheyenne-Arapaho land opening. In addition, Cloud Chief was also honored by having a post office and county seat named in his honor. (Courtesy Washita County Museum.)

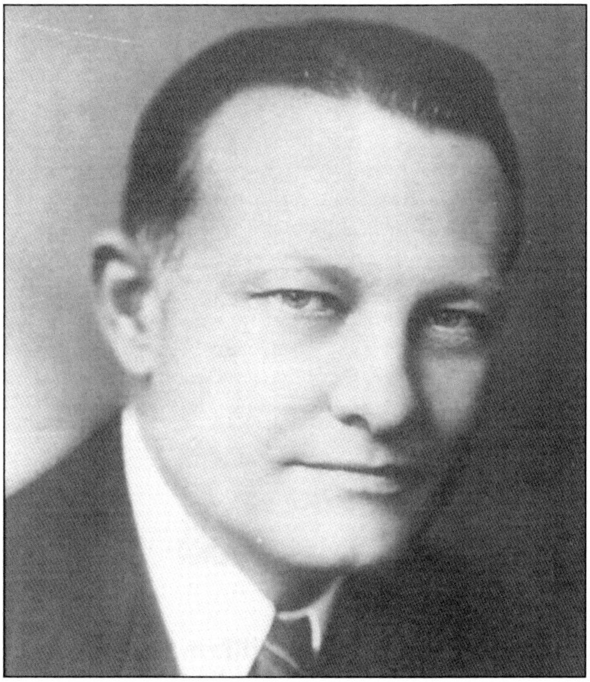

Josh Lee attended the Rocky school, his father was a medical doctor at Rocky. Lee was an outstanding speaker and won many speech contests. In 1934, Lee was elected to Congress and served only one term, as in 1936, he was elected to the U.S. Senate where he served until 1942. (Courtesy Washita County Museum.)

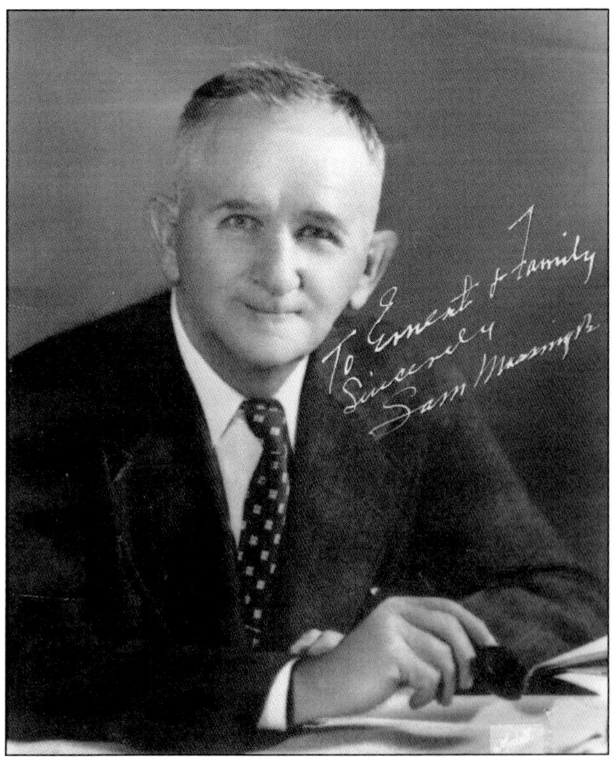

Sam Massingale was the Cordell attorney who was able to get Congress to pass a bill officially making Cordell the county seat of Washita County. Massingale served as a U.S. Congressman from 1936 until his death in 1941. (Courtesy Washita County Museum.)

Glen English was born and raised in Cordell. Glen was the third man to be elected to the U.S. Congress from Washita County when he won the election in 1974. English served in the U.S. Congress until his resignation in the 1990s. (Courtesy Washita County Museum.)

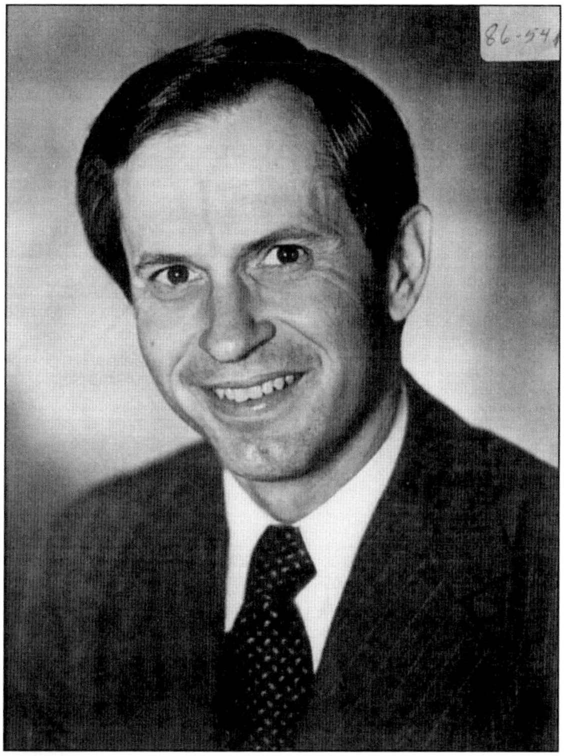

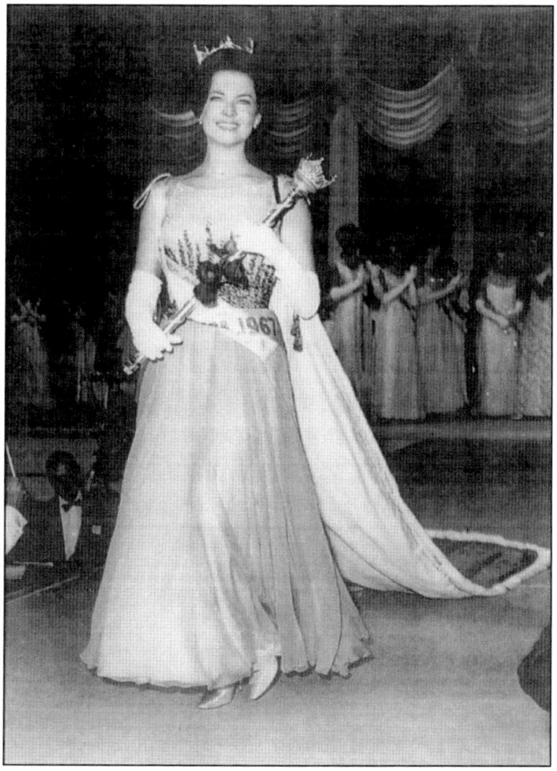

Jane Jayroe, 1976 Miss America, was born in Washita County at Sentinel, where her parents and grandparents lived. In 1967, as a student at Oklahoma City University, Jayroe was named Miss America. (Courtesy Washita County Museum.)

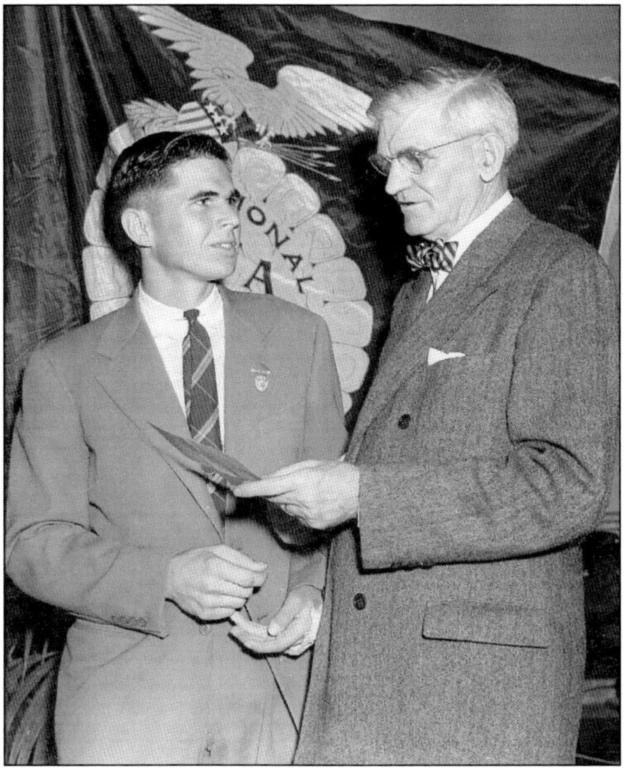

Wayne Boothe was born in Washita County and attended Cordell school. This photograph was taken in 1943, when Boothe was Oklahoma State Future Farmers of America (FFA) president receiving the Star Farmer of America award from W. A. Cochel, editor of the *Kansas City Star*. Boothe was the first Star Farmer of America from Oklahoma. (Courtesy Washita County Museum.)

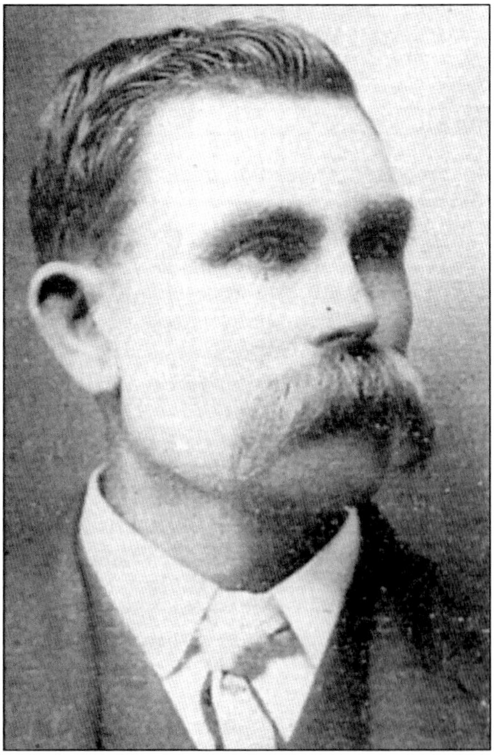

J. C. Harrel was one of the founders of the city of New Cordell in 1897. The homestead of Harrel is where the north half of Cordell is located today. Harrel gave the land for the north half of the town square. He built the first brick building in Cordell and gave the land for the Cordell Christian College and the Church of Christ. (Courtesy Washita County Museum.)

A. J. Johnson was cofounder of New Cordell with Harrel. The Johnson homestead was where the south half of New Cordell is located today, and he gave the land for the south half of the town square. J. A. White was the editor of the *Cordell Beacon* newspaper in 1902. White wrote an editorial that riled Johnson, who told White that if he did not retract the editorial he would whip him on the courthouse square. White met Johnson on Monday morning December 22, 1902, where he shot and killed Johnson on the southeast corner of the square. The *Cordell Beacon* got a new editor. (Courtesy Washita County Museum.)

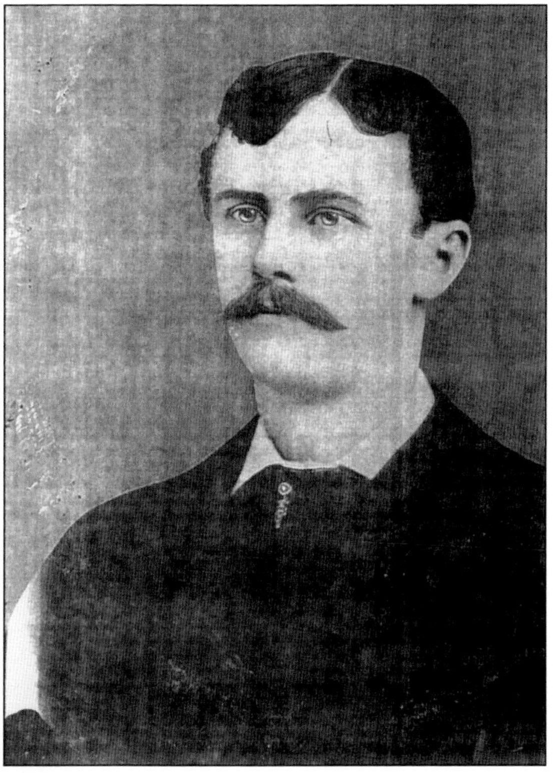

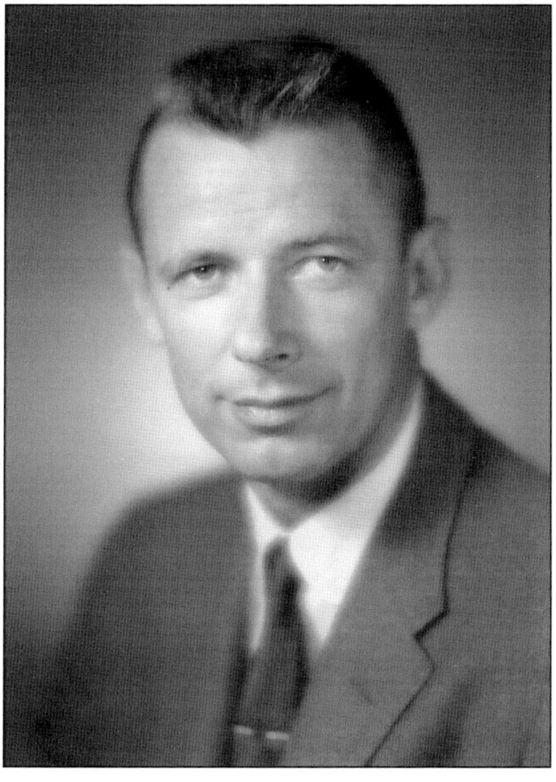

Bob Taylor, nationally known photographer, was born and raised in the town of Cordell in Washita County. Taylor, a registered pharmacist, returned from World War II interested in photography. With determination, he became one of the nation's best-known agricultural photographers. Hundreds of Taylor photographs have been used as cover pages for state and national magazines and by national companies. (Courtesy Washita County Museum.)

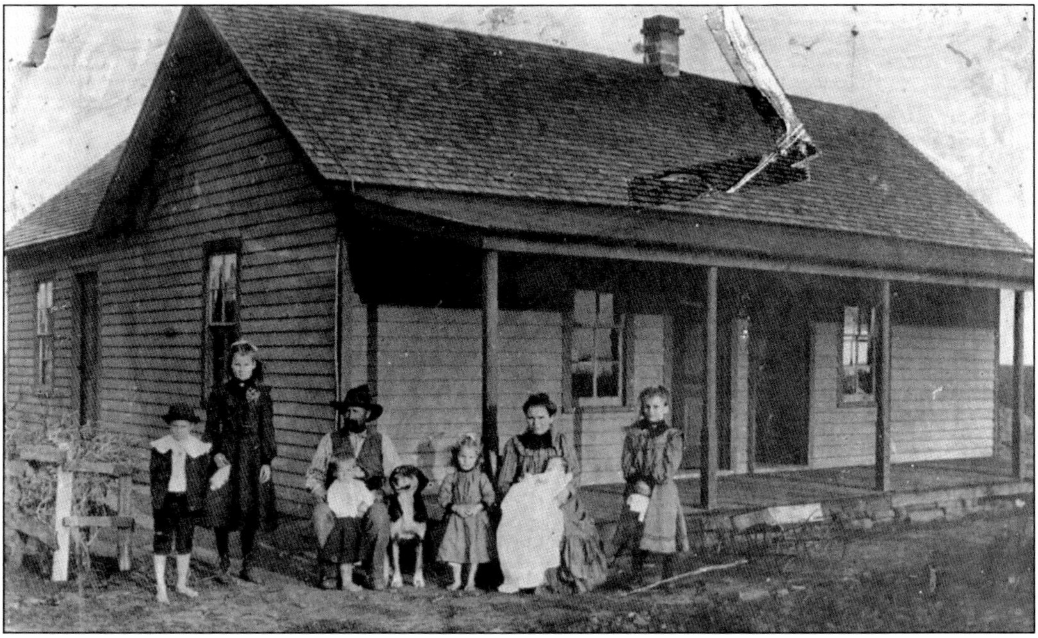

This is the T. H. Armstrong family in 1902 in the North Burns area. Armstrong ran a freight line, using mules and wagons, from 1887 until about 1904, hauling freight from El Reno to North Burns, about 160 miles round-trip, which required five to six days. (Courtesy Washita County Museum.)

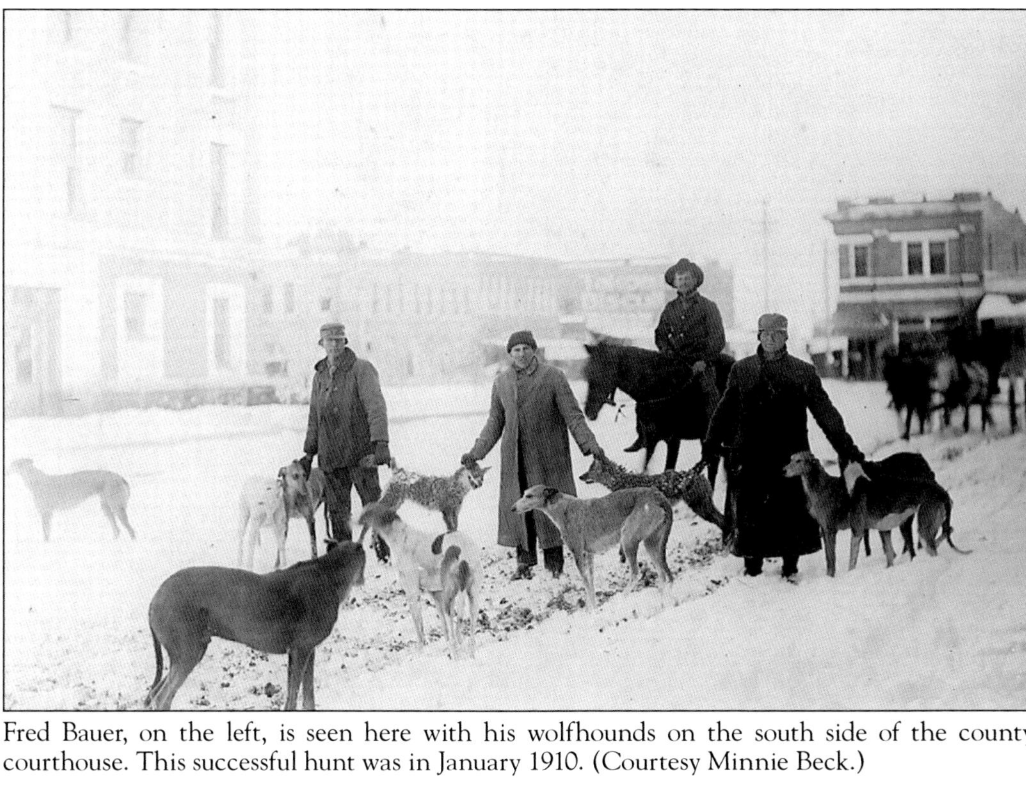

Fred Bauer, on the left, is seen here with his wolfhounds on the south side of the county courthouse. This successful hunt was in January 1910. (Courtesy Minnie Beck.)

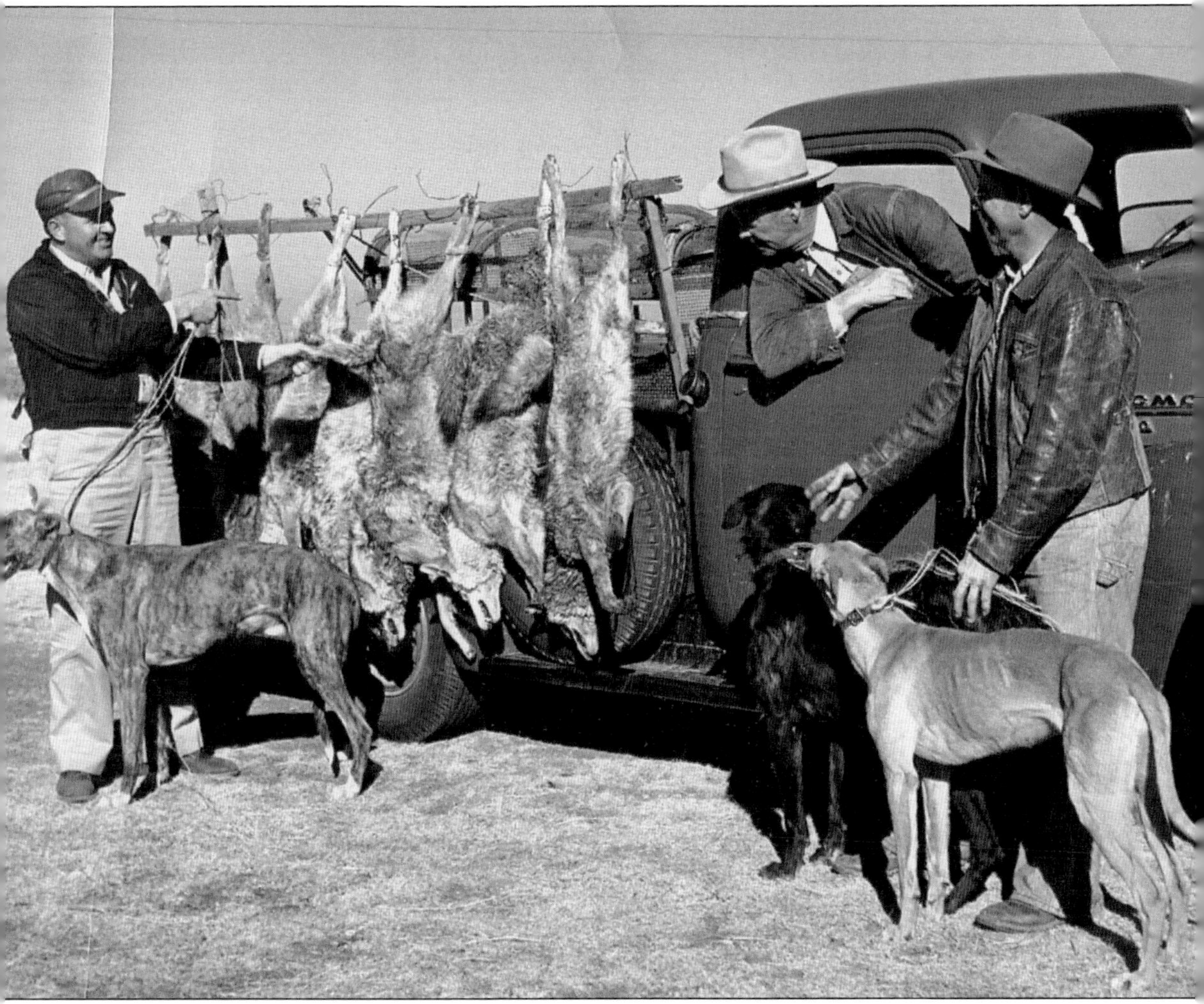

John Best, at the back of the pickup; Bill Gregory, in the pickup; and Ronald Vaniman show off their catch for the day in the late 1940s. The hunt that drew the most attention of any hunt in Washita County was in March 1945. Lord and Lady Halifax of England came to the Washita County area for a wolf hunt. Dr. V. C. Tisdal of Elk City had met Lord Halifax in Scotland at a famous foxhunt in 1928 and invited him to come to the United States for a wolf hunt. On March 20, 1945, a very large airplane landed on the long runway at the Burns Flat Airbase with Lord and Lady Halifax. Millard C. Milstead of Canute had arranged for about 50 Oklahoma quarter horse mounts and more than 250 hounds from four states. A large crowd of onlookers gathered. As mounts were selected and stirrups adjusted, the hunt was on. Yes, several wolves and coyotes were caught, but no foxes. Lord Halifax said he had never ridden a mount that was as easy riding as the one he rode that day. Looking back, Canute and Washita County are one of the few areas in the United States that can boast about hosting a "Royal Wolf Hunt." (Courtesy Bob Taylor.)

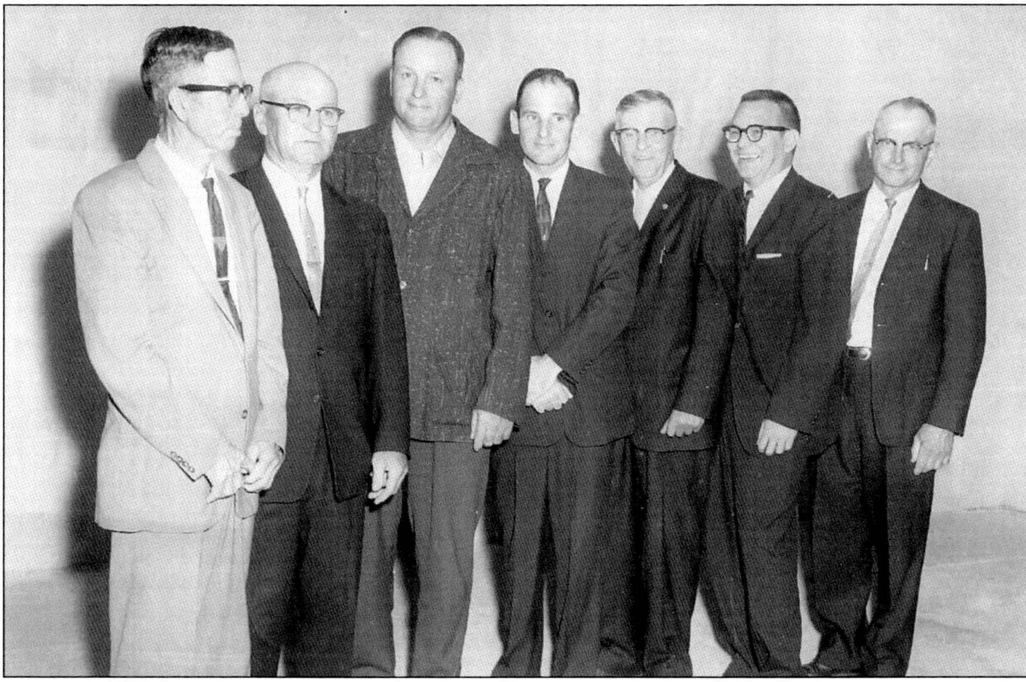

Washita County's first soil conservation board is seen here in the early 1940s. From left to right are Bill Nash, Ed Bose, Maurice Huls, Eldred Sasseen, Augie Sewell, associate member Frank Kliewer, and Sellers Archer, conservation manger. The Washita County SCS (Soil Conservation Service) is still very active today. (Courtesy Washita County SCS District.)

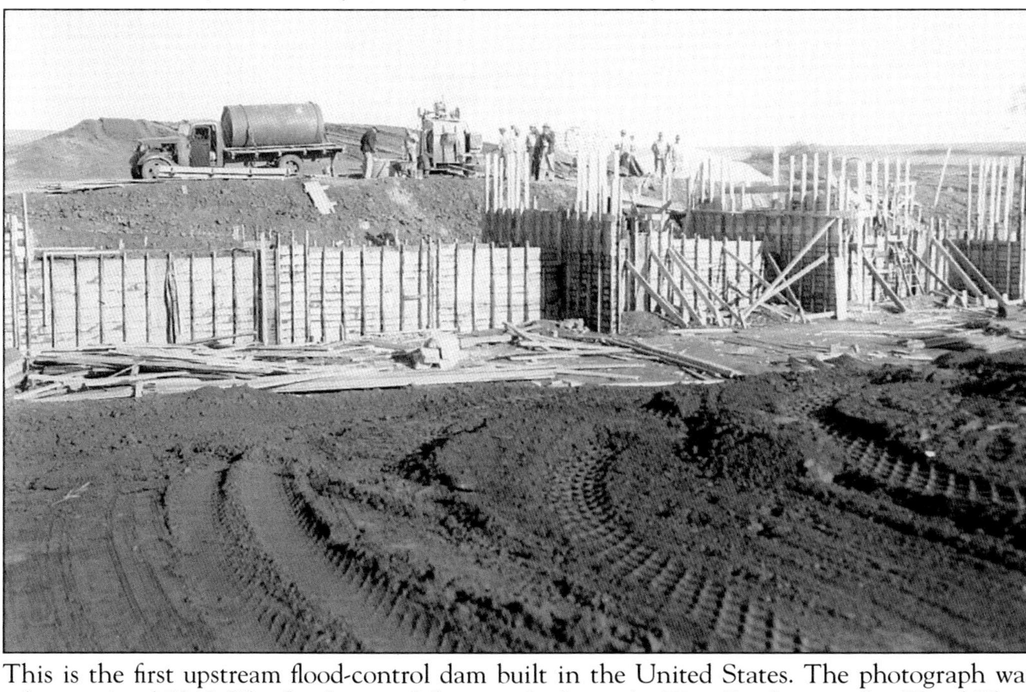

This is the first upstream flood-control dam built in the United States. The photograph was taken in April 1948. The flood-control dam was built on the Troy Orr farm in the Cloud Chief area in 1948. (Courtesy Washita County SCS District.)

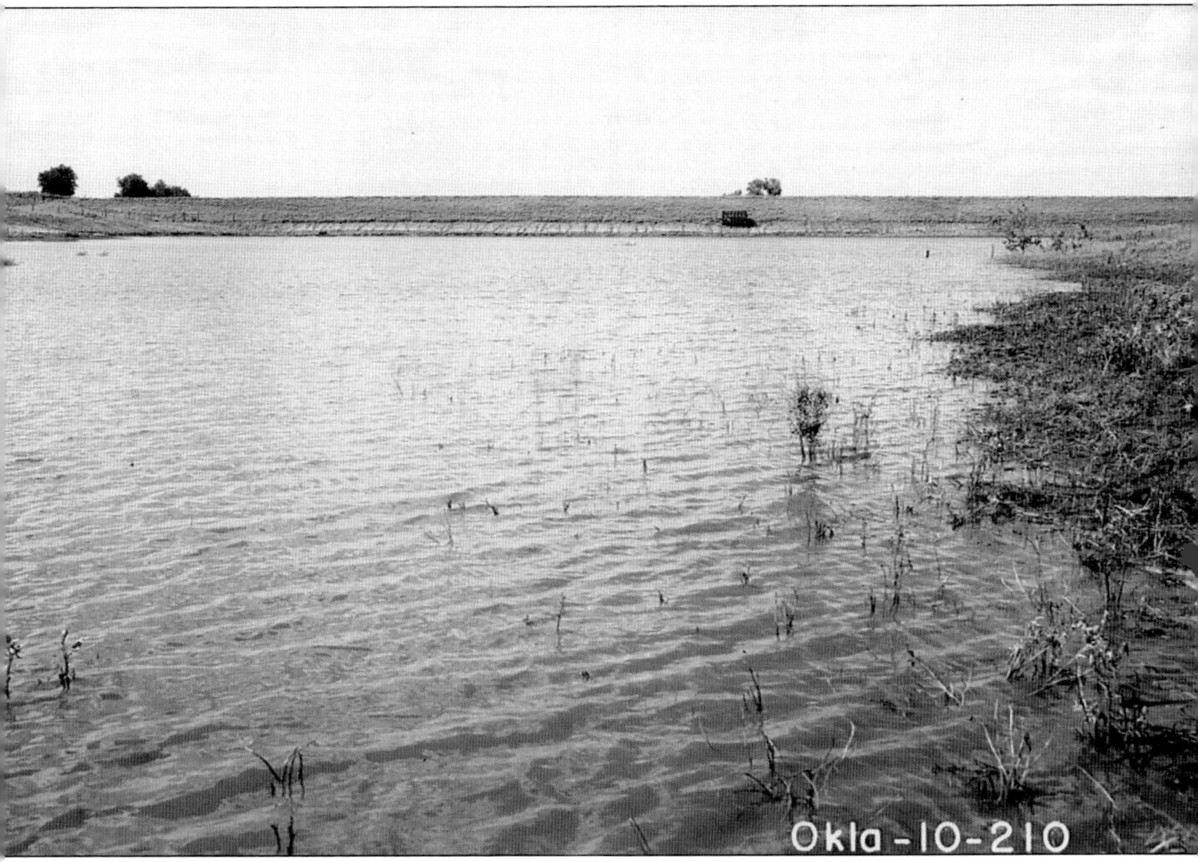

The first upstream flood-control dam built in the United States was located in Washita County. It was built in 1948, and by June 1949, the lake was about half full. The national upstream flood-control program's first structure was built in Washita County on Cloud Creek. Today over 10,000 upstream flood-control structures have been completed in the United States. The Washita County Soil Conservation District has 144 of the flood-control structures. The projected life of the flood-control dams was 50 years. Many of the county structures are now 50 years old and still functioning very well. (Courtesy Washita County SCS District.)

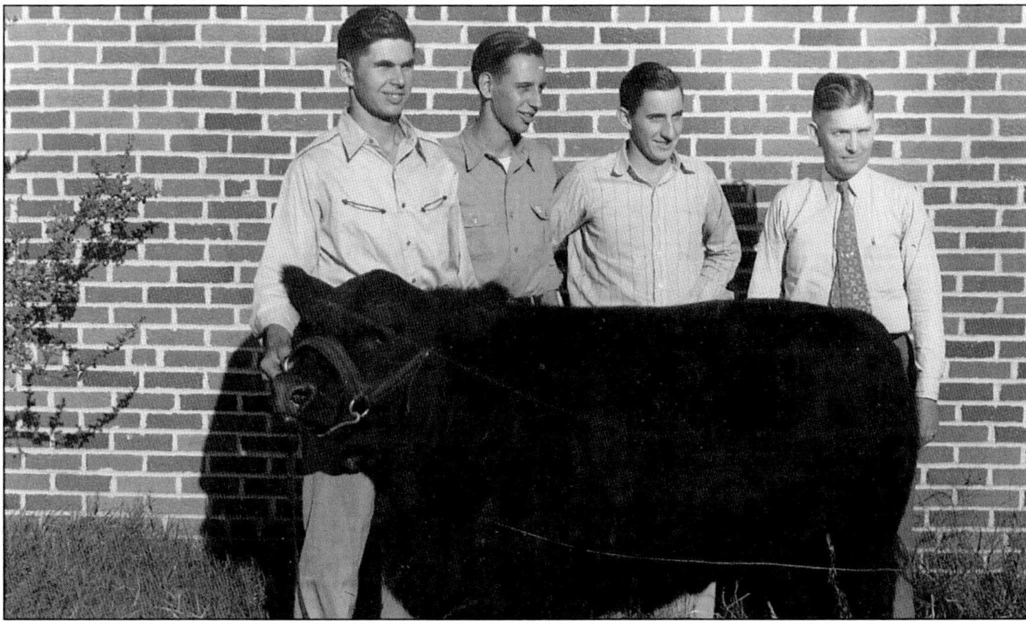

Seen here is the Cordell FFA livestock judging team, which won the National FFA and 4-H National Livestock Judging Contest in 1942. Team members are, from left to right, Wayne Boothe, Jerold Smith, A. J. Green, and instructor G. E. Gaines. Of the 63 teams competing in the national contest, the Cordell team won first, and Wayne Boothe was top individual of the 252 contestants in the national contest. (Courtesy Cordell FFA.)

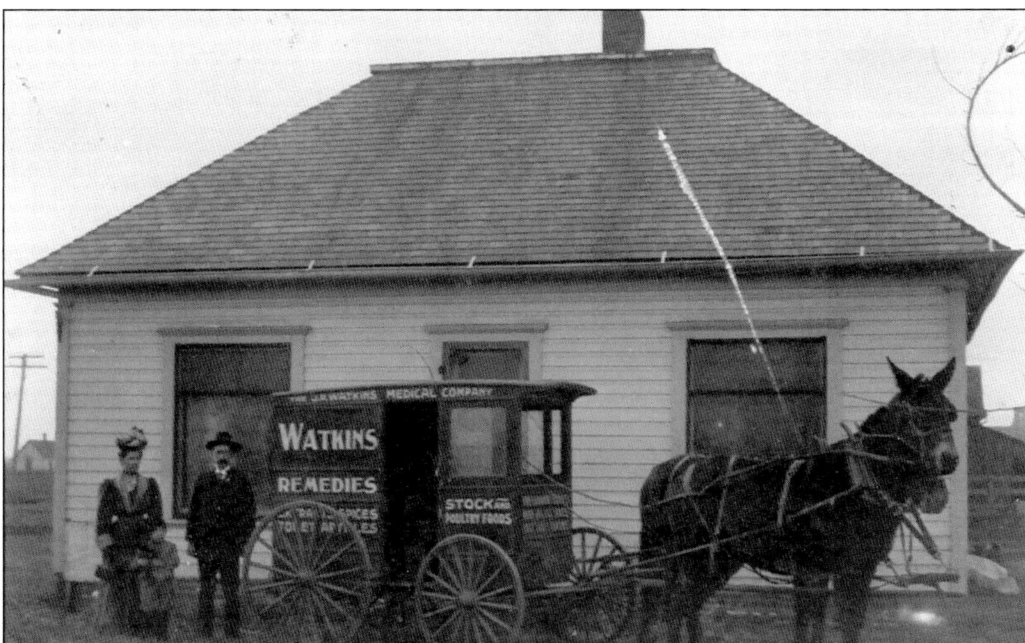

Marvin Sheets from Cowden traveled thousands of miles with his team of mules and his Watkins wagon selling Watkins products to the people of Washita County. (Courtesy Washita County Museum.)

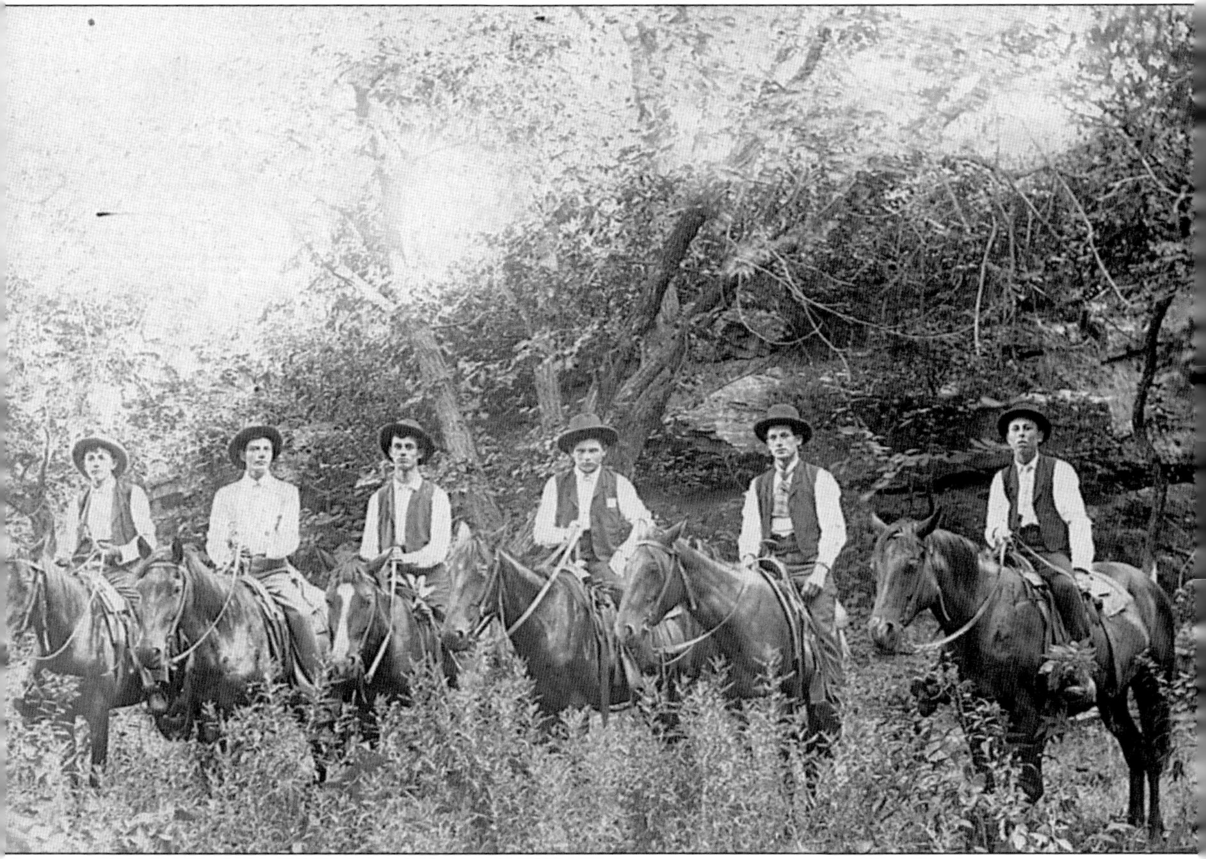

A special posse deputized by Washita County sheriff Neal Morrison in 1899 entered the Hughes Ranch on the Washita River in search of Ben Casey and Cole Younger. The posse, from left to right, includes John Stewart, Bill Stewart, Jim Meeler, Will Meeler, Paul Ward, and Claude Meeler. The Hughes Ranch was a well-known hideout for outlaws on the run. The ranch headquarters was located about six miles southeast of Cloud Chief in the Washita River bottom. By 1905, the Hughes Ranch was about 20,000 acres of owned and leased land. The ranch extended east about 12 miles, almost to the Caddo County line. Both Ben Hughes and his brother Jim Hughes served time for train robbery and bank robbery. (Courtesy Washita County Museum.)

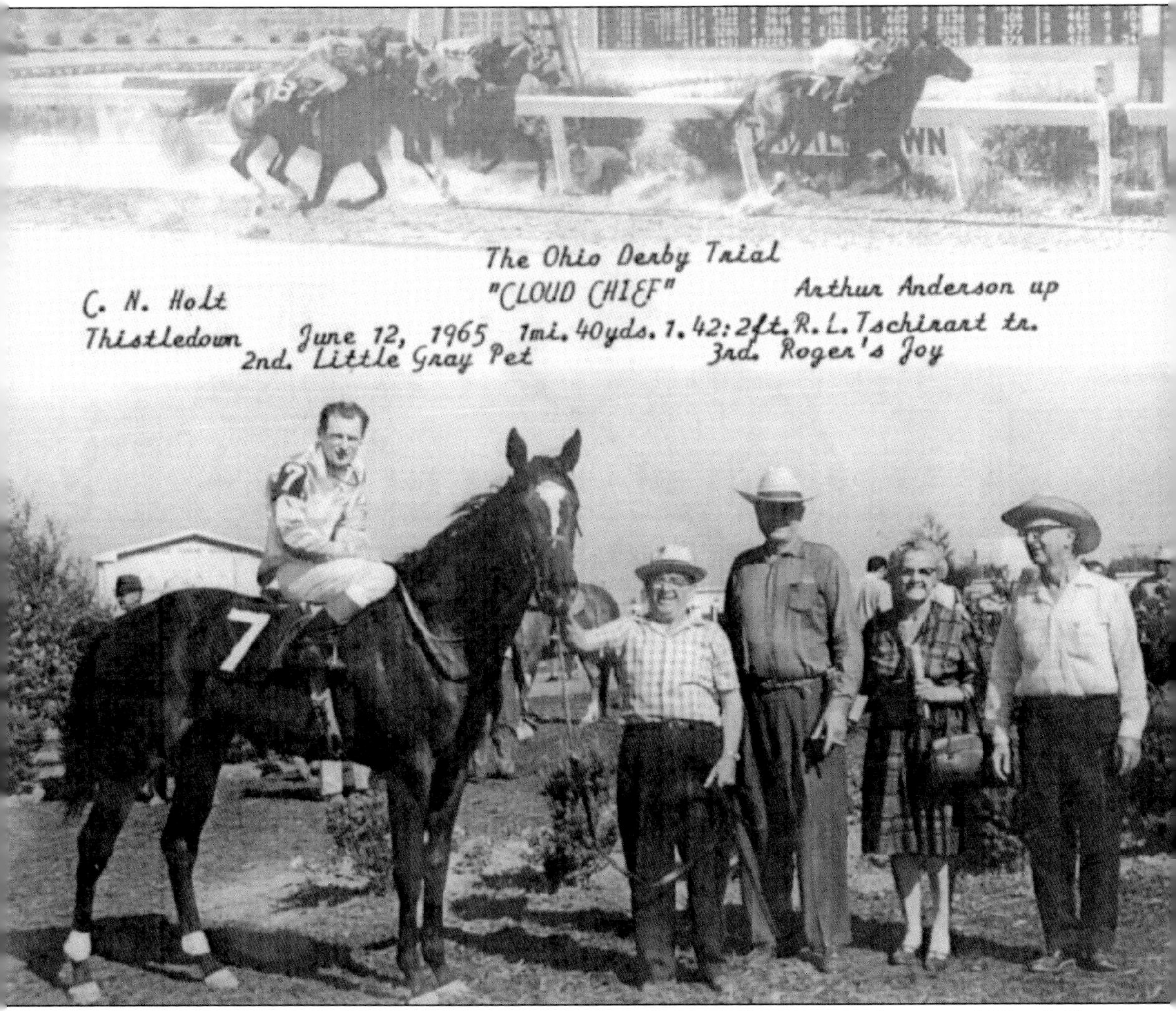

Cloud Chief, the racehorse, was born in 1962 on the Holt farm one mile west of Cloud Chief in Washita County. This photograph is from when he not only won but set a track record at the Ohio Derby. From left to right, Arthur Anderson, jockey on Cloud Chief; R. L. Tschirart, trainer; Charley Holt; Mrs. Holt; and an unidentified gentleman are seen here. The racehorse Cloud Chief was undefeated as a three year old and was entered in the 1965 Kentucky Derby. He had the fastest time of any horse entered in the derby. A week before the race, Cloud Chief was disabled in a suspicious accident and was unable to run in the Kentucky Derby. His injury was so bad he had to be destroyed. (Courtesy Ed Holt.)

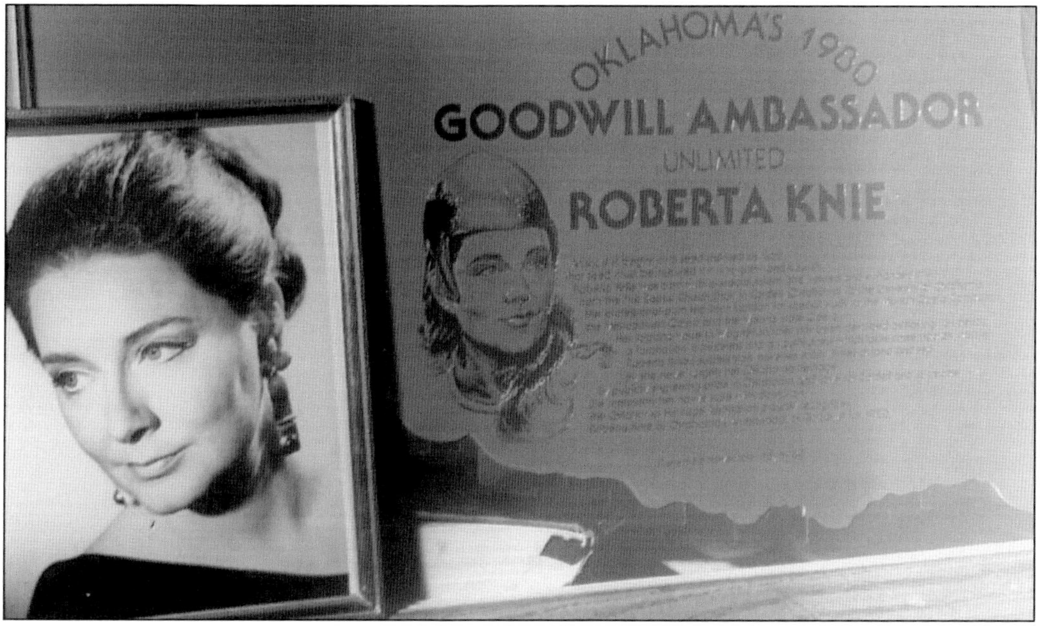

Roberta Knie was born and raised in Cordell. Knie always had a love for music and as a high school student won many state and national music awards. She spent many years in Austria and preformed in many countries around the world. Knie is in a who's who list of well-known and important opera performers in both world opera and American opera. She represented the state as "Oklahoma's Ambassador of Good Will" during the 1980s. (Courtesy Washita County Museum.)

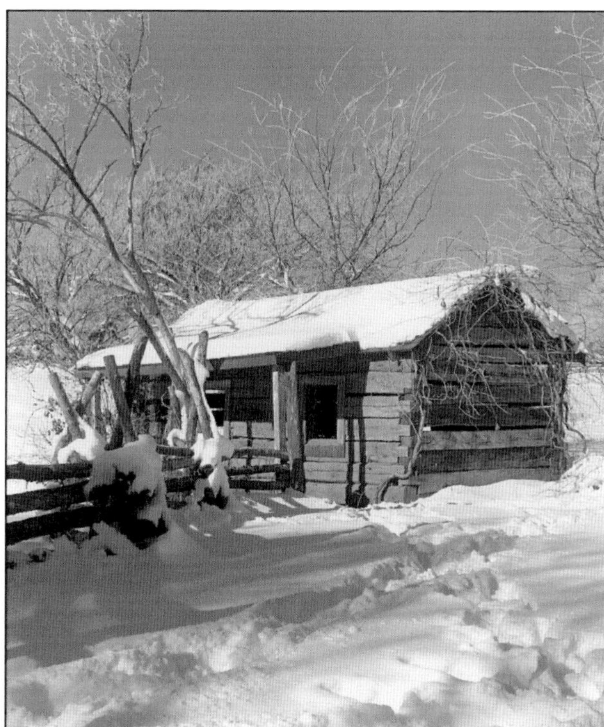

The log cabin was constructed about 1916 by Dr. A. H. Bungardt, who was born in a log cabin. It still stands today in the backyard of Mary and Wayne Boothe. (Courtesy Bob Taylor.)

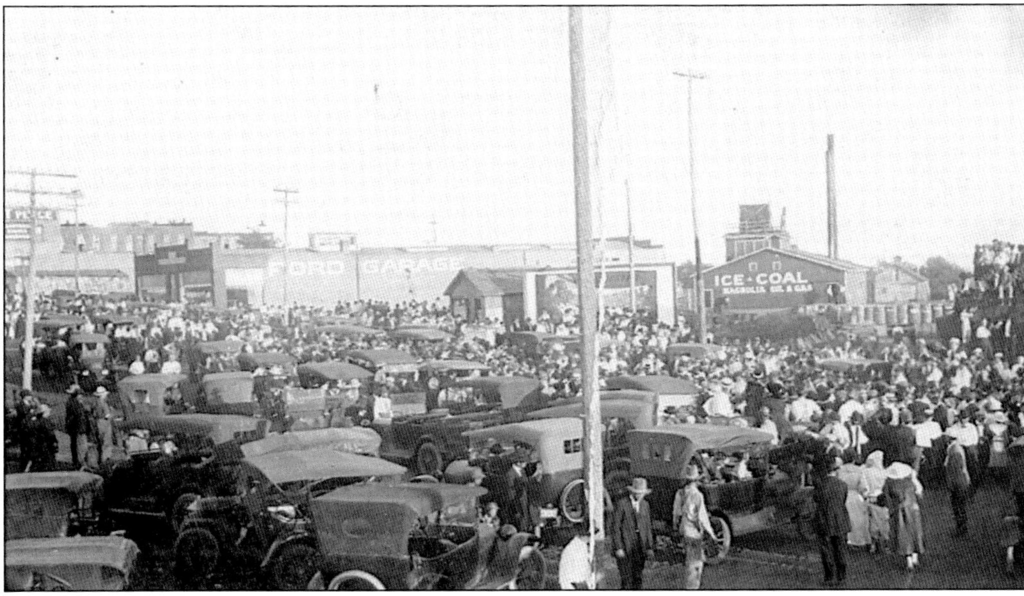

This 1917 World War I photograph was taken at the railroad depot at Cordell when the draftees were boarding the train to leave for army camp. (Courtesy Nora Diffendaffer.)

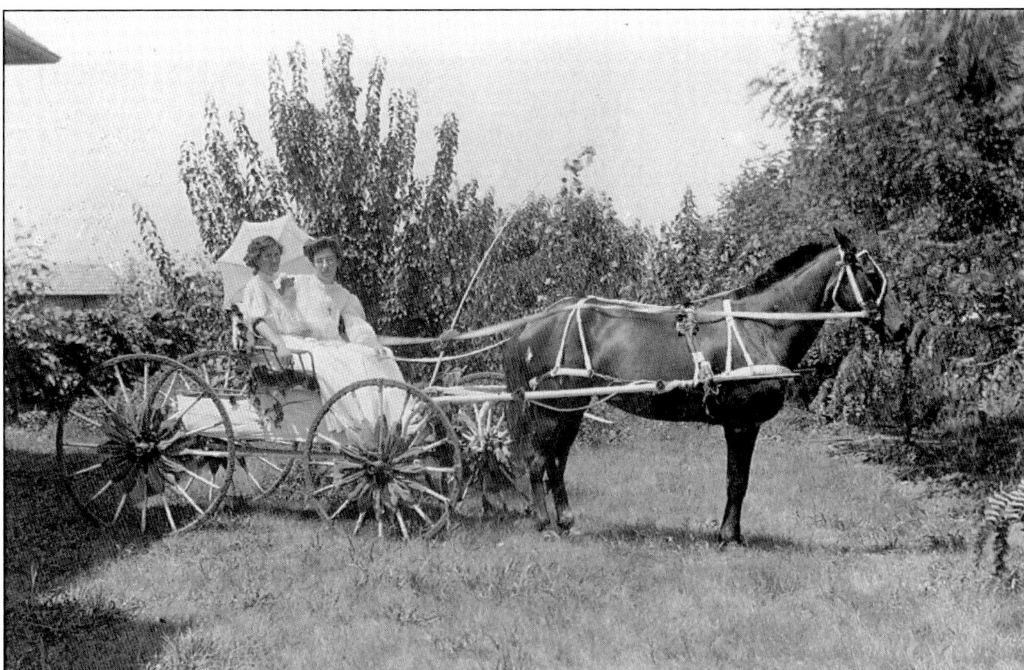

Laura Corley and Maud Haeberly are all dressed up in the apple orchard on their way to town in the summer of 1896. (Courtesy Washita County Museum.)

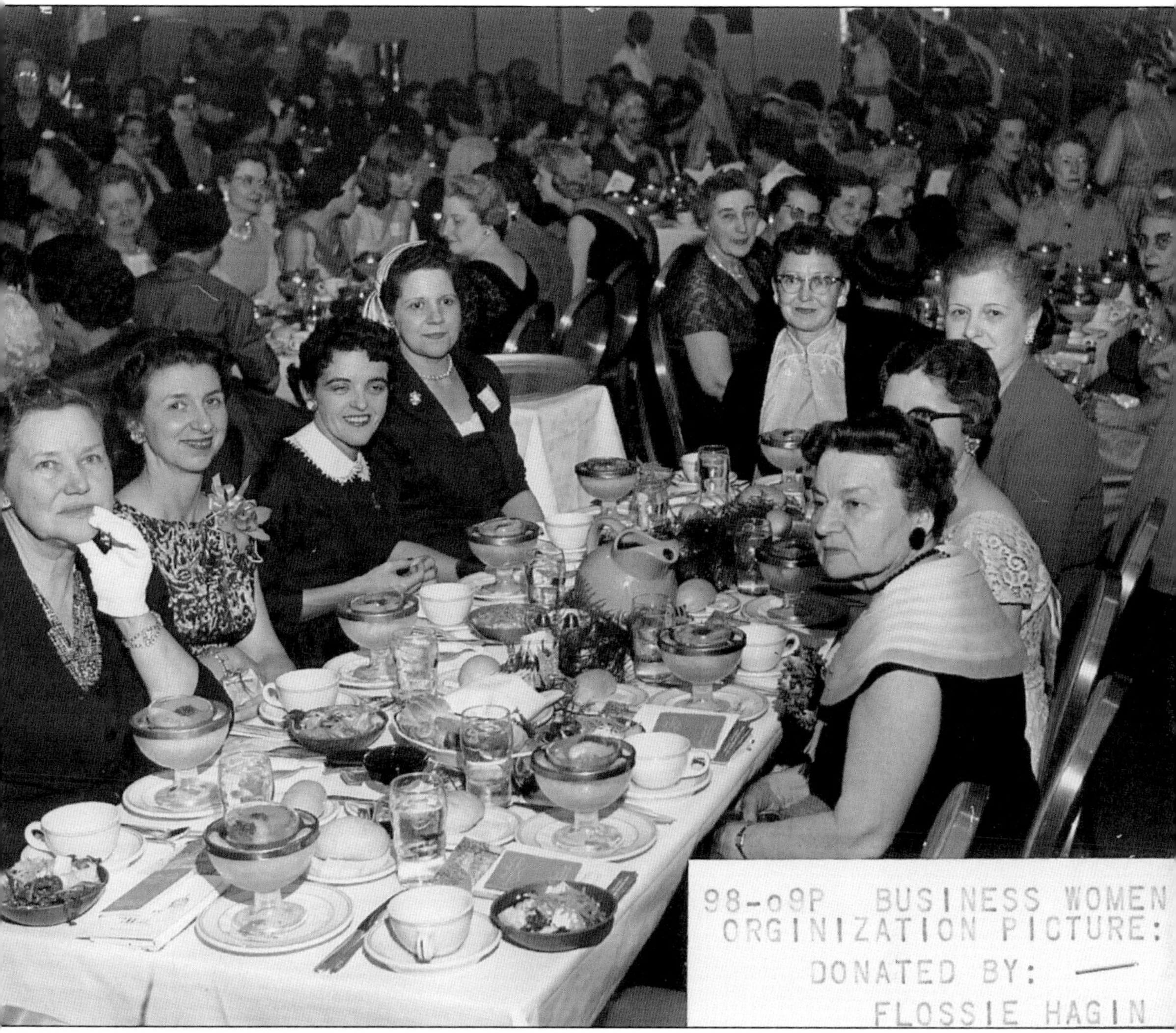

Seen here is a Cordell Business and Professional Women's Club dinner meeting. The Cordell club was organized on October 25, 1928. The charter members were Floy Armfield, Florence Austin, Lois Armstrong, Olivetta Bruce, Alta Carder, Ollie Cochran, Emma Dysurt, Pearl Donald, Vivian Gibson, Alma Kerley, Marianne Klingman, Rena Ledbetter, Lena Lain, Esta Lamb, Gertha Molen, Frankie Moore, Beda Simpson, and D'eilah Symcox. The Business and Professional Women's Club is still active today. (Courtesy Washita County Museum.)

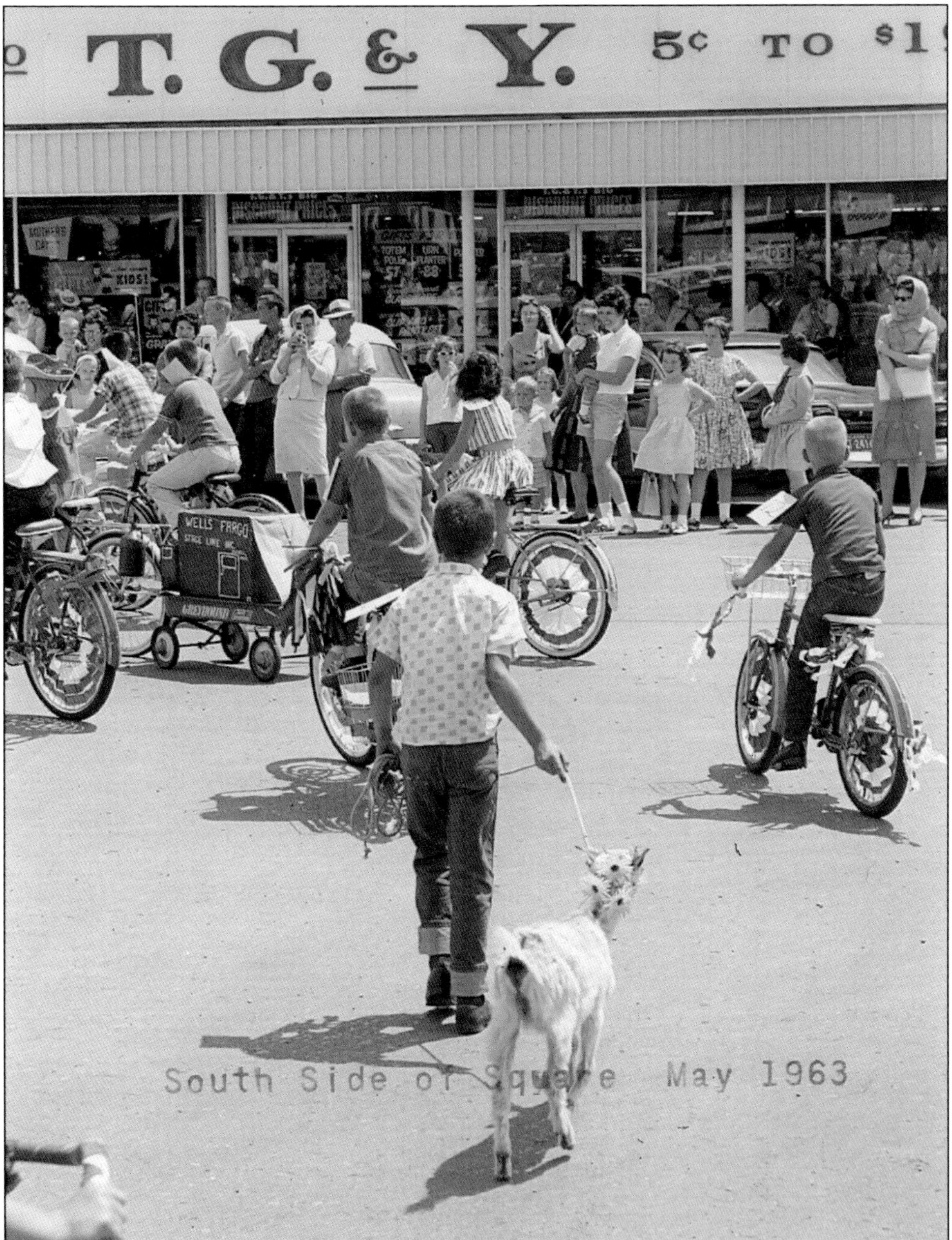

Participants of the Kids Day parade received a free ice-cream cone for taking part in the parade from TG&Y. Cordell was part of the start of TG&Y. Les Gosselin opened Gosselin's Variety Store in Cordell in 1922. In 1925, he opened his second store in Carnegie, and in 1925, he opened his third store in Mangum and fourth at Sentinel. He later added stores at Elk City and Hobart. In 1935, Gosselin was joined by R. E. Tomlinson of Fredrick and R. A. Young of Watonga to form a partnership for central purchasing and warehouseing. The three men founded the TG&Y Company with headquarters in Oklahoma City. In 1984, the company recorded $2 billion in sales in their 940 TG&Y stores located in 29 states. Those free ice-cream cones must have paid off. (Courtesy Bob Taylor.)

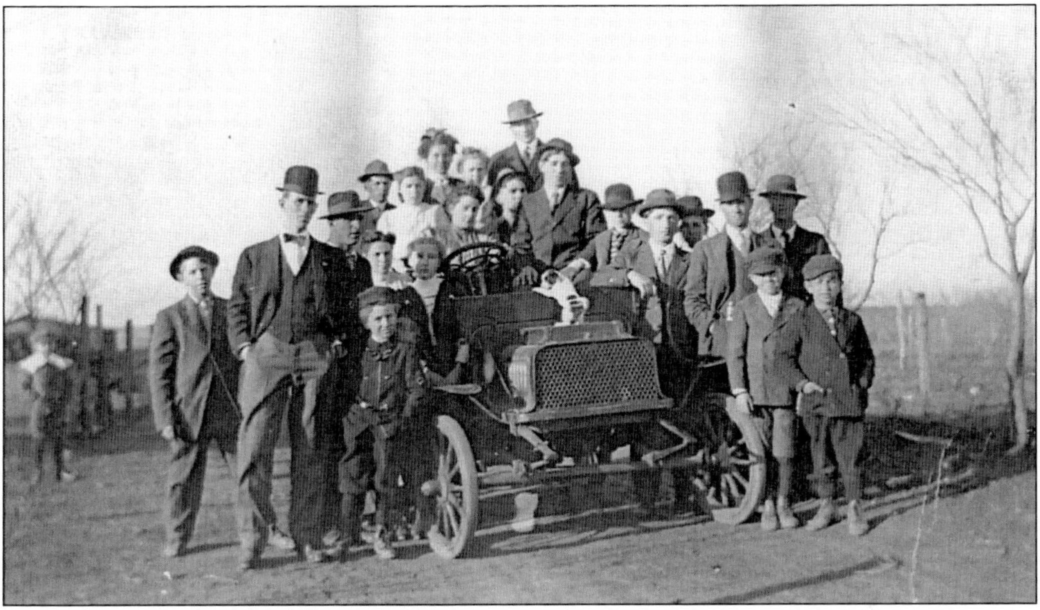

This is the Lenaburg family and their new Ford car, one of the first automobiles in the Bessie area. (Courtesy Washita County Museum.)

Horseshoes has always been an enjoyable game in Washita County. Bill Lowber, on the left, and Earl Wilkerson, pitching, are seen in 1949 in a county horseshoe-pitching contest. (Courtesy Bob Taylor.)

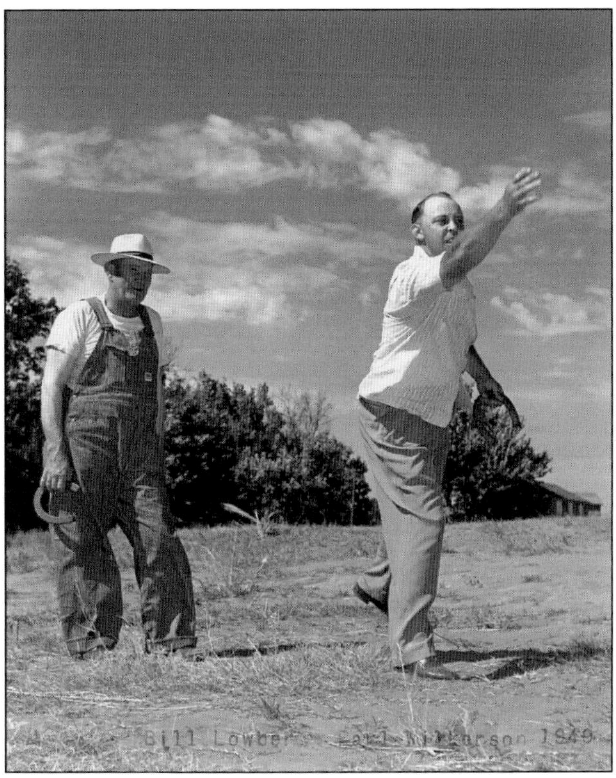

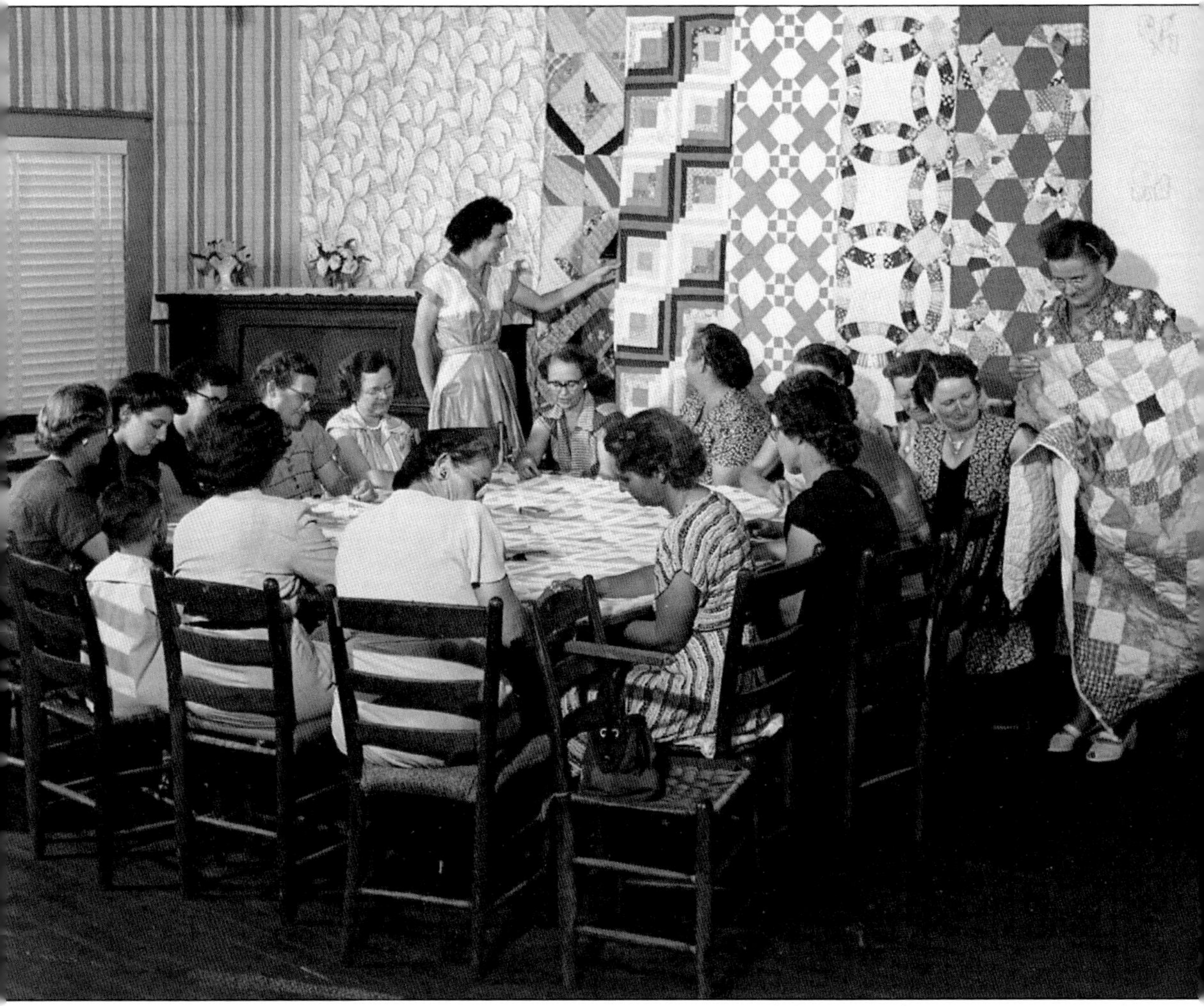

This is the Cloud Chief Extension Home Demonstration Club at a quilting meeting in 1957. The president Edith Sturgeon (fifth from left, in white blouse) and Gladys Maynard (seventh from left), club secretary, are seen here. The first Extension Home Makers Club was organized at Foss in 1929. By 1957, Washita County had 21 active Extension Home Demonstration Clubs. Today the name has been changed to Home and Community Education Club (HCE). The HCE will have hundreds of items in competition at the Washita County 100th annual county fair this fall. (Courtesy Bob Taylor.)

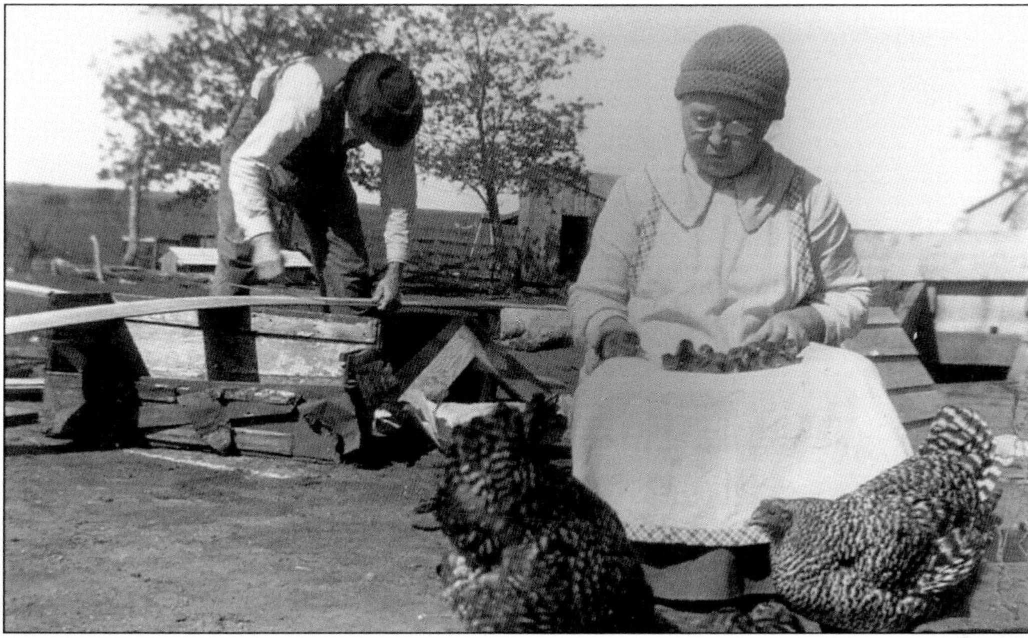

J. W. and Fanny Boothe came to Washita County in the late 1890s and established their home. This photograph shows J. W. building a chicken house about 1910 for Fanny's bard rock chickens, which were an important part of their farming operation. (Courtesy Washita County Museum.)

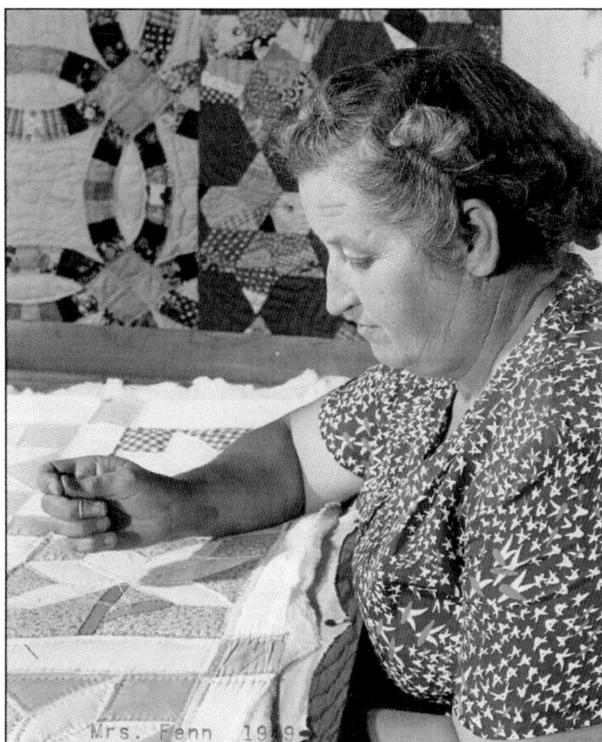

Florence Fenn of Cloud Chief is getting her quilts ready for the 1949 Washita County Fair. (Courtesy Bob Taylor.)

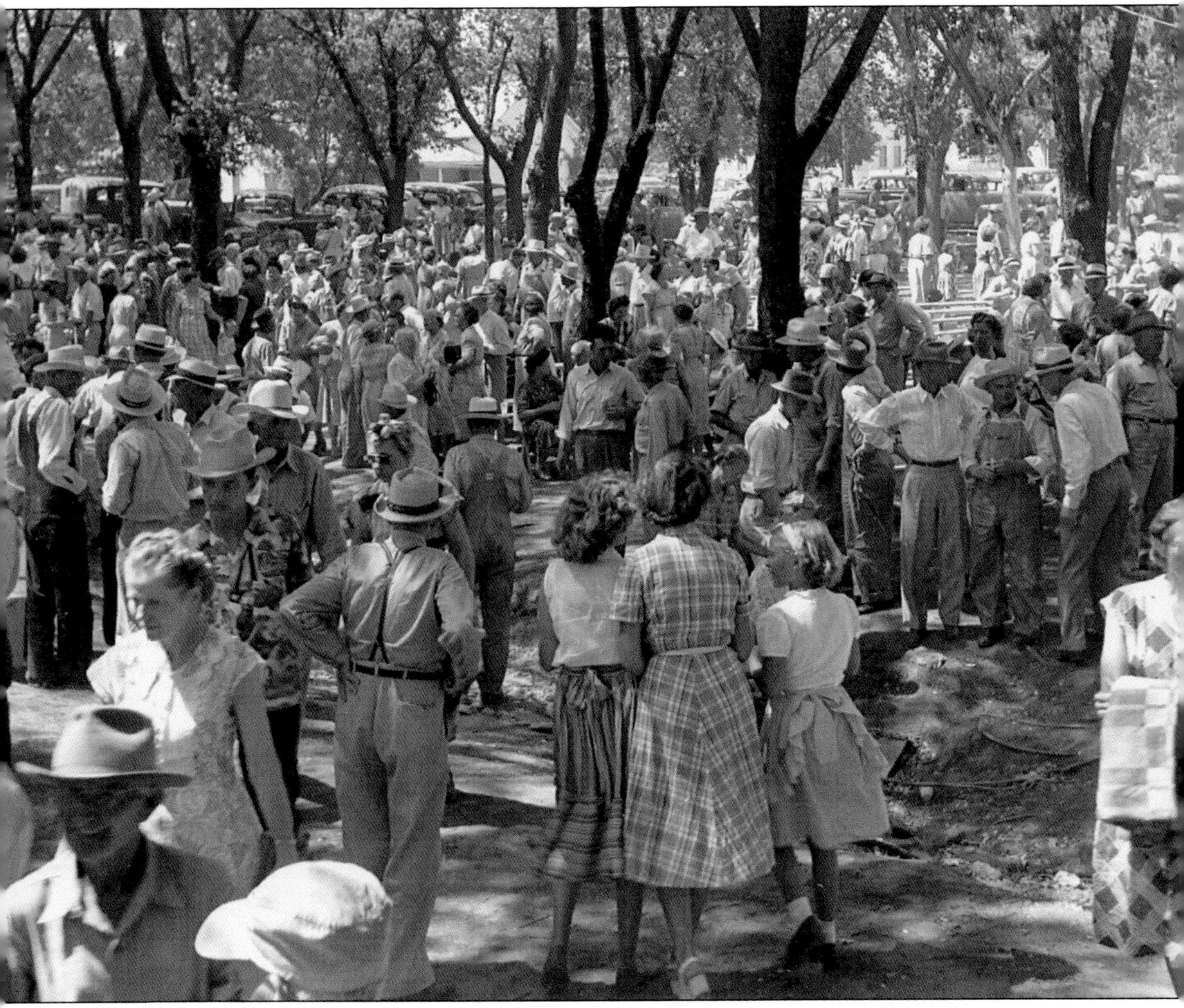

The August 1951 Kiwash REC (Rural Electric Cooperative) annual meeting at the Cordell City Park brought 5,000 members to Cordell. Kiwash Electric Cooperative was organized in 1938. It took a year to build about 50 miles of electric line to serve less than 50 members. At noon on December 6, 1941, the late Congressman Sam Massingale threw the switch and turned on the power for Kiwash REC's first service. The first power was bought from the City of Cordell. In 1947, the Kiwash REC started buying power from Western Farmers Electric. Cordell today buys its power from Western Farmers Electric. Kiwash REC today furnishes electric power to some 5,800 members who utilize more than 2,780 miles of electric line in a five-county area, Washita, Kiowa, Custer, Dewey, and Roger Mills Counties. Kiwash is a far cry from the less than 50 members it served 69 years ago. The Kiwash annual meetings are still held in Cordell. (Courtesy Bob Taylor.)

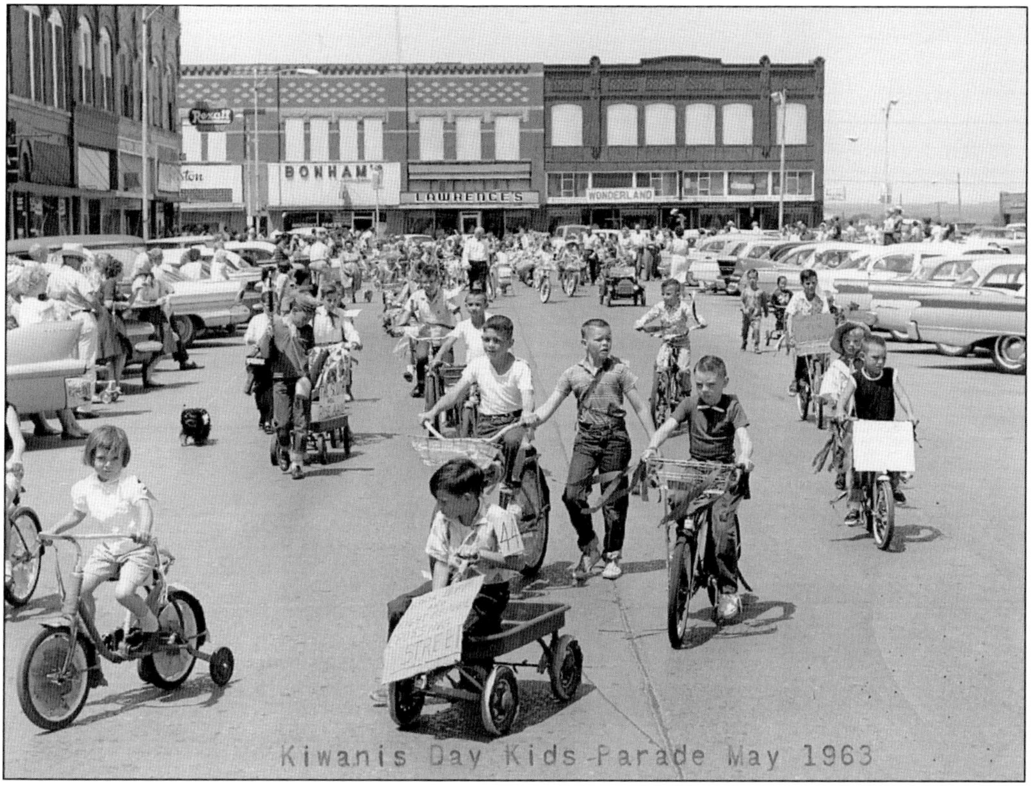

This is the Kiwanis Kids Day parade in May 1963. It was a big day for all the schoolchildren. (Courtesy Bob Taylor.)

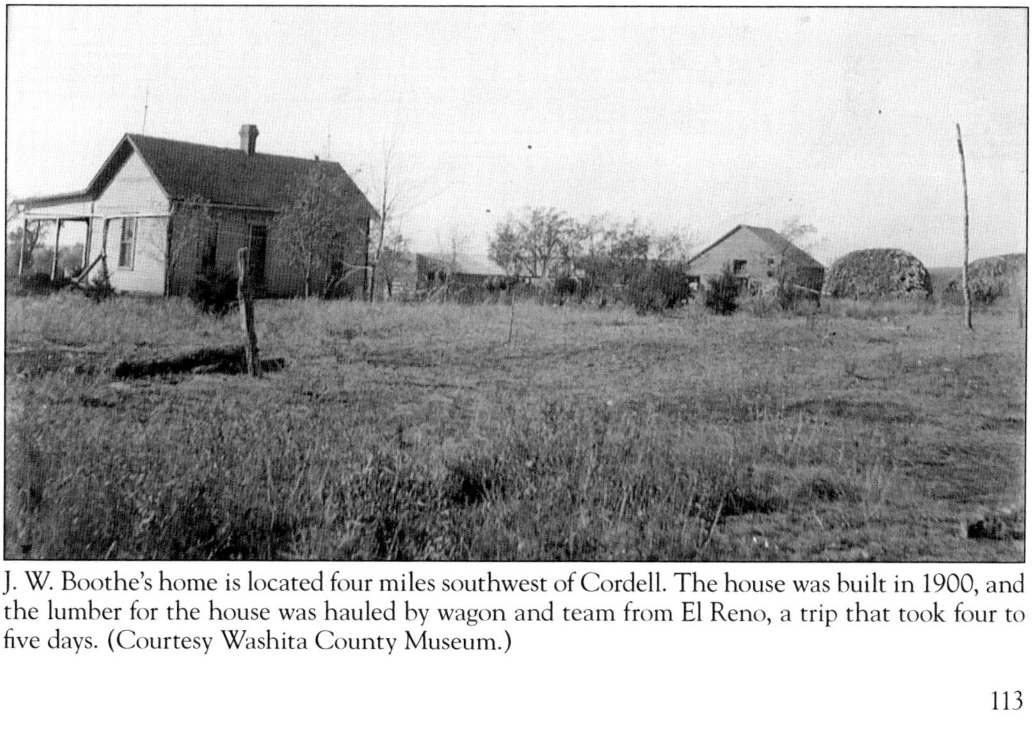

J. W. Boothe's home is located four miles southwest of Cordell. The house was built in 1900, and the lumber for the house was hauled by wagon and team from El Reno, a trip that took four to five days. (Courtesy Washita County Museum.)

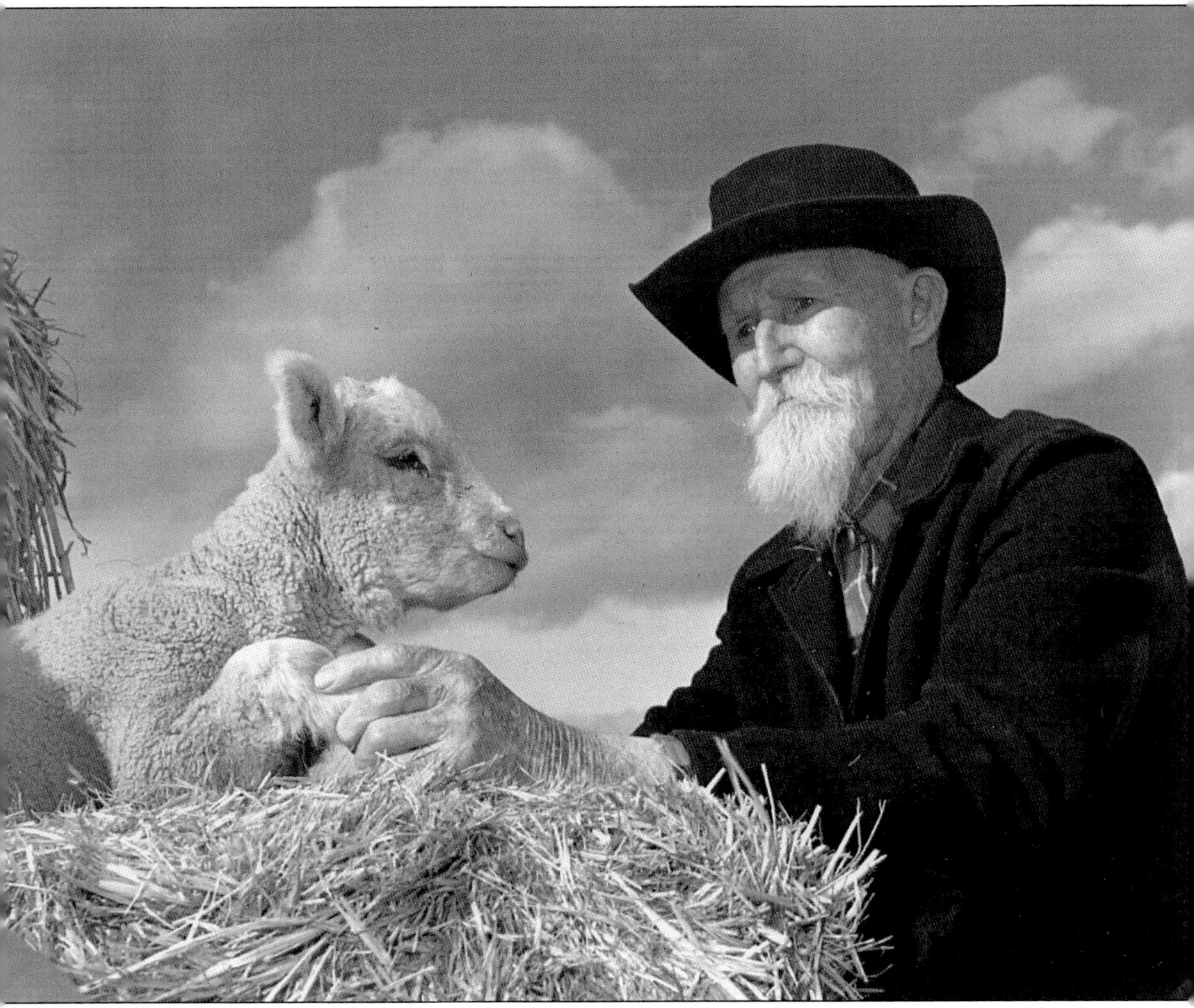

Sam McKee came to Washita County from Texas in 1900 with his wife, Idora, and their seven children. It took 16 days for the McKee family, with their two covered wagons, to make the trip. The McKees settled in the Salem community, nine miles southwest of Cordell, living in a half-dugout for several years. The dugout gave the family protection from one of their greatest dangers, prairie fires. The prairie grass was waist high. When one could see smoke and hear a loud crackle it was time to take cover in the dugout. Several neighbors lost their houses by prairie fires. Sam did well for a man with no formal education. Idora read the bible to Sam most every day. Although Sam could not read or write, he could add, subtract, and figure numbers faster in his head than most could on paper. The McKees did well in the new pioneer country, giving each of their seven children a farm. (Courtesy Bob Taylor.)

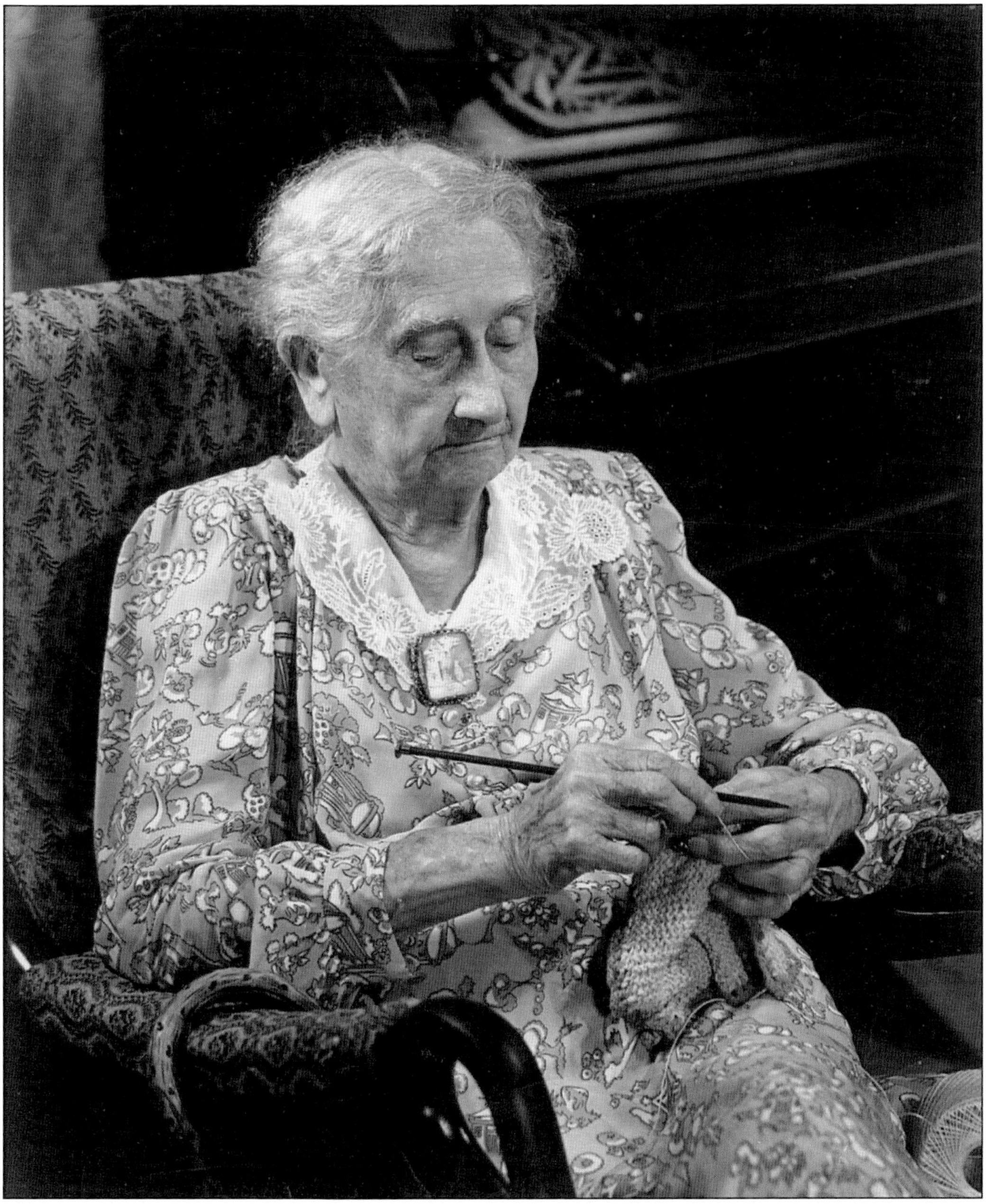

When Martha E. Gregory was 100 years old, she could read her bible or knit without glasses. She was born in Missouri in July 1850. When she was born, Abraham Lincoln had not yet been elected president of the United States. She was 10 years old when the guns at Fort Sumter severed the Union into two nations, plunging them into the bloody Civil War. Gregory had a strong memory of the Civil War. She said that she believed that people were much happier in the earlier days, before they had so much concern with the ways of the world. "Our needs were simpler and we took care of friends and neighbors in times of need." Gregory's death, before she reached 101 years of age, was due to a fall. (Courtesy Bob Taylor.)

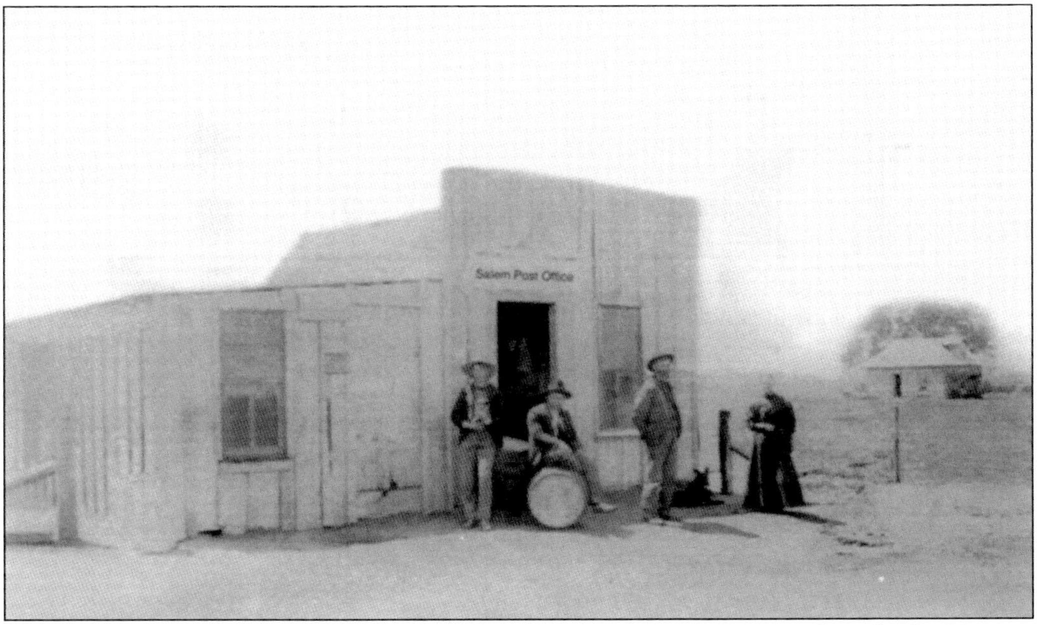

The Salem post office started in a dugout in 1893. In 1897, it was moved to the building in this photograph. Sarah Wood, the postmistress on the right, is seen here with Henry Wood, her husband, next to her. The two men on the left are unidentified. The rock house in the background, which was built in 1892 by the Woods, has been taken apart and reassembled at the Washita County Farm Museum. (Courtesy Ethel Miller.)

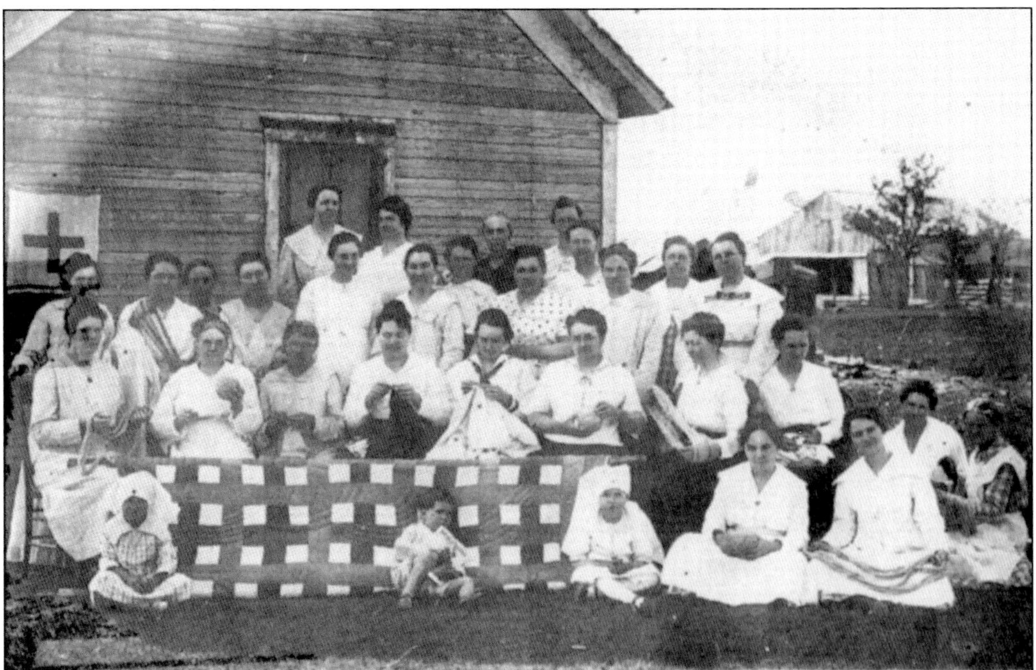

Seen here in Port are Red Cross workers on May 7, 1918. Each week these ladies met to make bandages, knit socks, cut squares of cloth for gun cleaning, or whatever was needed from the home front. (Courtesy Leonard Taylor.)

John Seger was the first white man to establish a home in Washita County when, in 1883, he built his home on Cobb Creek where Colony is located today. It was Seger who brought the Native Americans to establish Colony in 1889. Seger fired the shot at noon on April 19, 1892, to start the run for the settlement of homesteaders establishing Washita County. (Courtesy Washita County Museum.)

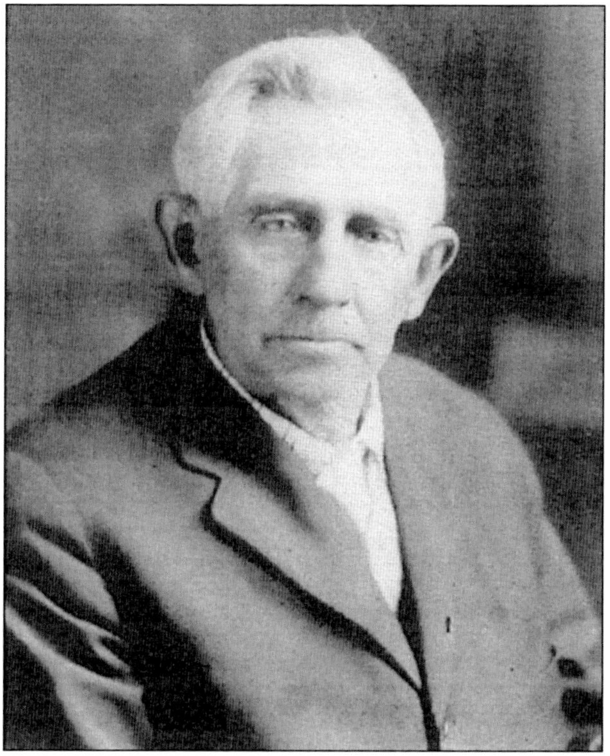

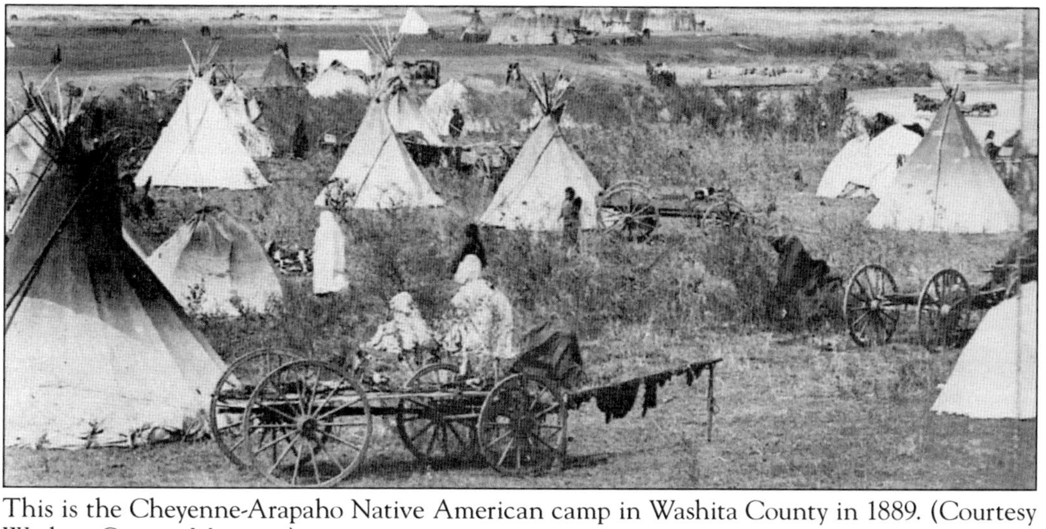

This is the Cheyenne-Arapaho Native American camp in Washita County in 1889. (Courtesy Washita County Museum.)

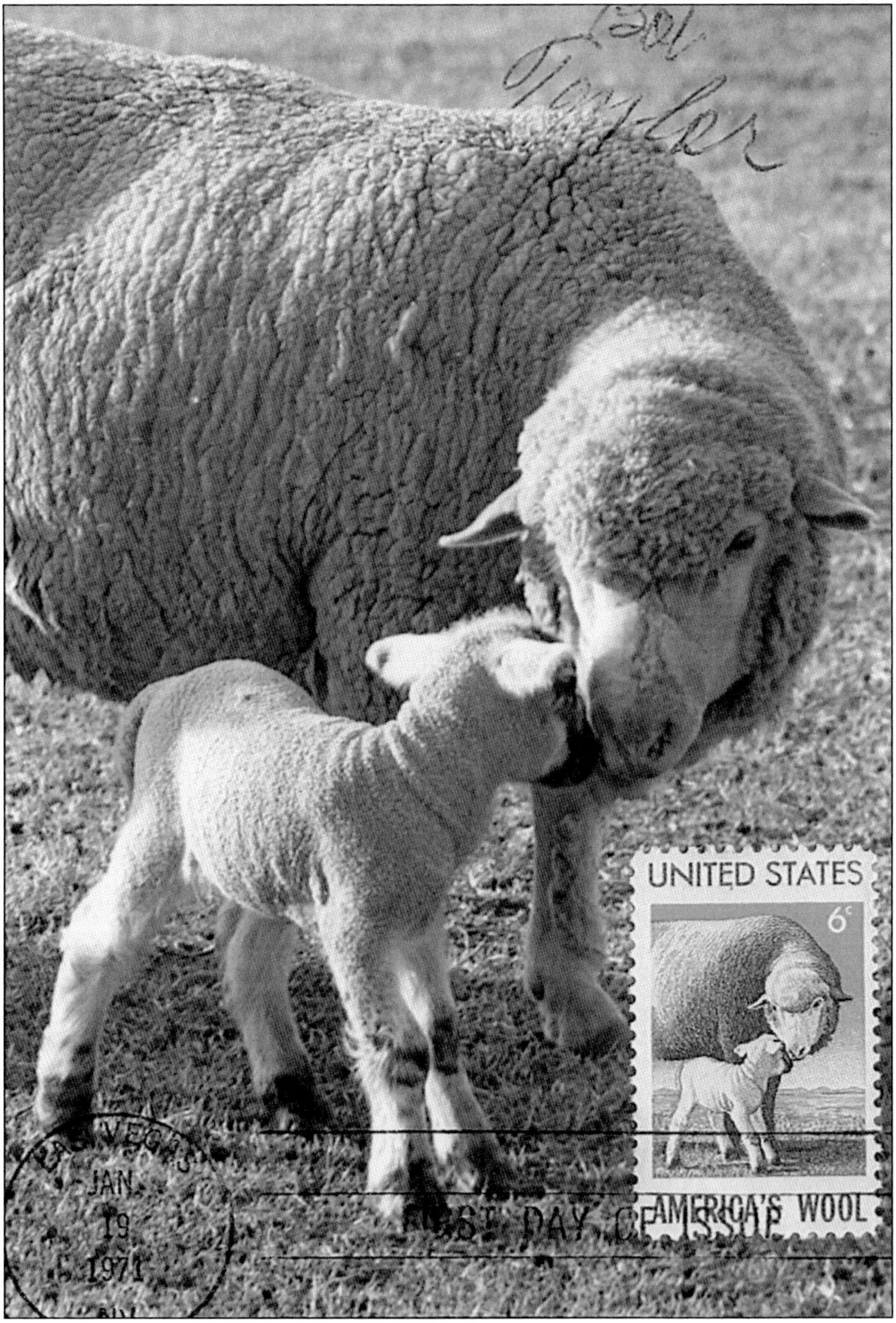

This is a 6¢ postage stamp, which was based on a picture of a Washita County sheep taken by a Washita County photographer, Bob Taylor. The National Sheep and Wool Growers Association was holding its annual meeting in Las Vegas, Nevada, when the U.S. post office department issued the stamp on January 19, 1971, at Las Vegas, commemorating 450 years of sheep and wool production on this continent. The sheep stamp was designed from a Bob Taylor photograph that appeared in the May 1970 issue of the National Wool Growers magazine. (Courtesy Washita County Museum.)

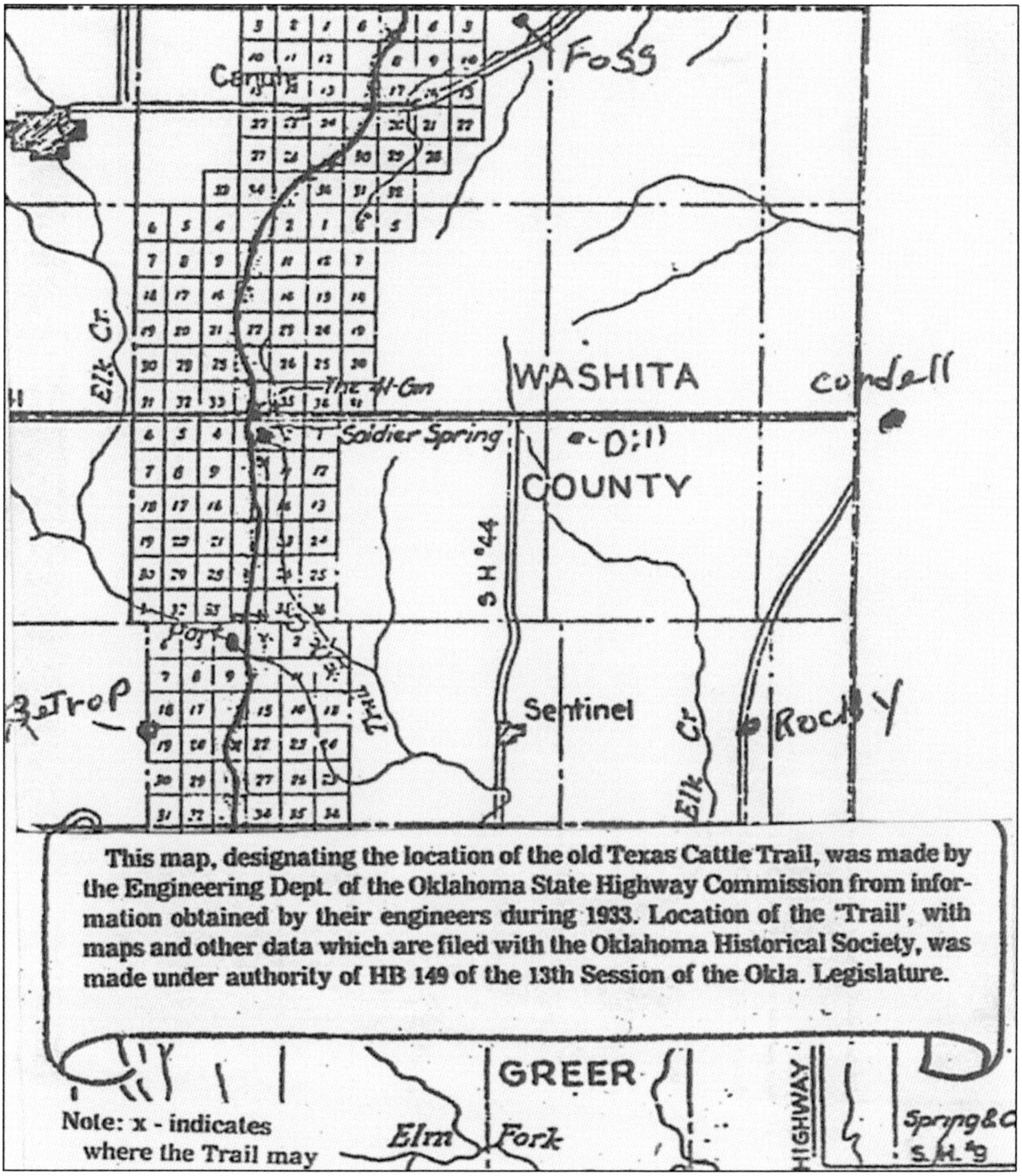

The great western cattle trail entered Oklahoma just south of Altus and left the state just north of Buffalo. The cattle trail entered Washita County in section 33, six miles south of old Port town. The trail exited the county through section 5, northeast of Canute. During the last half of the 1870s and the first half of the 1880s, over seven million head of cattle and horses crossed through Washita County going to the railroad at Dodge City. The cattle would leave the Texas ranch area around Liano and Fredericksburg in the early spring and graze their way north, arriving at Dodge City about three months later and much fatter. The grass was excellent grazing in the Port, Soldiers Springs, and Canute area, and the cattle would move only five miles or so a day where the grass was good grazing. Most herds along the trail numbered about 3,000 head. The value of a three-year-old steer on the ranch was about $6 to $8 while at the railroad at Dodge City the value jumped to around $40 to $50 and at the packinghouse in Kansas City or Chicago that same steer would be worth about $60 to $70. (Courtesy Washita County Museum.)

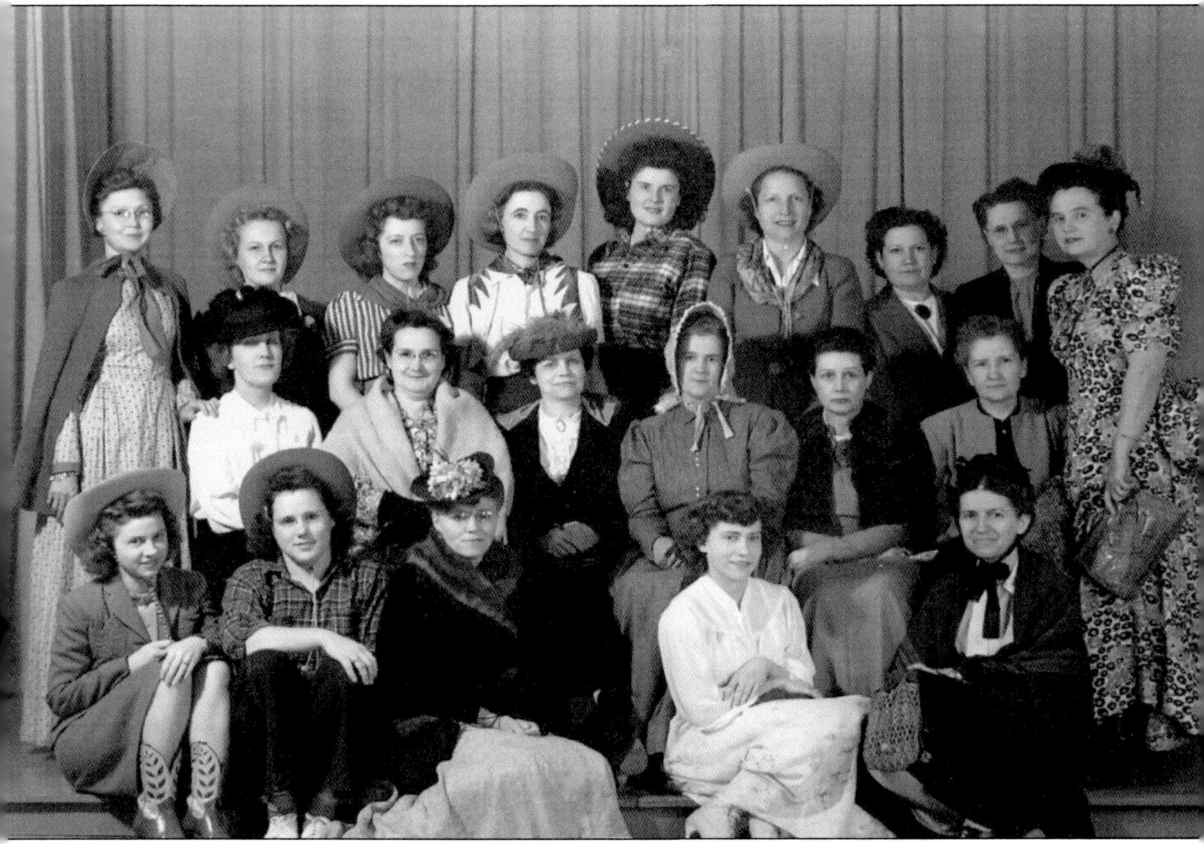

Cordell business and professional women are at a pioneer celebration in 1940. From left to right are (first row) Oleta Megli Colvin, Juanita Richards, Anna K. Wyatt, Ruth Allen, and Kathryn Kraus; (second row) Hattie Gilchrist, Elsie Bell, Zana Bish, Ellen Olsen, Elwyna Smith, and Gertha Molen; (third row) Flossie Hagin, Emma Jo Stafford, unidentified, Mattie Sue Carroll, Felive Brannigar, Ruby Klassen, Elsie Beaucamp, Ethel Monroe, and Ruth Hathaway. Everyone had a part in the pioneer celebration. (Courtesy Flossie Hagin.)

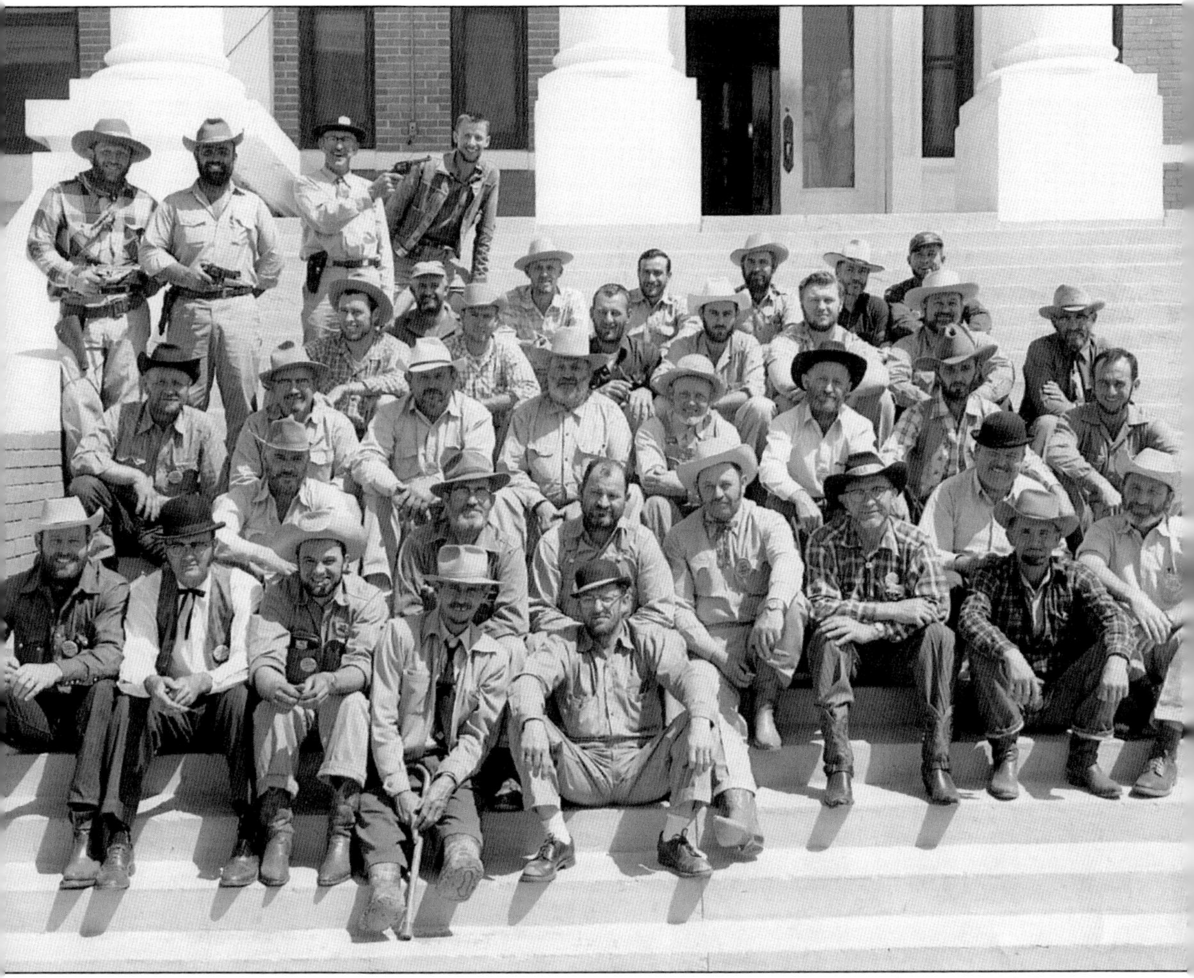

Washita County men pose for a picture on the courthouse steps for pioneer days. From left to right are (first row) Herman Jones, Kenneth Lowe, Bill Sewell, Larry Dean, and Tuffy Combs; (second row) Raymond Neeley, Les McDonald, Darwin Craig, Ed Piercey, Ralph Olsen, James Slatten, and Clifton McKee; (third row) George Klassen, Junior Kerley, Walt Krewall, Sam Holden, Dick Siemens, Otto Goeringer, Herold Brown, Charles Akers, and Johnney Wade; (fourth row) Bill Allen, Jerry Hawkins, Sid Marshel, Charles Sanders, Bob Phipps, O. L. Phipps, and Bill Banister; (fifth row) Edwin Kliewer, Harlin Hinds, Ed Delong, Dale Maddox, Shorty Bowman, and Eby Don Walters. Standing are Frank Flaming, Buck Merrill, Jiggs Botchlett, and Bob Taylor. (Courtesy Bob Taylor.)

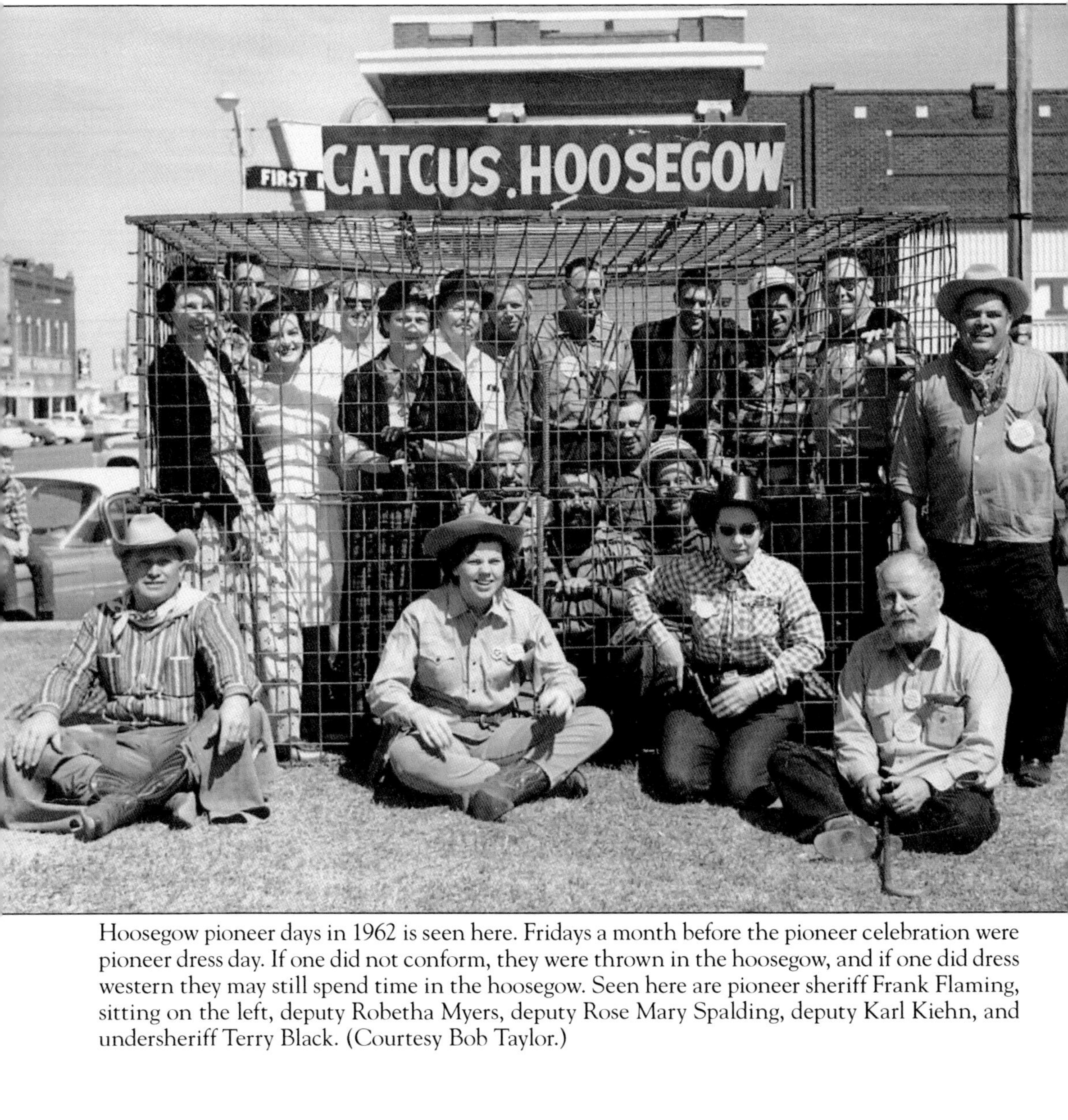

Hoosegow pioneer days in 1962 is seen here. Fridays a month before the pioneer celebration were pioneer dress day. If one did not conform, they were thrown in the hoosegow, and if one did dress western they may still spend time in the hoosegow. Seen here are pioneer sheriff Frank Flaming, sitting on the left, deputy Robetha Myers, deputy Rose Mary Spalding, deputy Karl Kiehn, and undersheriff Terry Black. (Courtesy Bob Taylor.)

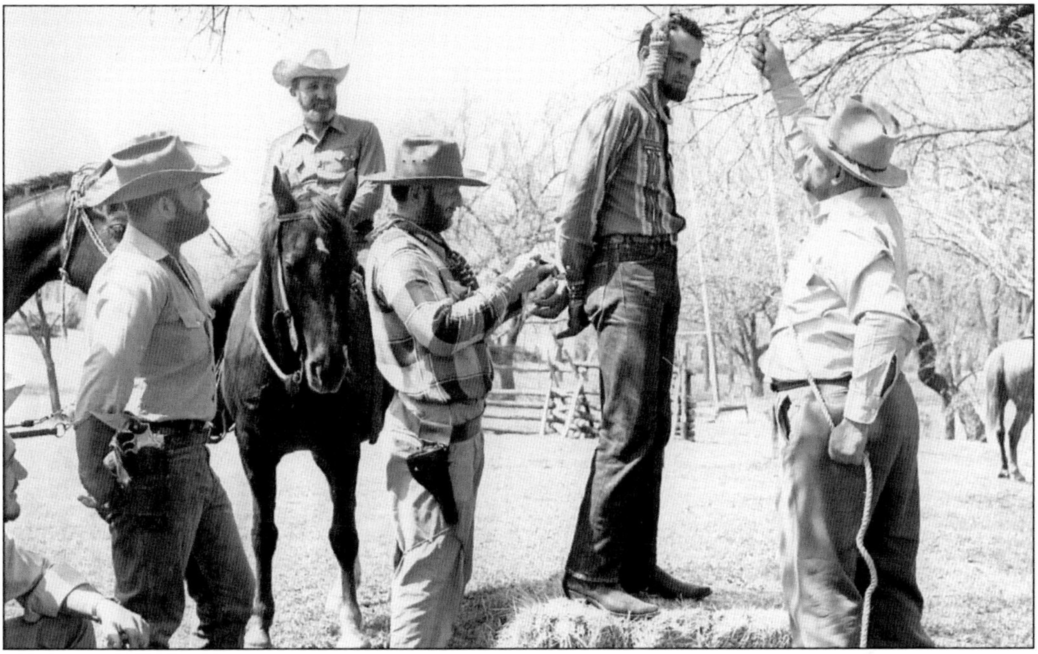

This culprit of a horse theft was caught red-handed and must pay the price by hanging. On the left is Buck Merrill, on the horse is Clifton McKee, tying hands is Frank Flaming, in the noose is Bill Sewell, and pulling the rope is Walt Krewall. The sentence was not carried out. (Courtesy Bob Taylor.)

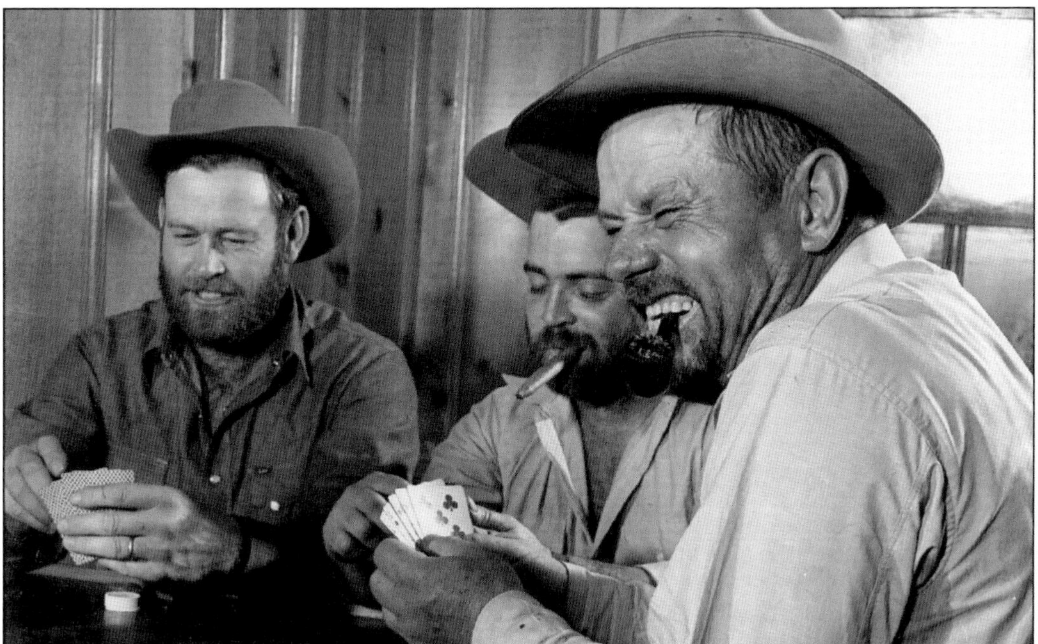

Seen here is pioneer poker in 1960. From left to right are Herman Jones, implement dealer; BuckMerrill, blacksmith; and Walter Krewall, farmer. Krewall must be winning, or maybe he is just a happy loser. (Courtesy Bob Taylor.)

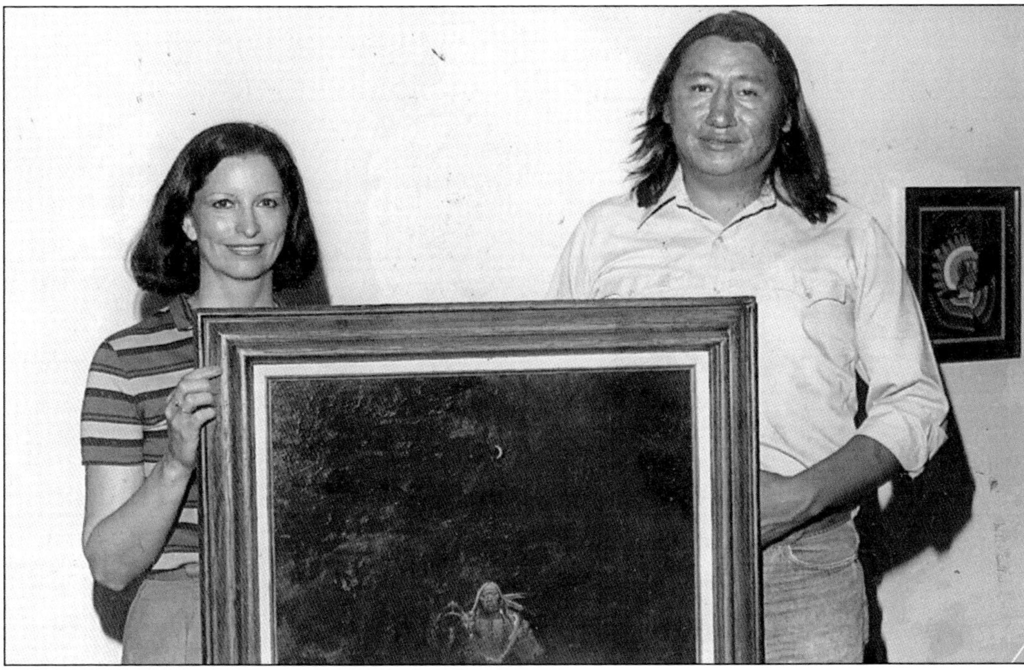

Yvonne Kauger, justice of the Oklahoma Supreme Court and a native of Colony, is seen here receiving some Native American art from Cheyenne artist Mivro Creep to be placed in the Colony Museum. (Courtesy Colony Museum.)

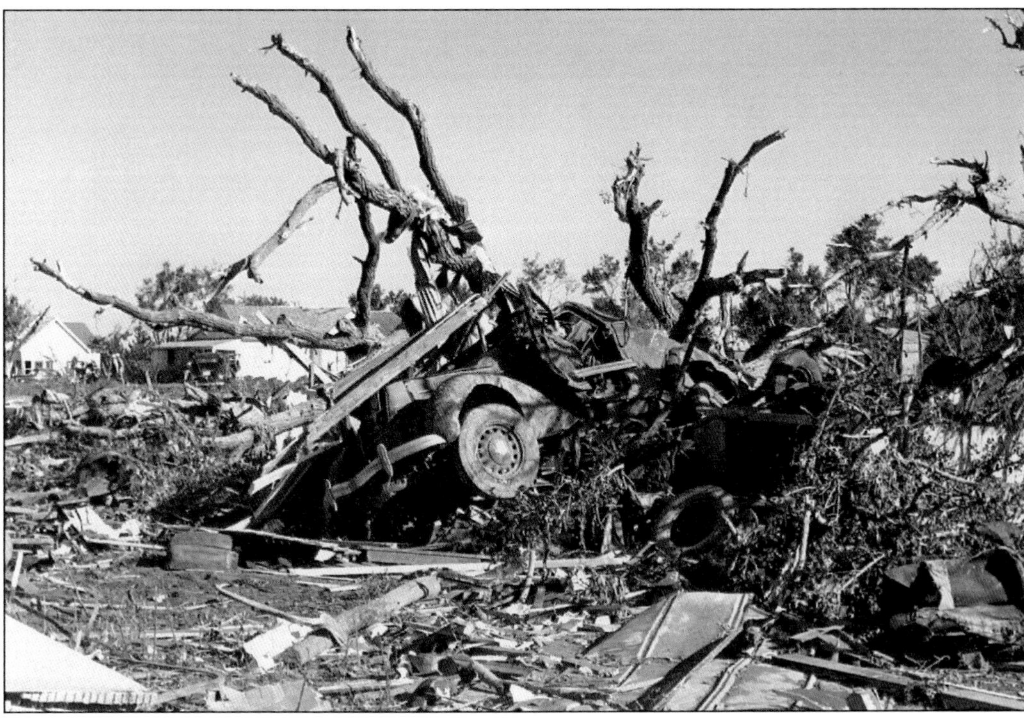

A tornado hit the southwest part of Corn in 1960. The school was damaged, and the new one-year-old school gymnasium was destroyed, as well as several homes. (Courtesy Bob Taylor.)

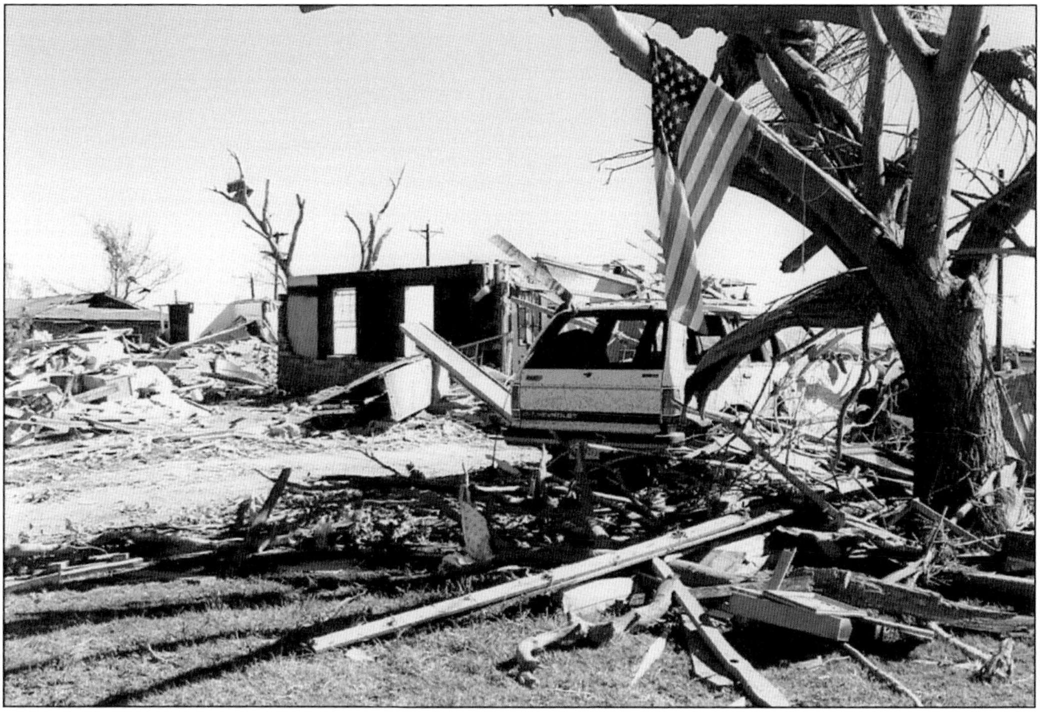

These two photographs were taken on east Ninth Street in Cordell. The picture above shows damage done by the October 9, 2001, tornado, while the picture below is down the street in the next block. It was reported that over 400 homes were destroyed or damaged. (Courtesy Bob Taylor.)

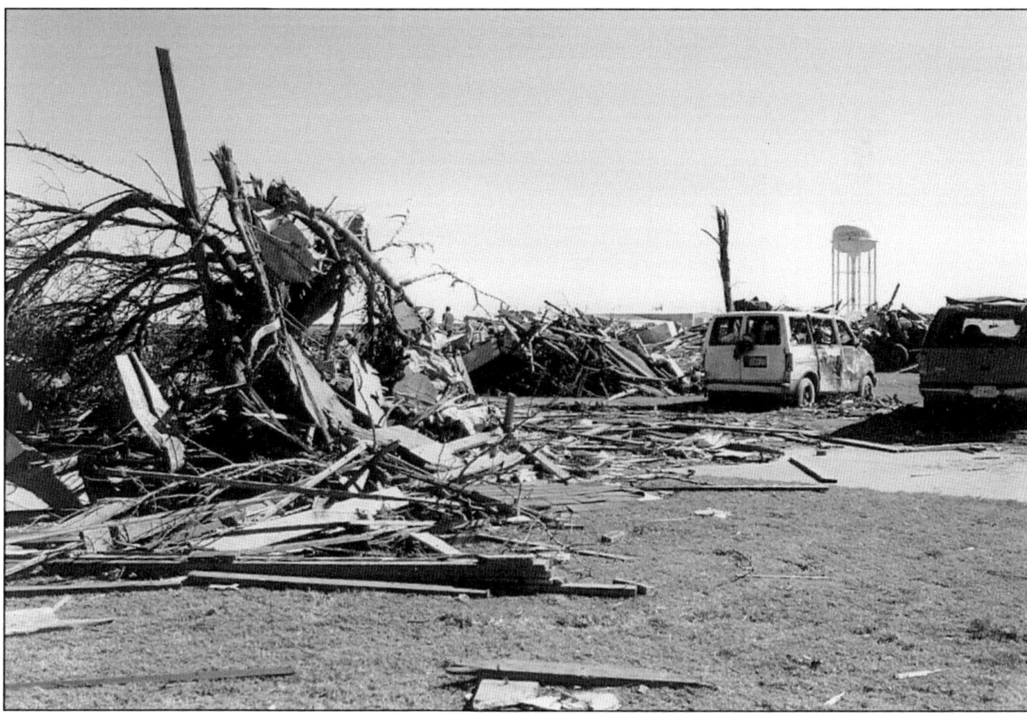

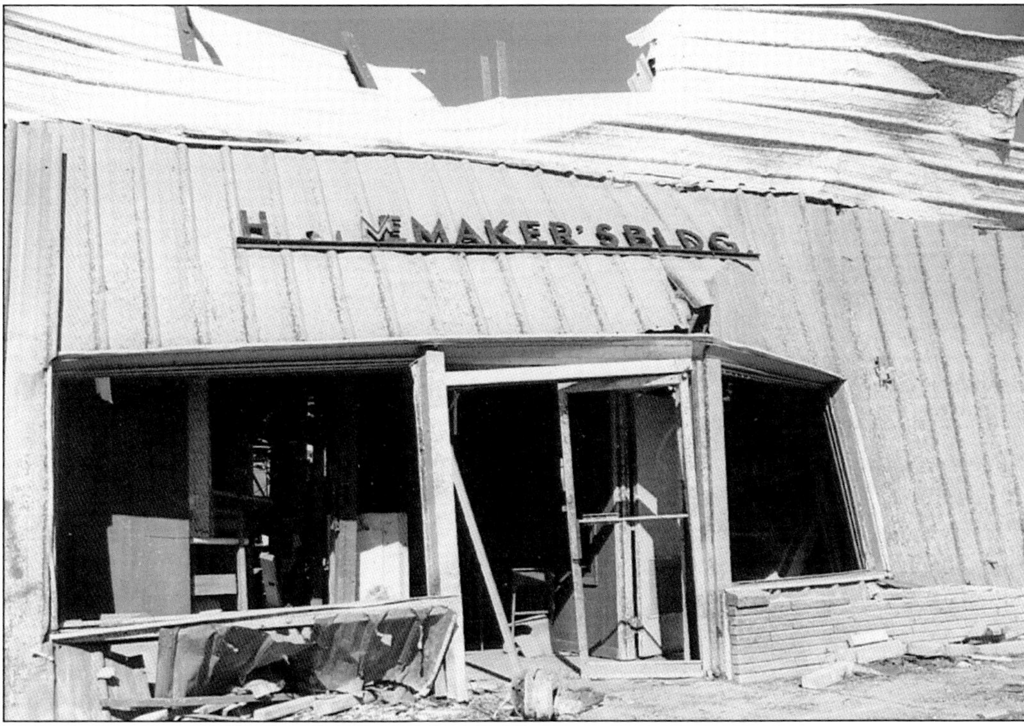

The photograph above is the homemakers building at the Washita County Fair grounds after it was destroyed by the October 2001 tornado. The photograph below is the livestock building at the Washita County Fair grounds after the tornado. A completely new Washita County fair complex was completed for the 2004 fair. (Courtesy Bob Taylor.)

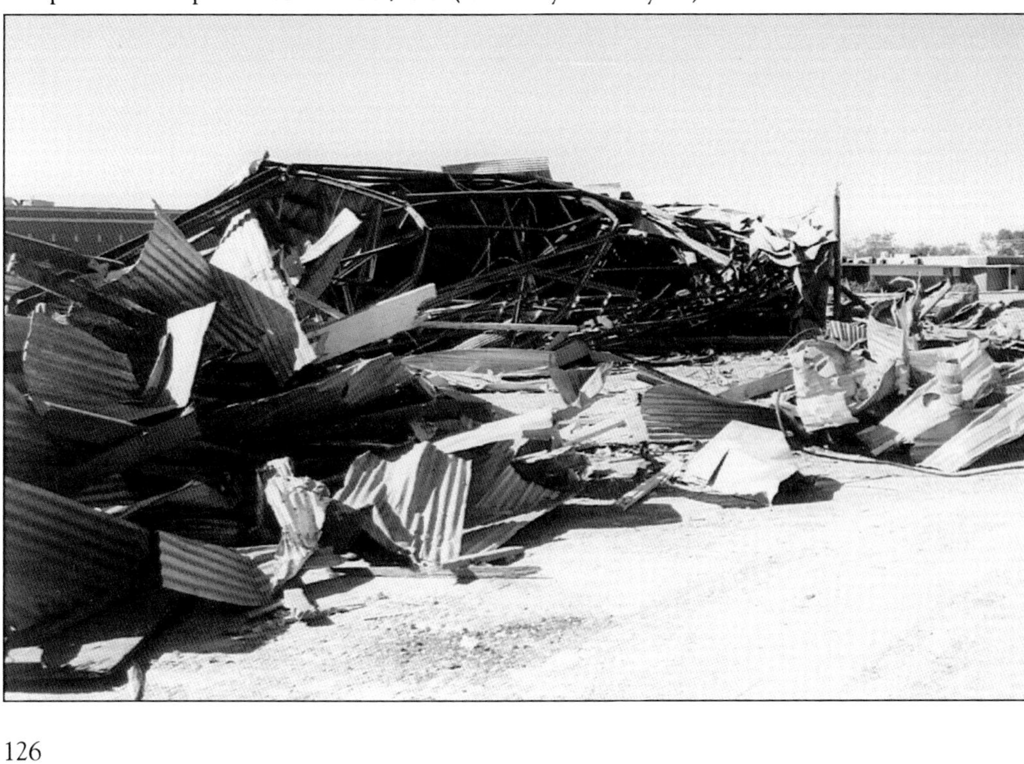

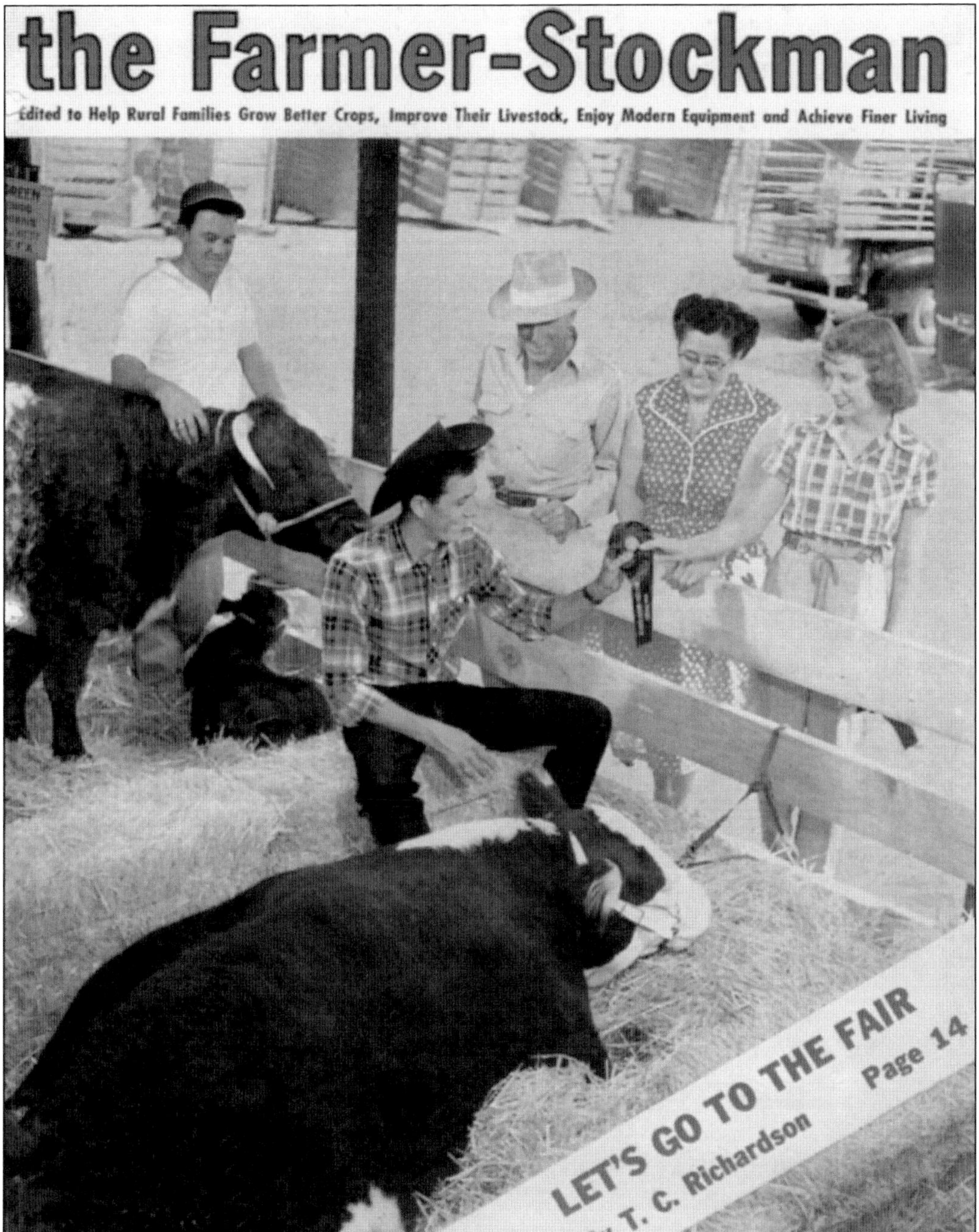

The Washita County Fair will hold its 100th annual county fair in August 2007. It is one of the top county fairs in Oklahoma. This photograph and a county fair story of the 1953 Washita County Fair were used on the cover page of the *Oklahoma Farmer-Stockman* magazine in 1954. Ted Green is in the black hat; his parents, Walter and Grace Green are standing behind him; his girlfriend Carol Hughes is at right; and Bill Sewell is at left. (Courtesy Bob Taylor and Oklahoma Farmer-Stockman.)

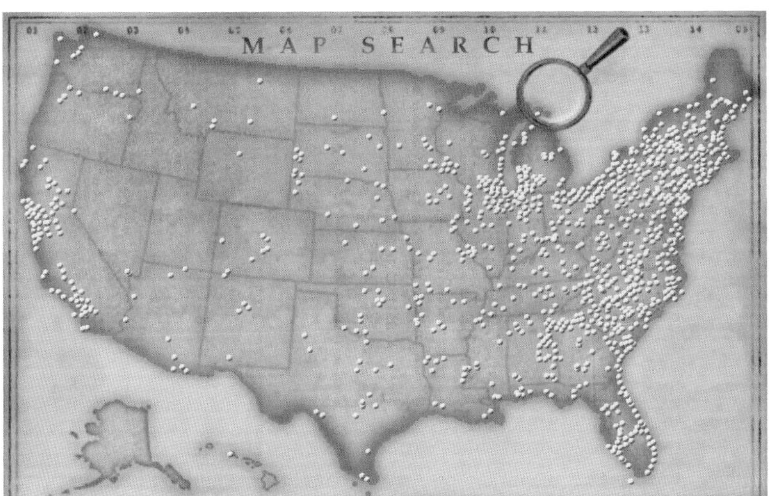
MAP SEARCH